Climate Change: Natural or Manmade?

Joe Fone has researched in depth contemporary tenets in the field of climatology in a freelance capacity over several years, alongside his role as an electronics technician and CAD designer for the solar inverter market. Prior to the present work, his analytical articles have appeared in the New Zealand journals *The Press*, *Dominion Post* and *Investigate*. He lives in Christchurch.

D0932327

CLIMATE CHANGE:
NATURAL OR MANMADE?

CLIMATE CHANGE: NATURAL OR MANMADE?

Joe Fone

STACEY
INTERNATIONAL

Climate Change: Natural or Manmade?

STACEY INTERNATIONAL
128 Kensington Church Street
London W8 4BH
Tel: +44 (0)20 7221 7166; Fax: +44 (0)20 7792 9288
Email: info@stacey-international.co.uk
www.stacey-international.co.uk

ISBN: 978-1-906768-95-9

© Joe Fone 2013

1 3 5 7 9 0 8 6 4 2

Printed in Turkey

CIP Data: A catalogue record for this book is available from the British Library

All rights reserved. No part of this publication may be reproduced,
stored in a retrieval system, or transmitted in any form or by any means, electronic, mechanical,
photocopying, recording or otherwise, without the prior permission of the copyright owners.

CONTENTS

Acknowledgements

Without the following people, I could not have written this book. I would like to thank them and acknowledge their help, advice and support, either directly or indirectly.

First and foremost, I thank my partner Clare whose patience and understanding helped me through the long task. Thanks too to my family who read some of the early drafts and who always encouraged me, and to my friend and colleague Arthur de Beun who read the first six chapters and offered many useful suggestions. But without the encouragement and advice of Paula Wagemaker at the very beginning, I might never have undertaken this project.

On the science, I especially acknowledge the New Zealand Climate Science Coalition members, many of whom offered tips and advice. My thanks specifically go to Terry Dunleavy, Bryan Leyland, Barry Brill, Richard Treadgold, Bob Carter for his many useful pieces and emails answering my questions; Timothy Ball and Paul V. Sheridan, both of whom read early drafts of the first five chapters and suggested some improvements; also the late Dennis Dutton whose encouragement and huge enthusiasm was utterly infectious; and of course my good friend Gerrit van der Lingen whose vast knowledge on climate matters and geology helped to fill the gaps in mine. In addition, I would like to acknowledge the many other scientists and members of the NZCSC who answered my frequent questions on the more esoteric points.

I wish to acknowledge David Archibald as well as Anthony Watts whose fabulous blog, wattsupwiththat.com, is a treasure trove of articles and data; and Joanne Nova, Steve McIntyre and Andrew Montford for the same. Their blogs (joannenova.com.au, climateaudit.org and bishophill.squarespace.com) are well worth a visit, as are a host of other science blogs of repute. The indefatigable Marc Morano's site, climatedepot.com, is a rich source of political and media information, sometimes dripping with humour and delicious sarcasm, as are the inimitable James Delingpole's articles in the *Telegraph*, both of which I frequently visited for anecdotal gems.

I also thank Tom Stacey, Struan Simpson, Elizabeth Holmes and Saba Ahmed of Stacey International whose tireless patience, advice and guidance brought the work to fruition.

That said, any errors and omissions are mine.

Author's Note

For the numerous quotes and sources used throughout this book, I have endeavoured to credit all work in good faith, fairly and accurately, and have used such quotes under fair use and scholarly use norms, applying for necessary permissions as far as reasonably possible, especially for quotes exceeding fifty words or so. All graphs have been redrawn manually by the author, as accurately and faithfully as possible, using a suitable CAD drawing package, with all due credit and acknowledgement given for the original in each case. Otherwise the originals have been reproduced with permission.

All statements, criticisms and viewpoints discussed in this book have been made honestly, using the material available in the public domain at the time. They reflect attitudes common to many writers, commentators and bloggers, and I have provided links and credits for such statements and views accordingly. Having said that, I admit to the occasional note of humour in some areas, though it arises from reasonably argued criticisms and observations based on readily obtainable information. However no individual offence is in any way implied or intended. Hence, this book reflects the situation within the climate science community and the political arena as the author honestly sees it, based on clear evidence available to all, and who has thus drawn the same conclusions that anyone might reasonably draw having accessed the same information available to the public. Indeed, the very same conclusions have been reached by many other writers and commentators whose work is similarly publicly available.

Joe Fone, January 2013

To my father, who set me on the right path.

Abbreviations

AGW	Anthropogenic Global Warming
AR4	Fourth Assessment Report of the IPCC
BoM	Bureau of Meteorology (Australia)
CAGW	Catastrophic Anthropogenic Global Warming
CCX	Chicago Climate Exchange
CERN	European Organization for Nuclear Research
CIA	Central Intelligence Agency
CNRS	Centre National de la Recherche Scientifique (French National Centre of Scientific Research)
CRU	Climatic Research Unit, University of East Anglia
ERBS	Earth Radiation Budget Satellite
ETS	Emissions Trading Scheme
FOIA	Freedom of Information Act
GCM	General Circulation Model
GIM	Generation Investment Management
GISS	Goddard Institute for Space Studies
HadCRUT	Hadley Centre/CRU gridded surface temperature dataset
IPCC	Intergovernmental Panel on Climate Change
KNMI	Koninklijk Nederlands Meteorologisch Instituut (Dutch Meteorological Institute)
LIA	Little Ice Age
MIT	Massachusetts Institute of Technology
MSM	Mainstream Media
MWP	Medieval Warm Period
NAS	National Academy of Sciences, USA
NASA	National Aeronautics and Space Administration, USA

NIWA	National Institute of Water and Atmospherics, New Zealand
NOAA	National Oceanic and Atmospheric Administration, USA
NZCSC	New Zealand Climate Science Coalition
PDO	Pacific Decadal Oscillation
ppm	parts per million
RSS	Radiodetermination Satellite System
RWP	Roman Warm Period
SEPP	Science and Environmental Policy Project
SO	Southern Oscillation
SOI	Southern Oscillation Index
TOGA COARE	Tropical Ocean Global Atmosphere Coupled Ocean Atmosphere Response Experiment
UAH	University of Alabama in Huntsville, USA
UHI	Urban Heat Island
UNEP	United Nations Environment Programme
USHCN	US Historical Climatology Network
VHEMT	Voluntary Human Extinction Movement
WMO	World Meteorological Organization

For more abbreviations, see www.ipcc.ch/publications_and_data/ar4/wg1/en/annexessannex-iv.html

Introduction

The heresy of one age becomes the orthodoxy of the next.

Helen Keller

Science is a cemetery of dead ideas.

Miguel de Unamuno

In the early 1970s I made a life-changing discovery: I encountered my first heretic. He was introduced to me by my father in the public library where we made a pilgrimage every Friday evening. My father had picked up a book so riddled with heresy it had even been blacklisted by the scientific community. Thanks to my youth, however, I was neither alarmed nor outraged at the heresy in its pages. I also failed to appreciate the far-reaching implications of the book my father was showing me. That lesson would come later. The book in question was a tragic tale of unimaginable fury being visited on one man by the closed ranks of the scientific establishment because he sought to challenge the scientific consensus on many disciplines at once, thus offending them all, an episode described in Chapter 2. His work was an unforgivable sin of unorthodox erudition. Yet that single book would later instil in me a keen sense of justice for the underdog and a healthy scepticism of so-called consensus science. But worse was to come because it encouraged me to be suspicious of the anthropogenic (manmade) global warming (AGW) movement, which entered the collective public consciousness nearly twenty years later. My suspicions were raised because this theory was also being trumpeted as consensus science and that immediately set warning bells ringing.

The penalty, however, was that this early discovery also turned me into an incorrigible cynic, which I freely admit is a profane pastime. But I blame my father for that because he taught me to question the basic tenets of any belief system and to be wise to fashions, especially in science, that ultimately become sacred cows – ideas and theories that become so entrenched that they pass unquestioned, are reproduced in textbooks and taught as unassailable truths. Anthropogenic global warming is but one of them.

Global warming is today's *cause célèbre*, promoted by an army of enthusiasts from scientists and politicians to environmentalists, celebrities and theologians, all of whom declare it to be the most pressing issue facing us since the last such scare – the 1970s ice age panic promoted by a similar army.

So AGW is a serious problem. Or is it?

One thing is certain: the global warming movement is a juggernaut of unprecedented proportions, an unstoppable monster threatening to engulf every facet of our lives. It masquerades as a self-evident scientific truth, yet it is wrapped in a cloak of political ambition while shielded from the darts of doubt with the armour plate of religious conviction. For a scientific theory, AGW is strangely polarizing, with belligerent defenders on one side and outraged sceptics on the other, and in between an assortment of teary-eyed celebrities tease the media with its message of climate doom.

The purpose of this book is to analyse all these aspects of the manmade global warming hypothesis, beginning with the history and origins of the scientific case in the nineteenth century and ending with the aggressive, quasi-religious fervour that today breathes life into its fragile frame in the face of fierce opposition.

1. The Problem Child

> There is something fascinating about science. One gets such wholesale returns of conjecture out of such a trifling investment of fact.
>
> *Mark Twain*

The theory of anthropogenic global warming (AGW), as it is known today, has a curious and troubled history. And it began with ice.

In 1836 the Swiss naturalist Jean Louis Rodolphe Agassiz was struck by a radical idea. He was one of the first scientists to realize the geological significance of ancient, 'erratic' boulders and scarred rock surfaces in the mountains and valleys of Switzerland which showed unmistakeable signs of past trauma. Earlier writers had suggested that these boulders had been carried by ancient glaciers, which had long since disappeared, but Agassiz took the idea further and theorized that the glaciers were part of an extensive ice sheet that once engulfed Switzerland. His research into glacial movements in Europe, and geology in the United States and Canada, advanced glacier science to such an extent that Agassiz became known as the Father of Glaciology. His ideas formed the basis of what is now known as ice age theory.

Thirty years later the Irish chemist and alpinist John Tyndall scaled the Weisshorn in Switzerland and realized that Agassiz's ice sheets were part of something even more extensive. From this and earlier field trips, Tyndall became convinced that the earth underwent periods of mass glaciation over many thousands of years. Colossal glaciers had at various times encased vast areas of the earth's surface, from the Arctic to mid-European latitudes, leaving evidence of their advance and subsequent retreat etched in the rock face, as Agassiz had correctly identified.

Tyndall, however, believed that over tens of thousands of years the climate must be changing for such massive volumes of ice to grow and then disappear, leaving only moraines, erratic boulders and rock abrasions as evidence. He surmised that changes in atmospheric gases might explain the phenomenon if it could be proved that these gases acted as an insulator, an atmospheric blanket, either trapping or transmitting solar radiation, and thereby warming or cooling the planet. Much later, a radical theory, developed by Charles Hutchins Hapgood, surmised that rapid pole-shifts due to movements in the earth's crust caused the ice ages which had nothing to do with variations in the atmospheric gases. Hapgood's theory of 'wandering poles' explained why today's ice-bound Siberian regions had once been lush, forested areas populated by mammoths, at a time when northern Europe was under ice, a mere 11,000 years ago.

Tyndall seized on the idea of a 'planetary hothouse', first proposed in 1807 by the French mathematician Joseph Fourier, who showed that some gases are more opaque to heat energy than others because they absorb infrared radiation more efficiently. Tyndall thus set about proving Fourier's theory experimentally with the known constituent gases of the atmosphere – particularly water vapour, 'carbonic acid' (carbon dioxide, or CO_2) and ozone – by measuring their infrared absorption ratios.

Tyndall was amazed to discover large differences in the ability of 'perfectly colourless and invisible gases and vapours' to absorb and transmit radiant heat, and noted that hydrogen, oxygen and nitrogen are quite transparent while other gases are more opaque. On the strength of his experiments, Tyndall concluded that water vapour was by far the most efficient absorber of radiant energy and that it was therefore the most important atmospheric gas affecting the earth's surface temperature; without water vapour, the earth's surface would be 'held fast in the iron grip of frost'. While CO_2 played a role in

Fourier's 'hothouse effect', Tyndall realized its influence was nugatory in comparison to water vapour and could therefore be ignored. He was correct, but in the meantime others were becoming just as obsessed with the idea of a CO_2-derived hothouse.

In 1895 the Swedish chemist Svante Arrhenius independently suggested that a relationship existed between atmospheric CO_2 and temperature. Like Tyndall, Arrhenius was looking for a cause to explain the ice ages and drew heavily on the work of his predecessors. However, he shifted his focus entirely to CO_2 despite Tyndall's conclusions. There were two reasons for this: first, Arrhenius was influenced by his colleague Arvid Högbom, who was investigating the effects of *industrial* CO_2 emissions on the atmosphere; and secondly, water vapour was far too variable, troublesome in equipment and impossible to factor reliably into energy absorption equations. It therefore tended to be ignored while CO_2 became the main focus of scientific interest.

The problem Arrhenius faced was what caused atmospheric CO_2 concentrations to change in the first place. He turned to Högbom, who had compiled estimates on natural CO_2 cycles, including the effects of volcanic eruptions which, he surmised, were the chief source of atmospheric CO_2. While compiling his data, Högbom had a radical idea. He conjectured that since industrial activity also released CO_2, its influence should be measurable and that, over time, its effect on temperature might become significant as levels increased. Arrhenius was impressed and decided to explore the hypothesis further. Industrial CO_2 was a variable that might be measured and accounted for more easily than emissions from volcanic eruptions which were assumed to have established the natural background level. CO_2 was also easier to factor mathematically than water vapour which was thought to be affected by changes in CO_2. Therefore CO_2 was considered appropriate for study of climate-changing gases while water vapour was not. This arbitrary discounting of water vapour and the single-minded focus on CO_2 as the principal climate-altering gas was the first false step in the development of the AGW hypothesis.

In 1896 Arrhenius calculated that earth's 'average' temperature was about 15°C and suggested that a doubling of atmospheric CO_2 would result in a temperature increase of 4°C– 5°C. This meant that humans could influence the climate. At the time, this was considered a real advantage. Arrhenius hoped that Sweden's cold climate would improve so that it might once again grow bananas. He imagined that by increasing the percentage of 'carbonic acid' in the atmosphere, the peoples of the earth would enjoy healthier climates and live longer. This idea was enthusiastically supported by the German chemist Walter Nernst, who suggested setting fire to coal seams in the mountains to release as much 'carbonic acid' into the air as possible in order to warm the planet. Like Arrhenius, Nernst thought more CO_2 was an advantage because of its fertilizing effect on plants. In his 1908 book *Worlds in the Making* Arrhenius predicted that the small amount of CO_2 in the atmosphere would increase in a few centuries as industrial activity advanced.

Despite his enthusiasm for the warming effect of 'carbonic acid', Arrhenius's early work was fundamentally flawed because he considered only a narrow band of the infrared spectrum[1] and his measurements relied on numerous assumptions and rough estimates which led him astray. As a consequence, his estimation of around a 5°C increase for a doubling of CO_2 was out by a factor of 10.[2] Nevertheless he continued working on the problem and by 1906 had completely reworked his calculations, reducing the theoretical warming effect of a doubling of CO_2 to only 1.6°C.

It made very little difference, though, for Arrhenius was largely ignored for the next thirty years, by which time the scientific world had moved on to other, more exciting and challenging theories. The atom was the next big thing. The pioneering work of J.J. Thompson, Ernest Rutherford and others into the structure of matter completely overshadowed Arrhenius's research into 'carbonic acid', and at the same time Albert Einstein dropped his relativity bombshell on orthodox scientific thought. At this point serious mainstream science was all about the atom, relativity and, later, quantum mechanics.

From 1914, in a world preoccupied by a world war and an economic depression, Arrhenius's theory remained little more than a scientific curiosity and was all but forgotten. It was not until 1938 that the greenhouse theory was revived by the British engineer Guy Stewart Callendar, who noticed that temperatures during the first forty years of the twentieth century had increased. Searching for an explanation, and like Tyndall, interested in why ice ages occur, he identified atmospheric CO_2 as the cause. Impressed by the work of Arrhenius, Tyndall and Fourier, Callendar assumed that the increase in temperatures over those forty years had been caused by a parallel increase in atmospheric CO_2. Because of the apparent correlation between the two, he concluded they were linked by industrial activity.

Callendar's interest in CO_2 was encouraged by the now widely held assumption that variations in solar output were too insignificant to effect changes in the earth's climate system. In the previous century, the idea of an energy-stable sun gave rise to the myth of the 'solar constant', that is to say that the sun's energy output is constant over time and in all directions, and so cannot account for variations in the earth's climate. That only left CO_2. This assumption would persist until the late twentieth century. Indeed, it is still considered by many adherents of the AGW hypothesis that major variations in the earth's climate are caused by factors other than the sun and that changes since the Industrial Revolution are the result of increases in atmospheric CO_2. The solar constant hypothesis has since been discredited.

The idea that climate change was caused by changes in atmospheric CO_2 became known as the 'Callendar effect', which was broadly defined as climate change brought about by the burning of fossil fuels, a term referring to the traditional 'biogenic' theory, which assumes that oil deposits are formed by biological material decaying over eons. (This hypothesis has been challenged by Thomas Gold of Cornell University, who argues that hydrocarbons in the earth's crust are 'abiogenic' and a natural function of the earth's core dynamics; they can therefore have nothing to do with decayed biological matter and never be depleted by artificial means.) Callendar's idea proved to be irresistible. For despite it still being considered fringe science, the notion of a human cause for rising temperatures through industrial emissions held a certain charm. Callendar himself was quite obsessed with it. He used many of his own CO_2 measurements, taken near his home in Sussex, and carefully selected a few nineteenth-century measurements that confirmed his hypothesis, rejecting the rest as unreliable. By ignoring the majority of the nineteenth-century measurements,[3] Callendar convinced himself that atmospheric CO_2 was increasing at an alarming rate due to the burning of fossil fuels and would ultimately raise global temperatures to dangerous levels (see Figure 1). The flaw in Callendar's approach was his assumption that atmospheric CO_2 prior to the Industrial Revolution had always been at a constant level because it was uninfluenced by human activity. The figure he arbitrarily settled on was 292 parts per million (ppm), which was supposedly increasing steadily from around 1870 due to industrial emissions.

However, some 90,000 measurements accurate to within 3 per cent and some to within 1 per cent, taken by nineteenth-century and early twentieth-century chemists, refuted Callendar's assertion. Instead, they showed that CO_2 levels from 350 ppm to well over 400 ppm were not unusual. For instance, 375 ppm was measured in Dresden by Walther Hempel in 1885; 390 ppm in 1866 by Eugen von Gorup (Eugen Franz Freiherr von Gorup-Besanez in Erlangen); while 416 ppm was measured in Innsbruck by von Gilm in 1857 and again in 1858. Similar measurements were taken across northern Europe, from India to Alaska and North and South America, and nearly all in rural areas uncontaminated by industry.[4] They were all rejected as Callendar considered only those measurements that allowed for an average of 290 ppm. Anything above that did not fit his hypothesis that pre-industrial levels were necessarily low and stable, while modern levels were much higher and steadily increasing.

It is easy therefore to suspect a hidden agenda in Callendar's approach. He seemed inordinately preoccupied with selective sampling and furthering the anthropogenic greenhouse gas hypothesis to the exclusion of all other possible causes for the temperature changes. However, mainstream science at the time was dominated by quantum theory and atomic physics – far more glamorous but very exclusive territory – while Callendar's fossil-fuelled greenhouse theory was hardly more than a curiosity of little interest to the scientific community. Only Callendar and a few fringe hobbyists cared about it.

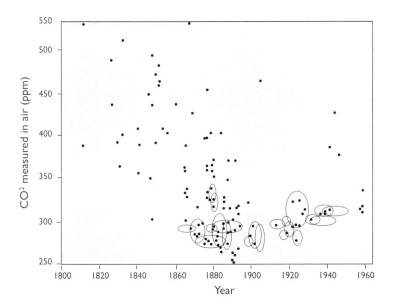

Figure 1.[5] Mean values of atmospheric CO_2 taken across Europe, North America and Peru between 1800 and 1955. The circled values, taken between 1860 and 1950, were arbitrarily selected by Callendar to arrive at his nineteenth-century average of 292 ppm. Otherwise the average is 335 ppm – only 50 ppm below today's mean level as determined at Mauna Loa, Hawaii. It is possible to discern from this plot a corresponding change in slope and trend between the raw data and Callendar's careful selections[6] (i.e. a downward slope changes to an upward slope). This helped establish the now common misconception that CO_2 rose sharply during the twentieth century due to the burning of fossil fuels.

Despite his efforts, Callendar's speculations were to suffer a similar fate to those of Arrhenius because by then scientists were preoccupied by another world war and global temperatures had started to fall. Indeed, they would continue to fall for the next thirty-eight years until around 1975, when once again they began to rise.

Following Callendar's selective techniques, monitoring methods changed with the establishment in 1958 of the world's first dedicated atmospheric monitoring laboratory on the Mauna Loa volcano in Hawaii. Under the direction of Charles David Keeling, Mauna Loa set the benchmark for all monitoring from then on, while the highly accurate chemical sampling methods used by nineteenth-century chemists like Walther Hempel and von Gilm were forgotten. Yet according to Ernst-Georg Beck, these earlier analytical methods 'usually achieved an accuracy rate better than 3 per cent' and 'modern climatologists have generally ignored the historic determinations of CO_2, despite the techniques being standard text book procedures in several different disciplines. Chemical methods were discredited as unreliable choosing only a few which fit the assumption of a climate – CO_2 connection.'[7] This mistake would lead to the biggest scientific fraud in history and culminate in the belief that CO_2 is a noxious gas inimical to life and has to be eradicated. It gave rise to the irrational idea that humankind's presence on earth is a scourge and that industrial progress, especially in the West, should be curtailed.

In 1956, two years before Keeling set up the Mauna Loa laboratory, the American physicist Gilbert Norman Plass made the first attempt at computer modelling the effects of a doubling of CO_2 on atmospheric temperature through its capacity to absorb infrared radiation. At best, this was a questionable undertaking because of the extremely limited and primitive nature of digital computers at the time. In order to cope with the multitude of unknown and complex variables associated with the performance of atmospheric gases at various altitudes, Plass was obliged to ignore all feedbacks and the effects of water vapour and clouds – some of the most important and significant influences on climate and far more potent as climate drivers than the CO_2 he was modelling.[8] Even today, with computer processing power and speeds many orders of magnitude greater than those Plass enjoyed, computer climate modelling, based on a doubling of atmospheric CO_2, is still highly unreliable. It cannot provide accurate climate forecasts even five years into the future, or even *retrospective data* of past climate and temperature when all the facts are known, without first being shaped, tweaked and adjusted in order to produce a match. But then once there, the models cannot be used to make any predictions about the future. It is inconceivable then that Plass could have achieved anything useful from modelling the absorption spectrum of CO_2 alone, and then extrapolating useful future climate information from the result.

However, Plass soon fell into the same trap that had misled Callendar a decade earlier. He confused *correlation* with *causation* by assuming that if atmospheric CO_2 appeared to increase at the same time as temperature, the two are necessarily linked, and that CO_2 is therefore the driving force. Plass believed Callendar's assertion that pre-industrial CO_2 was lower than the twentieth-century levels. He thus argued that 'if at the end of this century, the average temperature has continued to rise and in addition, measurement shows that the atmospheric carbon dioxide amount has also increased, *it will be firmly established* that carbon dioxide is a determining factor in causing climatic change'[9] (emphasis added). But nothing of the sort could be 'firmly established' on the grounds of a perceived correlation between atmospheric CO_2 and temperature trends. If such a correlation could so easily be interpreted as cause and effect, Plass might also have concluded that industrial CO_2 emissions were driving world population growth because both had been increasing since the Industrial Revolution, or indeed that increasing emissions since the turn of the century were responsible for the global decline in incidents of influenza over the same period. The correlation between all of these events is equally clear, but with the similar lack of *empirical* evidence irrefutably linking them as cause and effect they are just as open to arbitrary interpretation. Since there was no demonstrable link between industrial emissions of CO_2 and climate, Plass's conclusion may be regarded as specious.

Nevertheless it should have been apparent to Plass that increasing CO_2 could not be driving temperature up as the two were by then heading in opposite directions. If increasing CO_2 was really forcing global temperatures ever upward, how could this be? Plass though seemed undaunted. This may have been because he believed it had already been established by his own work, along with that of Callendar and others before him, that manmade CO_2 emissions were responsible for the observed overall increase in global temperatures since the end of the nineteenth century. Already this axiom was carved in stone.

The sharp decline in temperatures from 1940 was seen as an 'anomaly' that could be ignored on the grounds that the naturally driven decline was temporarily masking humankind's greater long-term influence, which would eventually be restored. Put simply, natural forces were merely superimposed on artificial forces. But this is a contradiction. If humankind's influence on the climate is generally greater and hence is the main driving force, how could it be overpowered by weaker natural forces, temporary or otherwise? According to Plass and his predecessors, the continued increase in CO_2 emissions should be *forcing* a corresponding increase in temperature. Ironically, this argument is a subtle yet unintended admission that natural forces are indeed easily capable of driving the earth's climate system without any help from humankind, whose influence clearly takes a back seat. But according to today's climate alarmists, this state of affairs occurs only when temperatures go in the 'wrong' direction; that is, downward and out of step with CO_2 emissions.

Plass therefore was wrong to conclude that continued industrial expansion into the foreseeable future would inevitably result in increasing global temperatures.[10]

At about the same time, ice cores taken from the Greenland and Antarctic ice sheets were being considered as proxies for determining CO_2 levels in the ancient and pre-industrial atmosphere. However, the results from ice core analyses carried out thirty years later were strongly influenced by the preconceptions shared by Callendar and Keeling that pre-industrial CO_2 was stable at around 290 ppm and consistently lower than twentieth-century levels which, according to Plass and Keeling, would continue to increase as a result of industrial expansion. Zbigniew Jaworowski, retired professor of atomic radiation at the Polish Academy of Sciences, has since pointed out that ice core analysis is vulnerable to misinterpretation due to a multitude of flawed assumptions. One of these is that CO_2 and other trace gases trapped within ancient ice remain stable for thousands of years, unaltered by deep ice pressure and the mechanical trauma and drastic pressure changes during the process of core extraction. Jaworowski writes:

> The basic assumption behind the CO_2 glaciology is a tacit view that air inclusions in ice are a closed system, which permanently preserves the original chemical and isotopic composition of gas, and thus that the inclusions are a suitable matrix for reliable reconstruction of the pre-industrial and ancient atmosphere.[11]

According to him, these assumptions fly in the face of evidence gained from other CO_2 studies, which suggests the opposite is the case.[12] Jaworowski further argued that extremely high sub-surface pressures result in artificially low CO_2 readings, with minimized variability and reduced maxima. Changes in the composition of gases trapped in ice over 200 metres in depth lead to a 'depletion of CO_2 in the gas trapped in the ice sheets',[13] which is why 'records of CO_2 concentration in the gas inclusions from deep polar ice show the values lower than in the contemporary atmosphere, even for the epochs when the global surface temperature was higher than now'.[14]

Current methods of gas analysis and core drilling techniques also alter the gases trapped within the ice due to infiltration of pollutants as a result of a combination of inward diffusion problems and pollution effects from the drilling process, especially as depth increases. Carbon dioxide concentrations detected in the ice cores, therefore, only *appear* to decrease and become more uniform and stable with age (depth), but are in fact unrelated to the pre-industrial atmospheric conditions at the time the gases were trapped. This problem was known about and identified by numerous researchers, but because it supported the AGW hypothesis as well as Callendar and Keeling's highly selective results, it was ignored. Indeed, it is still ignored today by the Intergovernmental Panel on Climate Change (IPCC). Even though the peaks and troughs in CO_2 levels are still evident from pre-industrial ice cores, they are substantially reduced, resulting in almost flat curves for ice cores 10,000 years old and older. This is why, explains Jaworowski, ice cores are an inappropriate matrix for determining absolute concentrations of pre-industrial atmospheric CO_2.[15] Ice cores are however still useful for determining patterns and trends in atmospheric CO_2 (a feature explored more in Chapter 3).

The low CO_2 readings obtained from these cores contradict other proxies for determining ancient CO_2, nearly all of which suggest that much *higher* values than today were common in the past, during periods of both high and low temperatures. But because ice core results suggest ancient levels were lower and stable, and support Callendar and Keeling, they are accepted by the IPCC as correct, and other proxies suggesting the opposite are ignored.[16]

The obsession with low atmospheric CO_2 before 1870 gave rise to a peculiar problem. In order to provide a continuous record of the earth's CO_2 history, it was necessary to meld the pre-industrial data from ice cores with the atmospheric data taken at the Mauna Loa laboratory. This in itself was a dubious, even illegitimate, process because it necessitated grafting one proxy series onto a completely unrelated one, while ignoring the many different assumptions and process adjustments inherent in both, a procedure that also gave rise to the infamous Hockey Stick graph (see Chapter 7). However, it turned out that analysis of the top few centimetres of ice deposited towards the end of the nineteenth century, and unaffected by high-pressure gradients, resulted in CO_2 values that were 'unacceptably high', at around 330 ppm. According to Keeling's reckoning and Callendar's hypothesis, these levels should not have occurred for at least another eighty-three years. This was an embarrassment to those who were defending the assertion that pre-industrial CO_2 never exceeded 290 ppm, attaining 328 ppm only in 1973. To get round the problem, it was arbitrarily decided that the ice taken at Siple, in Antarctica, was eighty-three years *older* than the CO_2 it entrapped, thus allowing the scientists to shift the age axis of the ice core data by that number of years and graft it seamlessly onto Keeling's atmospheric dataset taken on Mauna Loa.[17]

There was no other way to achieve the expected 'continuous CO_2 record' from 10,000 years ago to the present. However, as Jaworowski pointed out, 'this was not supported by any experimental evidence, but only by assumptions which were in conflict with the facts. The "corrected" proxy ice data [from Siple] were then smoothly aligned with the direct atmospheric measurements from Mauna Loa.'[18] The resultant graft is used as 'proof' of an anthropogenic source for increasing atmospheric CO_2 during the twentieth century because it *appears* to demonstrate that ancient CO_2 was much lower and remained more or less stable until the advent of the Industrial Revolution, when it appears to soar. Indeed, it has been used repeatedly in

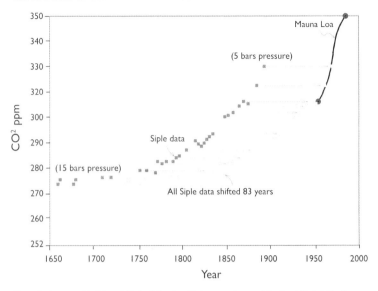

Figure 2. Ice core data taken at Siple, Antarctica (dark squares), are arbitrarily shifted eighty-three years to align with the Mauna Loa atmospheric data (solid black line), giving rise to an artificial 'continuous history' of CO_2 from pre-industrial times to the end of the twentieth century (black line plus light squares).[19]

numerous publications, including by the IPCC, without any justification.

This arbitrary shift in age might at first appear inconsequential in the scheme of things, but it is extremely significant when one considers the short period of warming attributed to humankind since the Industrial Revolution. Thus, in the years after Keeling set up his laboratory on Mauna Loa, the belief in low CO_2 levels before the Industrial Revolution has become a paradigm, largely because of Callendar's carefully selected data and Keeling's belief that his gas analysis techniques were superior to those of the previous century. Any data or empirical evidence that suggested otherwise were rejected – a fallacy that continues to be fostered by the IPCC.

Keeling's new measurements from 1958 onwards showed atmospheric CO_2 continuing on an upward trend. However, this was not in line with global temperatures, which were heading in the other direction. This should have alerted him at least to reconsider his sampling methods and those of the previous century. But, like Callendar, Keeling assumed that his techniques were superior to his predecessors' nineteenth-century technology.

This professional prejudice appears to have led Keeling to ignore two startling flaws in his own methodology. First, early CO_2 measurements of which he and Callendar were so dismissive were taken from around the globe in many diverse places, providing a far more reliable picture of global atmospheric CO_2 levels. Keeling, on the other hand, sampled from only one location and extrapolated his results to arrive at a global picture. Second, Keeling's observatory was located on an active volcano whose periodic massive CO_2 emissions would certainly have skewed his measurements. These would then have to be 'factored out' by some undefined and arbitrary means. Keeling's decision to site his observatory there is replicated in the practice of locating ground-based meteorology thermometers near airport runways and air-conditioning vents where measurements are biased by artificial heat sources. The results are then combined to provide 'evidence' of climate forcing by atmospheric CO_2. Following the formation of the National Oceanic and Atmospheric Administration (NOAA) in 1970, CO_2 monitoring sites were established in more than sixty sites around the world. However, measurements taken at Mauna Loa are generally considered the benchmark and are therefore normally quoted as the main authority for *global* CO_2 levels.

Ironically, it was during the thirty-year period of global cooling, from around 1940 to the mid-1970s, that scientists' attitudes to global climate completely reversed. Even though Callendar was viewed with respect by Keeling and others for his pioneering work a few years earlier, the assumption that CO_2 acted as a climate driver was temporarily marginalized. How could it be warming the climate when temperatures were falling?

Predictions were now being made of another approaching ice age, notwithstanding the gradual *rise* in CO_2.

During the first Earth Day in 1970, Kenneth E.F. Watt warned, 'The world has been chilling sharply for about twenty years. If present trends continue, the world will be about four degrees colder for the global mean temperature in 1990, but eleven degrees colder by the year 2000 . . . This is about twice what it would take to put us in an ice age.' Watt further warned that time was running out; he estimated there was about five years before it would be too late.[20]

In 1975, The US National Academy of Sciences (NAS) stated in its *National Research Council Report*, 'There is a finite possibility that a serious worldwide cooling could befall the Earth within the next 100 years.' NAS urged an immediate near-quadrupling of funds for research: 'We simply cannot afford to be unprepared for either a natural or manmade climatic catastrophe.'[21]

The clarion calls for global action and political awareness were becoming more extreme by the day as scientists became concerned and authors joined the new ice age bandwagon. In his 1976 book *The Cooling: Has the Next Ice Age Already Begun? Can We Survive It?*,[22] Lowell Ponte wrote, 'The NAS report was shocking' because it came 'from some of the world's most conservative scientists that an Ice Age beginning in the near future . . . was not impossible'. Ponte conjectured that the earth might be on the brink of a 10,000-year period of cooling and warned of the possibility of extreme weather events, an unstable climate and even nuclear war. 'The cooling is a fact,' he wrote, 'the cooling and all it represents is more than a threat of glaciers visiting our great-great-grandchildren. It threatens all of us right now.'[23]

The scientific community had already forgotten the work of Fourier, Tyndall and Arrhenius, and Callendar was shelved, because it was undeniable that CO_2 emissions and global temperatures were now heading in opposite directions. No scientist was promoting the greenhouse effect, at least not one based on CO_2, as all the evidence was against it. Temperatures continued to fall while the Mauna Loa observatory recorded increasing atmospheric CO_2.

According to Peter Gwynn writing in Newsweek magazine in 1975, there were 'ominous signs' that large and dramatic changes were taking place and that the evidence for the coming cold was accumulating so fast that meteorologists were finding it difficult to keep pace. There was no doubt in the minds of the meteorologists and climate scientists that the planet was sliding rapidly into an ice age and that it was imperative something was done to compensate and prepare for it. They were, however, 'pessimistic' that anything would be done in time.[24] Even the CIA in the early 1970s was concerned about the threat posed to the United States by global cooling.[25] The situation seemed serious, with no end in sight. The scientists were warning of the coming calamity, but the politicians weren't listening.

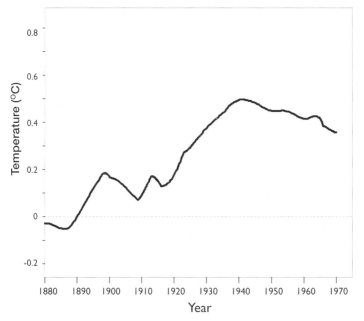

Figure 3. Global temperatures take a dive after 1940 and continue falling for the next thirty years, resulting in fears of an approaching ice age.

Some scientists who today are calling for urgent action to avert 'catastrophic global warming' due to CO_2 emissions were saying the very opposite in the 1960s and 1970s when CO_2 was still increasing. The late Stephen H. Schneider, one of the most prominent scientists of the twentieth century, was well known for his outbursts on global cooling in the 1960s and 1970s. 'A cooling trend has set in, perhaps one akin to the Little Ice Age,' he declared in 1965.[26] By 1989, he was wringing his hands over impending global warming linked to emissions of CO_2, methane and other gases: '[It] is a scientific phenomenon beyond doubt. It's only a question of how much warming there will be.'[27] Yet according to Fred Warshofsky in his book *Doomsday: The Science of Catastrophe*, Schneider was well aware ten years earlier that, 'after a certain increase in atmospheric carbon dioxide, temperature increases eventually level off' and that 'an eightfold increase in the carbon dioxide concentration – which he [Schneider] admits is unlikely – would raise temperatures less than two degrees',[28] thus *downplaying* its effect on temperature. In the space of ten years then, Schneider's view on the influence of CO_2 on temperature changed from 'negligible' to 'catastrophic'.

In an endorsement to Ponte's book *The Cooling*, Schneider had asserted that the earth was about to experience an ice age and that scientists and politicians needed to recognize the threat before it was too late: 'The dramatic importance of climate changes to the world's future has been dangerously underestimated by many.' Schneider put this down to the widespread belief that we have 'conquered nature' with technology, leaving us blind and unprepared for an ice age. Schneider worried 'that the climatic threat could be as awesome as any we might face, and that massive world-wide actions to hedge against that threat deserve immediate consideration'.[29] Then just fourteen years later, in a Channel 4 interview on global warming, he declared, 'The rate of change is so fast that I don't hesitate to call it potentially catastrophic for ecosystems'.[30] This *volte-face* is understandable given Schneider's view that 'Looking at every bump and wiggle . . . is a waste of time. I don't set very much store by looking at the direct evidence.'[31] '[I]t is journalistically irresponsible to present both sides [of the global warming debate] as though it were a question of balance.'[32]

In the end, in an interview for *Discover* magazine in 1989, Schneider reconciled the two extremes with some simple logic:

> we need to get some broad-based support, to capture the public's imagination. That, of course, entails getting loads of media coverage. So we have to offer up scary scenarios, make simplified, dramatic statements, and make little mention of any doubts we might have . . . Each of us has to decide what the right balance is between being effective and being honest.[33]

The British journalist and author Christopher Booker noted these contradictions. Writing in the *Daily Mail* he observed:

> And the cause of this [1970s] cooling, it was argued by the U.S. scientists, led by climatologists Stephen Schneider and James Hansen, was all the sulphur dioxide and other particulates being chucked out by burning fossil fuels – notably those from coal-fired power stations.
>
> Fifteen years later, the very same scientists were at the forefront of the great panic over global warming.
>
> Schneider, who became Professor of Environmental Biology and Global Change at Stanford University, argued this time that the damage was being done not by soot and sulphur preventing the sun's heat reaching the earth, but by carbon dioxide and other 'greenhouse gases', which were trapping heat.
>
> It was scientists such as Schneider and Hansen who, at the end of the 1980s, so terrified the politicians with their assertion that CO_2 equalled global warming that, within a few years, the world's leaders were gathering in vast conferences in Rio and Kyoto to sign treaties that committed us to massive cuts in the CO_2 emissions on which the global economy depended.[34]

Schneider and Hansen are by no means unique in this regard. Barak Obama's chief science and technology adviser, John P. Holdren, today warns of impending disaster by manmade global warming. Yet in his book, co-authored with Paul Ehrlich, *Global Ecology: Readings Toward a Rational Strategy for Man*, written in 1971,[35] Holdren held the opposite view and claimed 'a new ice age' was imminent, also as a result of human activity, because of the cooling effects of pollution, yet in 2009 he not only suggested that human activity was likely to cause catastrophic global warming, but that it could also save us from such perils by purposely injecting pollutants into the upper atmosphere to block the sun.[36] 'It's got to be looked at,' says Holdren, who was allegedly concerned that 'the United States and other nations won't slow global warming fast enough and that several "tipping points" could be fast approaching'.[37] *Several* tipping points? Wouldn't one be enough?

In any case, these views are clearly contradictory. Holdren might have recalled his earlier assertions that humankind's pollution could freeze the planet unless something was done to control industrial activity, which seems to be the crux of his reasoning. Yet here he was thirty years later blaming industrial activity, particularly the burning of fossil fuels, for having precisely the opposite effect, the only difference being aerosols and particulate pollution from burning fossil fuels on one hand and CO_2 emissions on the other. In both cases, Holdren held humankind's industrial activities responsible for either an ice age or for catastrophic global warming. Surely one would cancel out the other? It is easy to be cynical here and draw the conclusion that, provided the public are in a constant state of alarm, it is immaterial whether the climate is warming or cooling, or indeed what the cause might be, because the essential issue is sustaining this all-pervading need to be saved from whatever menace threatens our existence. The American writer and political commentator Henry Louis Mencken remarked on this in 1918 when he said, 'The whole aim of practical politics is to keep the populace alarmed – and hence clamorous to be led to safety – by menacing it with an endless series of hobgoblins, all of them imaginary.'

There was of course nothing new in these reversals of climate alarm. As early as 1895, *The New York Times* was warning of an approaching ice age as a result of which Canada would be 'wiped out' and that 'billions would die' due to widespread crop failures. *The Times* on 24 February 1895 reported, 'Geologists Think the World May be Frozen up Again' and in 1912 the *L.A. Times* reported, 'The fifth Ice Age is on the way'.

By 1922, however, the opposite was being reported. On 10 October, George Nicolas Ifft, the US consul to Norway, was concerned that the Arctic was warming and losing its ice. He submitted a report to the State Department advising that 'Reports from fishermen, seal hunters, and explorers who sail the seas about Spitzbergen and the eastern Arctic, all point to a radical change in climatic conditions, and hitherto unheard-of high temperatures in that part of the earth's surface . . . In fact, so little ice has never before been noted. The expedition all but established a record, sailing as far north as 81°29' [81 degrees 29 minutes] in ice-free water.' Where vast quantities of ice once were found, only moraines and bare earth remained. Ifft added that a certain Captain Ingebrigtsen, after sailing into the area, 'pointed out that formerly the waters about Spitzbergen held an even summer temperature of about 3° Celsius; this year recorded temperatures up to 15°, and last winter the ocean did not freeze over even on the north coast of Spitzbergen' because of increasing temperatures.[38]

A *Washington Post* article on 2 November 1922 reported further on Ifft's story, 'The Arctic Ocean is warming up, icebergs are growing scarcer and in some places the seals are finding the water too hot . . . Within a few years it is predicted that due to the ice melt the sea will rise and make most coastal cities uninhabitable.' But the *Chicago Tribune* was behind the times and announced the following year: 'Scientists say Arctic ice will wipe out Canada all the way down to the Great Lakes.' A year later, the *New York Times* also warned of 'Signs of a New Ice Age'.[39] Throughout the 1920s, stories of a new ice age continued, helped along by wide public interest in the adventures of the Arctic explorer Donald MacMillan who also reported 'Signs of a New Ice Age'.

It seemed no one could make up their minds, least of all the scientists for by 1929 the warnings had reversed yet again. The *L.A. Times* declared, 'Geologists believe the world is growing warmer and will keep getting warmer.' Clearly responding to the new warm phase which brought about the hottest period of the twentieth century, known as the 'Dust Bowl Era' in the United States, most newspapers were trumpeting a new global warming period. In 1932, the Associated Press reported, 'The earth is growing steadily warmer' and the following year the *New York Times* reported, 'The longest warm spell since 1776'.

Then, after the next cooling spell between 1940 and 1975, global temperatures began trending upward yet again, back in step with atmospheric CO_2. Carbon dioxide was back in fashion and the previous thirty years of steadily declining temperatures and all the warnings of an impending ice age made during the 1920s and 1970s were quietly forgotten. *TIME* magazine warned of an imminent ice age on 24 December 1979, but in its 9 April 2001 edition was announcing the opposite climate doom[40] – a warning it repeated on 3 April 2006, 'The climate is crashing, and global warming is to blame.' Global warming yesterday, ice age today, global warming tomorrow. This is not unusual in the scientific community as each generation has its own fads – theories embraced as unassailable truths are overthrown by a heretic who tomorrow will be considered a genius. As Albert Einstein observed in his discussions with Immanuel Velikovsky, 'Generations of scholars have a "bad memory". Scientists generally have little historical sense, so that each single generation knows little of the struggles and inner difficulties of the former generation.' They forget last year's craze the moment the wind changes direction and ushers in a new one.

As the planet emerged from the 1940–75 cool phase, the scientific establishment refocused its attention on the possible link between CO_2 emissions and temperature. The 'Callendar effect' was dusted off and embedded into mainstream science as a seriously advanced idea. Now, thanks to Keeling, his reputation as the father of the modern greenhouse theory was finally established and his data on pre-industrial CO_2 concentrations were accepted without critical analysis.

Keeling's conclusions from the Mauna Loa data were thus poisoned by the same assumptions Callendar made: that atmospheric CO_2 before the Industrial Revolution was necessarily stable and hovered around 290 ppm, and that CO_2 was a significant climate driver. Both assumptions are incorrect; the former was proved wrong by Ernst-Georg Beck in 2007[41] and the latter has been discredited by many scientists and climatologists, as we shall see. According to Beck, 'during the late 20th century, the hypothesis that the ongoing rise of CO_2 concentration in the atmosphere is a result of fossil fuel burning became the dominant paradigm. To establish this paradigm, and increasingly since then, historical measurements indicating fluctuating CO_2 levels between 300 ppm and 400+ ppm have been neglected.'[42] Beck compared 90,000 accurate chemical analyses of CO_2 levels in the air recorded between 1812 and 1961 which show a different trend from the literature published by the IPCC.

Fringe scientists who had clung to the greenhouse theory during the 1970s' cooling period were back in favour. The Swedish scientist Bert Bollin, who had been derided as a crank for suggesting we could avert an ice age disaster and increase temperatures by burning fossil fuels, was now respected, even admired, for his insight. In the 1970s, Bollin must have read about Walter Nernst's hare-brained scheme to set fire to coal seams in order to increase the temperature, since here he was a hero for coming up with the same idea. But the resuscitated greenhouse theory also received a potent new symbol, a bright emblem from an unexpected source: planet Venus.

2. Sagan's Problem Planet

> In questions of science, the authority of a thousand is not worth the humble reasoning of a single individual.
>
> *Galileo Galilei*

> It is dangerous to be right in matters on which the established authorities are wrong.
>
> *Voltaire*

> All truth passes through three stages. First, it is ridiculed. Second, it is violently opposed. Third, it is accepted as being self-evident.
>
> *Arthur Schopenhauer*

Behind the scenes, a venomous controversy was unfolding which helped rekindle serious scientific and public interest in Callendar's previously overlooked greenhouse theory, just as temperatures were bottoming out and beginning to rise again.

The trouble started with a scandalous book. Written in 1950 Immanuel Velikovsky's *Worlds in Collision* unleashed one of the most noxious and shameful episodes in science history – one that still has repercussions today. In the 1950s, Velikovsky shook the foundations of modern astronomy by theorizing that Venus was a relative newcomer to the solar system and that its surface temperature, atmospheric pressure and density would be extremely high due to its recent past. He calculated these conditions at a time when it was supposed they would be similar to those on earth – a balmy, tropical climate. His ideas were anathema to the scientific establishment at the time and would have been dismissed as the ravings of a lunatic had he not been so thorough in his research and compelling in his arguments. Velikovsky was clearly not a typical charlatan peddling a half-baked idea. As one commentator put it, his theory 'was not run-of-the-mill heresy, but a thesis that presented a genuine threat to the very ego of science'.[1] Later measurements taken by the US space programme in the early 1960s and 1970s proved Velikovsky correct, reporting temperatures on Venus in excess of 400°C and atmospheric pressures some ninety times those on earth. Ben Bova wrote of these findings, 'The first radio measurements of Venus's surface temperature startled astronomers so much that they refused to believe them.'[2] Venus suddenly became a problem – and so did Velikovsky for pointing it out.

Because of these successes, however, Velikovsky was gaining a reputation and developing a cult following among university students who saw him as a refreshing maverick, an unconventional fox among the conformist chickens, but he was perceived as a threat by his more orthodox colleagues. Velikovsky and his outrageous theories had to be swept under the scientific rug as quickly as possible. So, hasty efforts were set in motion to explain away the anomaly of Venus, while at the same time undermining Velikovsky, whose argument that the accepted theories on the origin of the solar system were wrong was an abomination. His book was blacklisted despite becoming an immediate bestseller and the textbook division of his US publisher, Macmillan, boycotted by the astronomical fraternity. Michigan astronomer Dean B. McLaughlin demanded in a letter that Macmillan must not only cease publishing Velikovsky's book, but that they publicly recant and admit having made a grave error. Macmillan was subsequently forced to relinquish the publishing rights to a rival publisher, Doubleday, who were immune to such boycotts, despite threats by astronomer Fred Whipple to withdraw his support from them too if they took the book on. Doubleday ignored him and published it anyway, seeing the obvious benefits in taking on a bestseller. The handover to Doubleday had no effect on the fury, which continued unabated.

A month before Velikovsky's book was published, Gordon A. Atwater, curator of the Hayden Planetarium, New York, planned to write a favourable preview of *Worlds in Collision* for *This Week* magazine, sparking a violent reaction from his fellow astronomers. Harlow Shapley, the influential Director of the Harvard College Observatory, was so outraged that he insisted the piece be withdrawn prior to publication, as did other astronomers in aggressive letters to Atwater. Shapley then organized a campaign to have Atwater fired for not only supporting Velikovsky, but for his recommendation to Macmillan that they publish *Worlds in Collision*. Shapley got his way, despite Atwater's article appearing the day before *Worlds in Collision* hit the shelves. Atwater was later 'blacklisted' and, for the rest of his career, blocked from finding work in science education for having supported Velikovsky. He later confessed to Velikovsky that he had been mistaken in his view of establishment scientists, thinking them open-minded in their search for truth, but discovering instead that they would grind anyone among them into the dust who questioned the fundamentals.[3]

Atwater knew full well that Velikovsky's work would threaten received wisdom on the origin of the solar system, and in particular Venus, and would result in a scientific backlash. But Atwater pressed ahead because he foresaw the huge public interest it would generate, especially for the Hayden Planetarium for which he even planned to hold a *Worlds in Collision* sky show. Previous shows were so successful they had saved the planetarium from bankruptcy,[4] so he saw no reason why his proposed *Worlds in Collision* show would be any less popular. In the journal *Pensée*, the New York writer Clark Whelton wrote of the affair:

Atwater agreed to supply a quote to Macmillan: 'If Dr Velikovsky is right, the underpinnings of modern science will have to be re-examined'. It was a modest statement, given the revolutionary nature of Velikovsky's book, but Atwater's words provoked an instant furore. Harlow Shapley sprang into action, writing menacing letters to Macmillan, hinting at the boycott of its textbook division, which became a reality several months later. Atwater was at the focal point of a growing hysteria, as friends and colleagues tried to persuade him to recant and join the crusade against *Worlds in Collision*. Atwater refused to back down. But when it became known that he planned to review *Worlds in Collision* for *This Week*, all hell broke loose. 'There was sheer terror and panic at Hayden,' Atwater recalls. 'A member of the staff even walked into my office and spat in my face'. Atwater also knew that the written promise to him from Macmillan, pledging to publish *Worlds in Collision*, was impeding Shapley's campaign to have the book quashed.[5]

Then Shapley's colleague Cecilia Payne-Gaposchkin joined the campaign against Velikovsky by deliberately misquoting him in the popular press in order to make his ideas seem ridiculous. Using a review of *Worlds in Collision* by Eric Larrabee and published in *Harper's Magazine*, she strung phrases together from sentences on different pages of the review and set them in quotation marks as though citing Velikovsky. She then presented them as 'Dr Velikovsky's astronomical assertions'.[6] This stratagem of fabricating quotes and then attacking them as absurd was frequently used by Velikovsky's detractors in order to discredit him. Yet neither Shapley nor Payne-Gaposchkin had seen Velikovsky's book. Neither had they considered or checked any of the evidence amassed in its pages. Their criticisms were based entirely on a paraphrased review written by someone else in a periodical. According to McLaughlin, *Worlds in Collision* was 'nothing but lies'.

Astonishingly, McLaughlin then boasted he would never read it.[7] One newspaper even suggested the book was a propaganda ploy by the Russians, while others across the country were sent abusive letters denouncing Velikovsky.[8] When Velikovsky protested about the distortions and deliberate fudging of astronomical data to bring it into line with what was expected by orthodox science, it was claimed they were no more than misprints and therefore of no consequence.[9]

When Victor A. Bailey, professor of physics at Sydney University, published astronomical data in 1960 which inadvertently supported Velikovsky, he was approached by Donald H. Menzel of Harvard, who argued he had made a mistake and that Bailey's theory was therefore wrong. Menzel then asked him to withdraw his findings which were not helping the campaign against Velikovsky. Bailey was incensed and pointed out that it was Menzel's calculations that were incorrect, not his, thus obliging Menzel to publish a correction to his own data. This he did, while neglecting to acknowledge Velikovsky.[10] Menzel then claimed that since Velikovsky's ideas were not generally accepted, 'any seeming verification of Velikovsky's predictions is pure chance'.[11] And so it went on.

In his book *Doomsday: The Science of Catastrophe* Warshofsky wrote, 'It remained for the scientific community to launch the most vicious and unreasoning attack on both the ideas and the author of *Worlds in Collision*.'[12] Moses Hadas, professor of Greek at Columbia University, wrote, 'what bothered me was the violence of the attack [on Velikovsky]. One after another the reviews misquoted him and then attacked the misquotation.'[13]

The orthodox scientific community panicked right from the start and went into damage control because of increasing public and media interest in the controversy. According to the political scientist Alfred de Grazia, 'Efforts were made to block dissemination of Dr Velikovsky's ideas, and even to punish supporters of his investigations. Universities, scientific societies, publishing houses, the popular press were approached and threatened; social pressures and professional sanctions were invoked to control public opinion.'[14]

Analysing the hostility in his later book *Stargazers and Gravediggers*, Velikovsky wrote,

> The great displeasure with my forthcoming book, not yet read or seen, was the natural consequence of my being unorthodox. Anybody who resolutely steps off the beaten track and walks uncharted trails trespassing the fields owned by congregations of specialists, must be disciplined; his ideas must be invalidated before their scent poisons the good thinking and the loyal behaviour of the rest of the camp.[15]

Macmillan's senior editor, James Putnam, who drew up the original contract with Velikovsky on Atwater's recommendation, was sacked as a gesture to the establishment, while the unsold copies of *Worlds in Collision* were destroyed. Scientists, journalists and publishers were threatened with dismissal or boycotts if they associated with Velikovsky or supported him and his ideas in any way. Einstein, appalled at the hostility, which began almost immediately following the publication of *Worlds in Collision*, wrote to Velikovsky, 'It may be difficult finding a sensible publisher who would take the risk of such a heavy fiasco upon himself' and, referring to the vicious attacks by Shapley who was responsible for organizing the boycott of Macmillan without even reading *Worlds in Collision*, 'this is the intolerance and arrogance together with brutality which one often finds in successful people'. In reply Velikovsky wrote, 'Shapley, in a relentless effort, made me "out of bounds" for scientists.'[16]

Things were getting out of control and all because the conventional wisdom on the origin of the planets was being questioned by an iconoclast who could not be dismissed as a crank. Warshofsky summarized the tumult, that Velikovsky weathered:

storms of unbelievable fury and savagery as the entire
scientific community has mounted assault upon attack,
ridicule upon scorn and vituperation to discredit his
theories. For Velikovsky was attacking the very rules by
which such towering figures as Galileo, Copernicus,
Newton and Einstein had said our solar system was
governed.[17]

Yet Velikovsky proved himself more than a match for his critics in
public debates. But this merely added insult to injury for he was at
the same time threatening so much that had been taught in schools
and universities and had been accepted without question ever since
Galileo committed the same offence against the Church. The
orthodox understanding of the universe was carved in stone, but it
was being vandalized by an obscure polymath from the Russian
outback.

Then CO_2 came to the rescue.

In 1960, Velikovsky's ideas came under attack from the science
populist Carl Sagan who revived Callendar's almost forgotten
greenhouse theory to explain the extremely high surface
temperature on Venus. By this time, the vendetta against Velikovsky
had been running for at least ten years. And, like Payne-Gaposchkin
before him, Sagan went to extraordinary lengths to discredit him.
He managed to restore the public image of the scientific
establishment and repair the damage caused by Velikovsky's attack
on orthodox thinking, but the balm he applied merely covered over
the cracks, for the problem of Venus's high surface temperature still
remained. The Velikovsky controversy rumbled on for the next
twenty-five years, with Sagan dominating the scientific campaign
against him throughout the 1960s and 1970s.

Although Sagan is generally credited with establishing the
'enhanced greenhouse effect' hypothesis for Venus as early as 1960,

he actually borrowed the idea.[18] In an interview with Joseph Goodavage in 1976, Sagan admitted, 'Rupert Wildt wrote a paper in 1940 which proposed that the carbon dioxide content of the Venus atmosphere [detected spectroscopically in the 1930s] would produce a greenhouse effect which would make it much hotter than people had thought', which pre-dated Velikovsky by ten years and well before Venus's surface temperature was known. There was, of course, no empirical evidence at the time that a greenhouse effect existed, so Wildt suggested an upper limit of around 275°F (135°C) – a figure based entirely on his own calculations.[19]

However, according to Juergens, 'even this moderately high estimate was not accepted by Wildt's colleagues. Gerard Kuiper later refined the calculations and came up with 170°F [77°C] as the maximum temperature likely to be due to a greenhouse effect on Venus'.[20] Everyone was guessing. Wildt had no idea what the actual surface temperature was and, since he had nothing else to go on, his calculations were necessarily based on the theoretical work of Arrhenius, Tyndall and others who understood, and even emphasized, the limited warming effect of CO_2 on its own. Wildt's interest in a possible greenhouse effect was sparked by the discovery of CO_2 in the upper cloud tops. It was a radical suggestion. A 'Venusian greenhouse' was, in effect, Wildt's assumption, which was adopted by Sagan two decades later as a counter to Velikovsky. However, the theory immediately became popular and was taken further by S. Ichtiaque Rasool and Catheryn de Bergh in 1970[21] who postulated a 'runaway greenhouse' – a thermal runaway of the atmosphere – after it became known temperatures were extreme. The idea has since become the dominant paradigm, giving rise to 'runaway climate change' as today's *cause célèbre*.

Like Shapley and Payne-Gaposchkin then, it is easy to suspect that Sagan had an ulterior motive and that his intention was to undermine and refute Velikovsky who had become a thorn in the establishment's side. Velikovsky argued that the high surface temperature on Venus was due to its extreme youth and internal core heat, rather than to solar radiation alone, as expected in a 'uniformitarian' universe. But establishment science was in a bind. Nothing in the orthodox model could explain Venus, while Velikovsky's idea was heresy because the solar system was supposedly an ordered place of unimpeachable predictability. There could be no exceptions. According to this view, we live in a solar system of perfect order and it was this that Sagan and his orthodox colleagues were striving to protect. Ironically, this naïve concept harked back to the days when it was an article of faith that the earth was somehow special, at the centre of the universe, while any theory repudiating this view was treated as heresy. Isaac Asimov, referring to Velikovsky, asked Sagan 'What does one do with a heretic?'[22]

The problem was that astronomy, the queen of the sciences, was invested with theories considered to be sacrosanct, and here was an interloper revealing them to be spurious. The fact that his predictions were being verified one by one and his ideas quietly adopted by other scientists did not mitigate the fury.

However, the extreme surface temperature of Venus was only part of the problem. The massive density of Venus's atmosphere was also highly problematic because, according to accepted wisdom, it was thought to be little different from earth's. It was generally assumed that the two planets were formed at the same time from the same material and in approximately the same area of the solar system, an uninterrupted process lasting billions of years from which it was supposed all the planets were formed. Why then would Venus be different? Yet Venus is different, it even appears to exhibit a gravitational lock with the earth instead of the sun, turning the same face towards the earth at every inferior conjunction, suggesting the two planets had interacted in the past.[23] But these discoveries only supported Velikovsky's explanation, while confounding accepted wisdom on its nature and origins. Orthodox explanations were necessarily ad hoc so it was similarly assumed by Sagan and others that some form of 'greenhouse effect', as defined by Callendar, must be operating. There was no other explanation, once Velikovsky's hypothesis was excluded.

Despite uncertainty over the actual composition of Venus's atmosphere, Sagan seized on CO_2[24] while also insisting that the clouds of Venus are 'made of water', and that 'ice crystals [exist] in the colder cloud tops' with 'water droplets in the bottom of the clouds',[25] which extend almost to the surface of the planet. This assumption contradicted all spectroscopic measurements of the planet's atmosphere in the search for water in any quantity. None was found. To prove this, Velikovsky compiled a list of spectroscopic analyses carried out by astronomers looking for water vapour in the Venusian atmosphere, all of which proved negative.[26] Yet Sagan was not deterred and continued to defend his hypothesis for water vapour in quantity in the Venusian atmosphere. It was vital if his greenhouse effect was to work.[27]

The astronomer James Pollack pointed out that Sagan's 'enhanced greenhouse effect' on Venus requires at least 0.1 per cent water vapour, in addition to 96 per cent CO_2, in the atmosphere.[28] However, as Charles Ginenthal pointed out, 'There is practically no water on Venus. This is based on careful spectroscopic analysis of the clouds. Therefore, it is interesting to note that Sagan had just the opposite view based on his own brand of spectroscopic analysis.'[29]

Indeed, nothing has changed in this regard for forty years. According to a statement issued by the European Space Agency in 2010, 'Venus has very little water. Were the contents of earth's oceans to be spread evenly across the world, they would create a layer 3 km deep. If you were to condense the amount of water vapour in Venus' atmosphere [the only possible reservoir for it] onto its surface, it would create a global puddle just 3 cm deep.'[30] This is obviously insufficient to sustain a CO_2-based greenhouse.

In spite of the Russian and American Venus missions of the 1960s, 1970s and 1980s, the actual composition of Venus's atmosphere and clouds remains uncertain. In *Carl Sagan and Immanuel Velikovsky* Ginenthal writes, 'Does anyone know for certain the exact composition of the Venusian clouds? The answer is that no one really does know', yet Sagan 'was certain based on spectroscopic analysis that the clouds were made of water', while later insisting they were composed of sulphuric acid.[31] According to Ginenthal, the originator of the sulphuric acid theory, Andrew T. Young, contradicts Sagan by warning that 'a sound understanding of [the Venusian] clouds appears to be several years in the future'. Young further suggests,

> None of the currently popular interpretations of cloud phenomenon on Venus is consistent with all the data. Either a considerable fraction of the observational evidence is faulty or has been misinterpreted, or the clouds of Venus are much more complex than the current simplistic models.[32]

Of course, the discovery of CO_2 in the cloud tops, in addition to many other compounds, meant that Callendar's – and later Wildt's – greenhouse theory could be invoked. However, the penalty as far as Venus's age was concerned was that this idea inadvertently supported Velikovsky's theory of a very young planet, while repudiating Sagan's orthodox view that Venus was necessarily billions of years old. Sagan may not have known that Ulf von Zahn[33] had already pointed out that CO_2 would, in any case, very quickly dissociate into carbon monoxide and oxygen due to photo-dissociation by the sun and that CO_2 would then 'disappear from the upper atmosphere within a few weeks and from the entire middle atmosphere in a few thousand years'.[34] This suggests that Venus is a relative newcomer to the solar system since its atmosphere was still in its primordial state. Nevertheless, the Mariner II findings also confirmed Velikovsky's prior claim that the fifteen-mile-thick atmosphere would also be rich in hydrocarbons. So at the time, its composition was anything but certain. Sagan's suggestion that the CO_2 and the *assumed* presence of water vapour in Venus's thick atmosphere created an 'enhanced greenhouse effect' was desperate and specious, and completely backfired. His hastily conceived solution to the heat problem was also intended as a defence of the classic view that Venus was as old as the earth, while repudiating Velikovsky's claim that it was extremely young. It did precisely the opposite.

Despite these problems, Sagan's explanation gained enthusiastic support among the popular press thanks to his high media profile, while Velikovsky's hypothesis was relegated to the realms of science fiction and consequently ridiculed – an astonishing outcome considering Velikovsky's more consistent reasoning.

It did not take long for Sagan's quick-fix application of the enhanced greenhouse effect on Venus to be shown to be unworkable on other grounds. The planetary scientist Clark R. Chapman pointed out that simple atmospheric convection would prevent extremes of temperature at the surface of a planet heated only by the sun and would therefore act as a natural moderator. 'It was recently pointed out to embarrassed meteorologists . . . that this effect may not even be important for greenhouses' because, Chapman explains, the 'ground warmed by the sun heats adjacent air, which then floats upward to where the barometric pressure is less. The air parcel expands, cools and settles into equilibrium. Meanwhile at the ground the warmed air is replaced by cooler parcels from above.' The cycle continues while the air below is warmed by the surface. Chapman describes how this process of natural convection prevents 'air near the ground from getting too hot' and that the reason air inside a greenhouse is hotter than that outside is that it cannot mix with the outside air and thus succumb to the convection effect due to the glass roof. 'There is no lid on Venus and the dense carbon dioxide is free to convect,' he concludes.[35] Clearly, atmospheric CO_2 cannot be the cause of Venus's extreme heat.

These simple conclusions never occurred to Callendar when he was promoting his planetary hothouse model, and it certainly didn't deter Sagan. But worse was to come for Sagan because something very peculiar was happening on Venus that threatened his greenhouse theory even further, while at the same time supporting Velikovsky. The Mariner and Pioneer space probes discovered Venus's night side to be slightly warmer than its day side, its poles to be warmer than its equator and that it radiates up to 20 per cent more energy than it receives from the sun, which is incompatible with any greenhouse effect. In addition, Venus was found to have retrograde rotation, an entirely unexpected discovery that further supported Velikovsky who predicted its rotation would indeed be anomalous. Venus is a very strange place indeed, so strange that the source of its high surface temperature, and its other anomalous features, must be found elsewhere for classical theories could not provide a workable solution that explained them all together.

The British astronomer V.A. Firsoff, while no supporter of Velikovsky, ridiculed Sagan's greenhouse model[36] by arguing in *Astronomy and Space* that 'Increasing the mass of the atmosphere may intensify the greenhouse effect, but it must also reduce the proportion of solar energy reaching the surface.'[37] The total energy Venus received from the sun was obviously insufficient to heat the planet to the temperatures now known to exist there.[38] This is due to the planet's high albedo, which means that its reflective cloud cover results in 65 per cent of the sunlight it receives being reflected back into space.[39]

This view was reiterated by Juergens who wrote in the journal KRONOS:

If the surface of Venus has a temperature of 900°F, the only physically sound explanation is that an *outflow* of internal heat is taking place at a rate sufficient to maintain that temperature. It is quite likely that the dense atmosphere and clouds serve to inhibit the escape of heat from the surface. But in any case ground temperatures below the surface must be in excess of 900°F to provide a temperature gradient along which internal heat flows *outward* [emphasis added] . . .

> From any reasonable analysis of the available evidence, we appear to be left with Velikovsky's as the only viable explanation yet put forward: Venus is not billions of years old; it is apparently so young that it has not yet cooled enough for 'comfortable' surface temperatures to become established, and therefore solar-energy input has little or no influence upon its surface environment.[40]

Clearly, Venus's extreme heat is not the product of a greenhouse effect, enhanced or otherwise.

Fred W. Taylor of the Clarendon Laboratory, Oxford, theorized that Venus's heat was so extreme it must be coming from within the planet itself and not from the sun. This endorsed Velikovsky and refuted Sagan. *New Scientist* magazine ran an article describing Taylor's extensive observations which showed that Venus must be 'producing almost 10,000 times more heat than the earth'[41] which, like all the planets, produces heat from the radioactive decay of elements within its rocks. However, the article continued, it was 'inconceivable according to present theories of planetary formation, that Venus should have thousands of times more of the radioactive elements than earth does'.[42] There was no explanation from orthodox science for such a situation if both planets had been formed at the same time. According to *New Scientist*, Taylor himself could not explain his results. He first thought that the discrepancy was due to experimental error, perhaps a mistake or technical hitch, but even after 'more precise measurements' were taken 'it refused to go away'.[43] He suggested more measurements were needed 'before astronomers accept the result, and most planetary scientists are obviously expecting – and hoping – that the embarrassing extra heat will disappear on further investigation'.[44] They were to be disappointed. However, Taylor's theories on the source of Venus's heat 'met with scepticism – not to say outright disbelief – from other planetary scientists', who insisted that Venus's heat came from *outside* the planet, as on earth, because accepted theories on the origin of the solar system would not allow for any alternatives.[45]

Taylor, of course, would have been familiar with Velikovsky's controversial theories of only a few years earlier, which the scientific community was hoping could be dealt with by Sagan's enhanced greenhouse model, if only superficially. But as we have seen, supporting Velikovsky was a career-limiting move for scientists, academics and even students. However, Taylor's view that Venus must generate its own heat came uncomfortably close, so his ideas were also brushed aside as incompatible with 'accepted wisdom'.

According to Holden,

> Carl Sagan and Immanuel Velikovsky are the only two authors of theories which attempt to explain the intense surface heat of Venus. Velikovsky claims that Venus is simply a new planet, which has not had time to cool; a wealth of historical evidence supports him. Sagan claims that the < 2 per cent of solar energy which somehow finds its way through the thick CO_2 clouds of Venus to the surface is forever trapped there and cannot re-radiate as infra-red flux and thus escape. This he claims causes the intense heat; he even manages to keep a straight face.[46]

But things were going from bad to worse for Sagan's greenhouse. The problems with Venus's heat were so large the scientists involved with the Mariner and Pioneer programmes resorted to 'correcting' their instruments to deal with the unexpected temperature readings. They were simply unacceptable.

Every one of the American and Soviet Venus probes discovered temperature anomalies that contradicted both conventional wisdom and the floundering greenhouse hypothesis. They found that temperatures increased rapidly as they descended through the atmosphere and that the infrared flux was far greater from below than from above, the Soviet Venera Landers putting the difference at forty times higher.[47] By now it was clear to everyone, including Sagan, that a CO_2-fuelled greenhouse was incapable of causing such extreme thermal conditions. They were in a bind: Sagan's greenhouse model was untenable and Velikovsky's was unacceptable. So the problem was ascribed to 'instrument error'.[48] The Soviet Venera-13 Lander survived for only 117 minutes before being destroyed by the extreme heat and pressure at the surface, the very conditions predicted by Velikovsky.

But it was too late. No one was troubled by the anomalies because the idea of a planetary 'greenhouse' was so convenient and popular it stuck fast and would be used again in the near future. The theory *appeared* to deal with Velikovsky and it appealed to the wider public whose insatiable appetite for catastrophes required a new peril to replace the defunct ice age scare of the 1970s. Scientists were already beginning to issue dire warnings of climate doom due to industrial CO_2 emissions, using Venus as a vivid example of what might happen on earth if CO_2 increased unchecked. Where would it end?

Whether Velikovsky's theories on the origin of Venus are right or wrong is almost immaterial here. The point is that the greenhouse theory is hopelessly inadequate to explain the Venus heat problem, while the scientific community went into overdrive to shut Velikovsky down because he represented a serious threat to accepted wisdom with a wide-ranging and consistent hypothesis. Yet he could not be ignored. 'There is scarcely one of Velikovsky's central ideas . . . which has not since been propounded in all seriousness by a scientist of repute,' wrote Eric Larabee in *Harper's*.[49] Like many such 'heretics' Velikovsky ran headlong into professional hubris, entrenched ignorance and academic intransigence only to find that the boundary between science and dogma is not always clear. Such an offence generates the most hostile and irrational of reactions from the establishment whose institutionalized scientists have reputations and careers to protect as an industry builds up around the paradigms they themselves have created. Velikovsky was advised by a supporter and admirer to prepare for a siege from entrenched scientific bigots that would last ten years. It continued for nearly thirty. According to John J.

O'Neill who wrote one of the early reviews of *Worlds in Collision*, it was Shapley who started the 'campaign of ridicule and suppression against the book as nasty as anything that has befouled American science and scholarship' which began even before Shapley had seen the book.[50]

According to de Grazia, the suppression of Velikovsky's ideas included the 'techniques of denying and avoiding public discussion, of refusing access to scientific publications – via articles or letters of reply, or even advertising'.[51] To which can be added manipulation and distortion of scientific data and deliberate misquotations in order to give a completely warped idea of the scientific case. We witness these same ploys and scientific fraud today as so-called climate change 'deniers' are treated in the same way by establishment figures.

Despite his efforts, Sagan's Venus greenhouse theory failed to deal with all the inconsistencies. It was riddled with problems that still haven't gone away. But provided it gave the *appearance* of an explanation, everyone was content to leave it at that. Sagan's hypothesis was a cosmic gap-filler designed more to discredit Velikovsky than to deal seriously with the vexing Venus problem. By now, of course, Sagan had become something of a demi-god in popular scientific circles despite being repeatedly outclassed by Velikovsky in public debates. After the 1974 AAAS (American Association for the Advancement of Science) Symposium, NASA scientist Robert Jastrow wrote, 'Dr. Velikovsky had his day when he spotted a major scientific boner in Professor Sagan's argument.' Jastrow concluded that 'Here, Velikovsky was the better astronomer'. Yet Sagan was a media darling who could utter no wrong, so his solution to Venus's heat problem became the dominant paradigm for the next three decades and will no doubt remain carved in the granite of scientific dogma for decades to come until another 'heretic' like Velikovsky attempts to deal with the issues. Yet Velikovsky's opponents were well aware of the inconsistencies and contradictions with the standard model. They were conscious of the ad hoc explanations for them, but it was easier to live with these flaws than countenance any superior hypothesis that might undermine or destroy the accepted dogma. In the next chapters we will see this same attitude again within the climate science community as dissent against the 'manmade global warming' hypothesis is also ruthlessly suppressed.

The Venus greenhouse argument was a hasty and panicky attempt to protect the status quo, but it also lent apparent scientific legitimacy to the new social fad appearing on the political horizon: global warming.

By the late 1970s the greenhouse theory had earned its stripes. But just before it morphed into 'global warming' as the new *cause célèbre*, the theory entered the political arena. By the early 1980s, three events occurred that served to promote global warming in the media: temperatures were on the rise again, socialism in Eastern Europe had collapsed and, in the UK, the coal miners went on strike.

Prime Minister Thatcher saw the miners as a serious threat not only to the government but also to the national power supply. Repeated power cuts in 1974 following further strikes and the recent global oil crisis, led to the three-day working week and to bringing down Edward Heath's administration. Margaret Thatcher as the new Prime Minister had an added incentive to avoid the fate of her predecessor and so looked for a long-term solution to the political threat and to the problems of maintaining the power supply. She found it in CO_2 and global warming, becoming committed internationally to climate change issues.

In 1988, following the first meeting of the Inter-governmental Panel on Climate Change (IPCC), the Thatcher government commissioned the UK Meteorological Office to set up the Hadley Centre for Climate Prediction and Research, a climate modelling unit to investigate global warming as a possible consequence of industrial CO_2 emissions with the covert intention of undermining the coal industry.[52] If it could be proved scientifically that burning coal was causing dangerous global warming, there would be justification for limiting the country's reliance on it as its principal source of energy. As Richard Courtney reports in *Global Warming: How it All Began*, 'early in her global warming campaign – and at her personal instigation' the Science and Engineering Research Council was encouraged to prioritize the funding of 'climate-related research'.[53]

With government money pouring in for research, there was a strong incentive for scientists to produce politically favourable results. Thatcher's government expected these results to 'prove' the connection between increasing global temperatures and atmospheric CO_2. The miners' unions would then be undermined and the threat of further strikes reduced if not eliminated. However, the secondary purpose was to promote nuclear power as a more reliable alternative to both coal and oil in terms of supply. Nuclear power was immune to the kinds of external influences which routinely interrupted the supply of the other major energy supplies.

Then a happy coincidence occurred that oiled the political wheels: Thatcher was indirectly and inadvertently aided by the collapse of Communism in Eastern Europe. With this came a glut of disaffected political activists looking for a new anti-capitalist cause. The activism market was flooded with unemployed socialists who now swelled the ranks of the environmental movement. 'Environmentalism' became the new surrogate religion filling the void left by socialism and the slow decline of Christianity. It was grist for the global warming mill because it allowed the public to focus on a new surrogate devil: CO_2. It may have satisfied the psychological need for something always to fear and something to feel guilty about: the collective guilt of success and of enjoying a comfortable lifestyle. Environmentalism gave the Western world CO_2 to wring its hands over.

Ironically, CO_2 was the by-product and fossil fuels the means by which the West became what it is: wealthy, successful, thriving and free. It was oil and the combustion engine that helped liberate the West from the poverty and hardship that characterized the pre-industrial age, something everyone had forgotten. We now take our hard-earned freedom and prosperity for granted as though it has always been thus.

By the 1980s, out of the blue, Thatcher had a host of accidental allies supporting her crusade against fossil fuels. It was an unlikely alliance, but it served all agendas as carbon dioxide was singled out for hostile attention from politicians and their subservient scientists to radical environmentalists who still wanted to bring the capitalists down – an irksome fact Thatcher's administration chose to ignore.

Patrick Moore, co-founder of Greenpeace and one of the most prominent environmentalists of the 1970s, says:

> Communism failed, the Wall came down, and a lot of peaceniks and political activists moved into the environmental movement, bringing their neo-Marxism with them … [they] learned to use Green language in a very clever way to cloak agendas that actually have more to do with anti-capitalism and anti-globalisation than they do anything with ecology or science.[54]

It was a strange irony that such philosophically opposing forces found themselves actively supporting a common agenda, one that demanded a certain curtailment of prosperity and a tightening of the energy belt. The left-wing fanatics, however, wished to impose a far more radical solution to the sin of plenty, which they interpreted as unbridled greed. They demanded a return to a peasant lifestyle, close to nature. Use less, spend less, eat frugally, give up the combustion engine, get back to nature with the horse and cart and the yoke. Of course, the difference between Thatcher's right-wing government and the radical environmentalists was the food chain and the underlying motivations: money flowed from the politicians to the scientists to 'prove' the case against CO_2, the very lifeblood of their own prosperous future, while at the same time it legitimized and supported the anti-capitalist left-wing environmental cause by accident. The global warming hypothesis now served both. All it needed was proof.

In an audit of the Australian Climate Commission's 2011 report 'The Critical Decade – Climate Science, Risks and Responses', Bob Carter, David Evans, Stewart Franks and William Kininmonth explain how the global warming issue became fully politicized. They write that, at a UN-convened conference in Villach, Austria, in October 1985, 'invited participants reviewed the greenhouse effect, climate change and their effects on ecosystems. The ensuing Conference Statement declared that past climate data, without modification, were no longer to be viewed as a reliable guide to the future'[55] and that instead of utilizing past data for the purposes of projecting possible future climate patterns,

> Computer modelling (rudimentary though it was at the time) was to be relied upon, and indicated that increasing concentrations of greenhouse gases would warm the global climate significantly during the 21st century. The Villach statement was followed by a series of national and international public awareness-raising conferences and events sponsored by government and non-government organisations. In culmination, in 1988 the UN established the IPCC to provide advice to governments on the enhanced greenhouse effect and its impact on climate change.

The audit continues,

> IPCC advice has been known to be politically motivated since publication of the 1995 Second Assessment Report, in which the wording of the Summary for Policymakers was tampered with *after* the scientists had signed off on it. In 2001, the Third IPCC Assessment Report took as its

leitmotif a deeply flawed paper by Michael Mann and co-authors that falsely depicted Northern Hemisphere temperature over the last 800–1000 years as having the shape of a horizontal hockey-stick in which the upturned blade represented alleged dramatic warming in the twentieth century; this graphic was later exposed as false, and the result of statistical incompetence. Most recently, the Fourth Assessment Report, published in 2007, has been subjected to a blizzard of criticism subsequent to the revelations of the Climategate affair.[56]

By 2002, Thatcher had changed her mind on the alleged threat posed by global warming. She could now see the dangers posed by the 'romantics and cranks', as she called them, of the environmental lobby who were becoming increasingly vocal. According to Iain Murray, Thatcher was 'initially skeptical of the arguments about global warming, although she thought they deserved to be treated seriously' and by 1990, 'she had begun to recognize that the issue was being used as a Trojan horse by anti-capitalist forces'.[57] But again it was too late. 'Alas', writes Christopher Booker in the 12 June 2010 edition of the *Telegraph*, 'what she set in train earlier continues to exercise its baleful influence to this day. But the fact that she became one of the first and most prominent of "climate sceptics" has been almost entirely buried from view.'

Thanks largely to Sagan, the campaign against CO_2 as the devil's own gas had already benefited from the still smouldering Velikovsky affair. And no one wanted the earth to end up like Venus, the graphic symbol of our ultimate fate winking at us every evening.

Not much has changed since the late 1980s as government grants still flow in colossal amounts to finance the search for the so-called 'smoking gun' – the evidence that will establish the link between industrial CO_2 emissions and global temperatures beyond all doubt.[58] But as the atmospheric scientist John Christy of the

University of Alabama pointed out, 'We have a vested interest in creating panic because money will then flow to climate scientists'.[59] The new climate modelling unit of the UK Met Office flourished under its political benefactor and ultimately formed the basis of what would become the Intergovernmental Panel on Climate Change (IPCC) under the directorship of John Houghton, with Bert Bollin as its chair, the same man who just a few years earlier had been dismissed as a crank for peddling the same ideas.

According to the social anthropologist Benny Peiser, an outspoken critic of the IPCC:

> The climate hysteria created and perpetuated by Western government officials has opened Pandora's Box. What looked to be a valuable policy tool for green protectionism is now threatening to unleash political chaos and economic misery on its creators and their nations. Climate alarmism has turned into a Frankenstein monster that threatens to devour its own designers.[60]

The Western world was embarking on a cause of self-destruction and paying for the privilege, while the 'smoking gun' has yet to be found despite political enthusiasm and largesse.

3.   The Cart before the Horse

The great tragedy of Science: the slaying of a beautiful hypothesis by an ugly fact.

Thomas Huxley

Perhaps the most important of the fundamental assumptions of anthropogenic global warming (AGW) is that an increase in atmospheric CO_2 forces a corresponding increase in global temperature. This means that temperature change must *follow* a change in the quantity of CO_2 in the atmosphere. This assumption was implied in Al Gore's 2006 film *An Inconvenient Truth* where Gore, riding in a hoist for dramatic effect, showed his audience a graph of the earth's temperature history with corresponding changes in atmospheric CO_2. His demonstration showed that the two were inextricably linked and that changes in CO_2 necessarily *caused* the changes in temperature. By way of explanation Gore says: 'The relationship is actually very complicated but there is one relationship that is far more powerful than all the others and it is this. When there is more carbon dioxide, the temperature gets warmer, because it traps more heat from the sun inside.' His suggestion that more CO_2 necessarily causes the temperature to rise sounds very plausible. It should therefore be easy to prove.

The problem is that Gore's own graph suggests his theory is wrong. The glacial/interglacial pattern of the earth's history, as Gore shows, proves there is nothing unusual in periods of higher temperature or of large fluctuations in atmospheric CO_2. His graph also shows that prehistoric interglacial periods were frequently warmer than today's presumed 'average' global temperature, yet this seems to have escaped his notice. Indeed, the obvious question that should have occurred to his audience is this:

> *Why is the current warm period necessarily manmade if all previous such periods have been from natural causes and have even been warmer than today?*

And then there is the problem of the scale of Gore's graph. If the time axis is stretched (magnified), it becomes clear that changes in the earth's temperature have always *preceded* changes in atmospheric CO_2 by 800–1,000 years. However, this is not obvious in Gore's graph because of the coarse scaling, which masks which of the two occurs first. Instead, the temperature and CO_2 peaks appear to coincide, as Figure 4 shows.

Even if Gore's suggestion is correct that CO_2 is the primary driver, his audience might also have asked, *if atmospheric CO_2 is forcing temperature, what is forcing CO_2?* There is no easy answer for

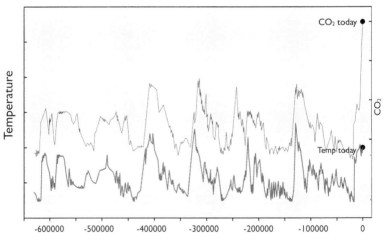

Figure 4. Al Gore's CO_2–temperature graph, from *An Inconvenient Truth*, showing temperature and CO_2 over the past 600,000 years. Closer analysis reveals CO_2 *lags* temperature by around 1,000 years.[1]

pre-industrial times because Gore cannot claim an artificial source. He can only account for this scenario from the Industrial Revolution until the present, where it is assumed from the work of Callendar and others (as described in Chapter 1) that increases in CO_2 are *necessarily* caused by industrial activities. So what did cause prehistoric CO_2 to rise and fall if we are to accept seriously the claim that CO_2 drives temperature? If the cause is not temperature, what is it? There is no answer from his perspective. Gore's 'CO_2 drives temperature' scenario raises more questions than it answers.

By the time Gore was making his film it was already well known from ice core samples taken primarily at the Russian Vostok station in eastern Antarctica, and others taken at Taylor Dome and Byrd in western Antarctica, that both increases and decreases in atmospheric CO_2 have always *followed* similar changes in temperature. The deepest ice core ever drilled was taken at the Vostok station in 1998. Reaching a depth of 3,623 metres, ice some 400,000 years old was extracted and analysed. Other cores of lesser depth were taken at Taylor Dome and Byrd in the 1980s. Each ice core indicates that atmospheric CO_2 lags temperature by up to

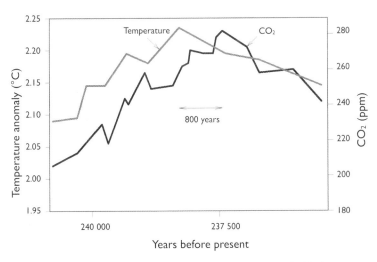

Figure 5. An 800-year lag (the lighter area between the two peaks) becomes noticeable after magnification of the time axis.[2]

1,000 years. Thus *temperature drives* CO_2, not the other way around as Gore implied. Why didn't Gore know this? Or, if he did, why did he suggest that the opposite was true when it had already been shown not to be?

To be fair to Gore, after initial analysis of the early ice cores, especially those taken at Vostok in 1974, it was clear that a close relationship between atmospheric CO_2 and near-surface air temperature did exist. This was seized on by advocates of the AGW hypothesis, including Gore, as proof that CO_2 was responsible for past and present temperature rises. However, Sherwood B. Idso and others[3] demonstrated as early as 1987 that the temperature peaked almost a millennium *before* CO_2. Idso argued that 'changes in atmospheric CO_2 content never precede changes in air temperature, when going from glacial to interglacial conditions; and when going from interglacial to glacial conditions, the change in CO_2 concentration actually *lags* the change in air temperature.' Hence, he concluded, '*changes in CO_2 concentration cannot be claimed to be the cause of changes in air temperature*, for the appropriate sequence of events (temperature change *following* CO_2 change) is not only never present, it is actually violated in [at least] half of the record' (emphasis added).[4] Later, in 1999, Petit and Fischer determined from higher-resolution reconstructions of temperature histories of the Vostok ice cores that CO_2 lag periods could be thousands of years behind temperature increases.[5] Then, in 2003, Caillon and others found by analysing air bubbles in the Vostok ice core that 'the CO_2 increase lagged Antarctic deglacial warming by 800 ± 200 years.'[6] This 'confirms that CO_2 is not the forcing that initially drives the climatic system during a deglaciation'.[7]

There is no known period in the earth's history when changes in atmospheric CO_2 have preceded and caused corresponding changes in temperature. It has *always* been the other way around. In fact, it has been pointed out by Beck and others that a five-year lag is also discernible between atmospheric CO_2 taken from Antarctic ice cores and temperatures in the northern hemisphere taken from historical measurements between 1812 and 1961. But here again it is clear that CO_2 *follows* temperature.

Immediately following this discovery, another bid was made to save the AGW theory. NASA scientist James Hansen, one of the most outspoken apologists of the theory, argued that slight changes in the earth's orbit around the sun, known as Milankovitch cycles, induce minor warming or cooling of the planet, which then causes a corresponding change in atmospheric CO_2. During a warm phase, carbon dioxide supposedly out-gases from the oceans as they begin to warm due to increased insolation (the amount of sunlight warming a given area of the earth at any given time). CO_2 then takes over and drives the temperature the rest of the way, with water vapour playing a positive feedback role, increasing temperatures further and releasing yet more carbon dioxide from the oceans. This was a desperate and strained explanation and one that was plagued with problems. But it did provide Hansen with the very high climate sensitivity he needed to justify pointing the finger at CO_2 today as a climate-forcing agent and it appeared to explain the embarrassing extended temperature lag. Carbon dioxide was once again brandished as the principal climate driver for all past, present and future glaciations and interglacial periods.[8] But the only basis for this explanation is that CO_2 is known to be a weak greenhouse gas which exhibits some warming properties, a fact earlier demonstrated by Arrhenius, Tyndall and others. Therefore, according to Hansen, once the warming has already been started by another agent, such as increased insolation due to the Milankovitch cycles, CO_2 encourages a positive feedback to follow, which amplifies it further. But Hansen was obliged to make two crucial assumptions to make it work: first, a very high climate sensitivity; and second, that Milankovitch forcing is sufficient on its own to trigger glaciation and glacial termination events in the first place. He is completely wrong on the first, and on very thin ice with the second.

It turns out that the Milankovitch cycles are not in step with past ice age cycles. The climatologist and former NASA scientist Roy Spencer has pointed out that 'there is no statistically significant connection between the two'[9] and that any apparent correlation is no better than chance. On its own, this is enough to undermine the hypothesis. But Milankovitch cycles are also out of phase with the southern temperature response in the Vostok ice core, because the forcing came from the north, not from the south,[10] raising the problem of why very small northern hemispheric solar forcings can result in huge southern hemisphere temperature changes.[11] Since the periods of glaciation occurred over the *entire* globe, and not just in the northern hemisphere, Milankovitch cycles could not be the cause, leaving CO_2 out in the cold. But it gets worse. Because Milankovitch effects are so minuscule they are unable to account for even the small variations in temperature, as discerned from the ice cores, let alone the large temperature swings over a 100,000-year cycle,[12] as the periods of glaciations for the past one million years appear to be. And as glacial cycles seem to have changed from a 41,000-year period to 100,000-year period about one million years ago, this compounds the problem for the Milankovitch-CO_2 hypothesis.

But the fatal blow came in 1992 in a paper written for *Nature* by the geochemist Wallace Broecker of Columbia University.[13] Broecker pointed out that, among many other potential problems for the Milankovitch hypothesis, oxygen isotope ($\delta^{18}O$) data from the Devil's Hole aquifer in Nevada indicate that northern hemisphere summer insolation had not reached the point it 'should' have in order to trigger a glacial termination,[14] specifically Termination II, the end of the penultimate ice age some 140,000 years ago, as predicted by Milankovitch theory. They are out of phase by up to 17,000 years, a difference far too great to explain away by reference to acceptable margins of error. Milankovitch cycles could not have triggered the glacial termination because the event appeared to precede its own cause.[15] This became known as the 'causality problem' and has remained unsolved by defenders of the Milankovitch hypothesis ever since, despite numerous attempts to address it. In Broecker's words, 'climate modellers should start preparing themselves for a world without Milankovitch'.[16]

Furthermore, Gerald E. Marsh of Argonne National Laboratory, Chicago, has shown that since past interglacial periods 'were much warmer than previously thought' and that CO_2 concentrations were at the same time *lower* than today's level of 385–390 ppm, 'carbon dioxide could not have been responsible'. He further argues that the 'data strongly imply that Termination II was initiated by a reduction in cosmic ray flux. Such a reduction would lead to a reduction in the amount of low-altitude cloud cover, (thereby) reducing the Earth's albedo with a consequent rise in global temperature.'[17] Clearly, CO_2 has played little or no part in the earth's past climate extremes, whether glacial or interglacial. Therefore, the commonly held assumption that atmospheric CO_2 'enhanced' the Milankovitch cycles to bring about such climate changes is unproven.

Yet none of this has deterred today's global warming alarmists from arguing that the large interglacial temperature changes throughout the earth's history are simply not possible to explain without carbon dioxide as the primary driver: it was CO_2 or nothing. 'We cannot explain the temperature observations without CO_2,' admits one prominent alarmist blogger.[18] A flat refusal to consider alternative ideas developed because the defenders of the anthropogenic global warming hypothesis were determined to vilify CO_2 as the principal climate-forcing agent, something that compels them to make numerous unfounded assumptions and employ convoluted, ad hoc explanations to make it work.

Milankovitch forcing was the fashion in the 1970s and was revisited in the 1990s, despite its many problems, because the CO_2 hypothesis had become the reigning paradigm and was useless without it. As there was no other explanation that had any hope of fingering carbon dioxide as the culprit for the earth's past warming phases once it became known that it *lagged* temperature, Milankovitch was shoehorned in. Reputations were now at stake and carbon dioxide had to be singled out from all other possibilities regardless of how flimsy was the evidence.

Meanwhile contempt for considering other natural causes for twentieth-century warming developed. The possibility that the sun was a climate driver was anathema because it did not suit political interests that have dominated the scientific method since the mid-1980s. Politics was in the driver's seat and catastrophic anthropogenic global warming (CAGW) became an investment opportunity.

Spencer argues that,

> the interpretation of the Vostok ice core record of temperature and CO_2 variations has the same problem that the interpretation of warming and CO_2 increase in the last century has: CAUSATION. In both cases, Hansen's . . . inference of high climate sensitivity . . . depends critically on there not being another mechanism causing most of the temperature variations. If most of the warming in the last 100 years was due to CO_2, then that (arguably) implies a moderately sensitive climate. If it caused the temperature variations in the ice core record, it implies a catastrophically sensitive climate.

He adds, 'the implicit assumption that science knows what the forcings were of past climate change even 50 years ago, let alone 100,000 years ago, strikes me as hubris'.[19]

But there was yet another problem. As the biotechnologist Frank Lansner pointed out in Anthony Watt's science blog wattsupwiththat.com, and as Figure 4 and Gore's film show, all the major temperature peaks exhibit large but steep temperature increases followed by similarly large but less steep declines.

However, there is a marked difference in the downward slopes of temperature and CO_2, where the temperature falls far more rapidly than does CO_2. If CO_2 was the driver and controlled temperature, why did it not force temperature to remain high and essentially follow the same slope? From the rapid divergence of the two graphs following the peak, it is clear that temperature is independent of CO_2 and is being acted on by another force.

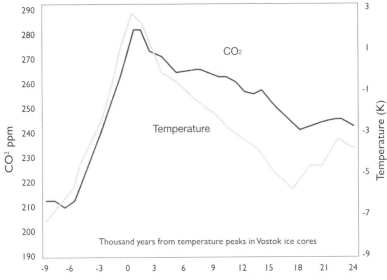

Figure 6. Lansner summed all the major temperature and CO_2 peaks into one. The result is a composite graph of actual data taken from the Vostok ice cores.[20]

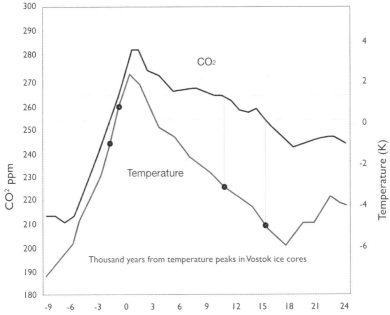

Figure 7. Temperature clearly falls earlier, faster and independently of atmospheric CO_2, which follows some time later, remaining near its maximum value for an extended period.[21]

Furthermore, as Lansner pointed out, it is clear from Figure 7 (derived from Gore's original) that two entirely different temperatures are possible for the *same* concentration in atmospheric CO_2: for example, at 253 ppm we have temperatures of −0.7K *and* −4.7K, and for 264 ppm we have temperatures of +0.7K *and* −2.9K.[22] How is this possible if CO_2 is the principal climatic driving force controlling temperature? It can only be possible if they are independent of each other or if temperature drives CO_2, which remains high (near maximum) for an extended period well *after* the temperature falls, but whose less steep downward slope is governed by hysteresis and physical inertia in the climate system. Changes in atmospheric CO_2 are therefore the *consequence* of temperature change and not the cause.

But it is also possible for CO_2 and temperature to be completely out of phase and to trend in opposite directions. It was during the post-Second World War economic boom (1950–75, see Figure 8) that CO_2 emissions increased while temperatures steadily declined. This disconnect, caused by the Pacific Decadal Oscillation (PDO) moving into its cool phase actually continued for about thirty years, from 1945, giving rise to the 1970s ice age panic. Cool PDO phases prevailed from 1890–1924 and from 1945–1976, while a warm phase predominated 1925–1945 and again from the mid 1970s until the mid-1990s.[23]

During the 1970s cool phase, CO_2 was temporarily forgotten while the political and scientific worlds concentrated on climate doom with the planet freezing up. They were of course unaware of the existence of the PDO, which shifted back to a warm phase and continued for the next twenty-three years or so, culminating in the 1998 El Niño temperature spike. Then, following the temperature spike, global temperatures once again started to decline, with the PDO reverting to a cool phase.

The trend has been for temperatures to decline ever since and this will probably continue for another twenty to thirty years according to some researchers, partly due to the periodicity of the PDO, albeit with the shorter Southern Oscillation superimposed

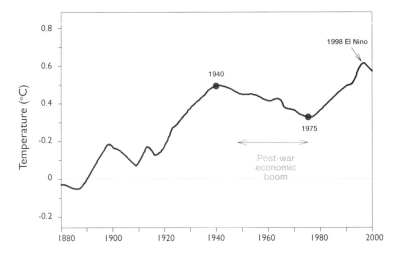

Figure 8. Temperatures declined during the post-Second World War economic boom (1950–75), the period when CO_2 output from industrial activities was accelerating.[24]

on it. Indeed, some scientists, including those working at the Russian Academy of Sciences, are now warning that the earth may be on the brink of another ice age.[25] Their evidence, besides the effects of the PDO now being in its negative (cool) phase, is the decline in solar activity (between solar cycles 23 and 24), a phenomenon that manifests itself in reduced sunspot numbers. This can last for many years and is known as a solar minimum and usually accompanies lower temperatures on earth. Sunspot number refers to the periodic appearance of sunspots on the surface of the sun. Depending on the counting method used (either the International Sunspot Number or the Boulder Sunspot Number used by NOAA) they range between approximately 90 and 200 sunspots per cycle over an average period of 10.6 years. The last Little Ice Age coincided with periods of low solar activity and long cycle lengths when sunspots were rarely observed. The earth has been emerging from this episode ever since.

Research carried out by Friis-Christensen and Lassen in 1991, David C. Archibald in 2009 and by the Norwegian physicists Jan-

Erik Solheim, Kjell Stordahl and Ole Humlum in 2012 found that temperatures are affected even more by the *length* of the solar cycle than by sunspot number alone. After monitoring a number of meteorological stations in the northern hemisphere, Jan-Erik Solheim and his colleagues concluded that

> No significant trend is found between the length of a cycle and the average temperature in the same cycle, but a significant negative trend is found between the length of a cycle and the temperature in the *next* cycle. This provides a tool to predict an average temperature decrease of at least 1.0°C from solar cycle 23 to 24 for the stations and areas analysed.[26]

On the strength of this, they predict 'a significant temperature decrease in cycle 24' due to the length of cycle 23 and that it may already have started.[27] This conclusion is supported by Girma Orssengo whose 'Mathematical Model for the Global Mean Temperature Anomaly (GMTA) Based on Observed Temperature Patterns' shows 'global cooling by about 0.42 deg C until 2030'.[28] These predictions are in direct opposition to the IPCC's projection of 'a warming of about 0.2°C per decade'.[29]

Yet the link between solar activity and temperatures on earth has been known for at least two centuries. In 1801 the English astronomer William Herschel noticed a close correlation between low sunspot numbers and high wheat prices. He realized that as temperatures dropped, wheat yields also declined and prices increased as a consequence.[30] But the opposite applies in periods of high sunspot number when global temperatures tend to increase, which historically has had a corresponding effect on productivity and economic wealth, especially in Europe. This occurred during the Medieval Warm Period when most of the great cathedrals were built. At the time, atmospheric CO_2 was lower than it is today and was obviously not affected by industrial emissions. It was also during this period that Eric the Red colonized Greenland before that country was encased in ice and its name became an oxymoron.

Needless to say these historical events have been largely ignored by the IPCC and its supporting scientists. To be fair, the IPCC legitimately rejected the effect of the sun on global climate on the grounds that *correlation does not equate to causation*. This is true. But when the causal link between solar activity and global temperature was indeed established by the solar physicist Bo Christiansen[31] of the Danish Meteorological Institute as early as 1991, and again by K. Lassen,[32] Eigil Friis-Christensen[33], also in 1991 and Henrik Svensmark[34] in 1997, the IPCC largely discounted it because it did not tie in with the manmade global warming paradigm.

In any case, the IPCC's argument that correlation does not necessarily mean causation must also apply to the temporary correlation between CO_2 and temperature since the Industrial Revolution. But here they draw the line. Any apparent correlation between atmospheric CO_2 and temperature always means causation when they are in step and increasing. When trending in opposite directions, as during the 1945–75 ice age scare and again since 1998, it is put down to a temporary 'lull'[35] in manmade global warming, 'masked'[36] either by natural forces or dust from Chinese industrial activity blocking the sun. Any reprieve, according to the alarmists, will not last and manmade global warming will return with a vengeance.

In an amusing twist to this story, Rob Soria of the International Centre for Radio Astronomy Research in Australia[37] recently highlighted the absurdity of always interpreting a causal link between atmospheric CO_2 and temperature when the two appear to correlate. Anthony Watts, writing in wattsupwiththat.com, remarked that Soria 'plotted the number of supernovae (dying stars) discovered versus the HadCRUT temperature data [the combined sea and land surface temperature data from the UK Met Office and CRU] since 1960. There's a good correlation.' Soria sardonically explains that he was studying supernovae discovered in the last fifty years and says, 'I discovered that the number of [supernovae] discovered per year correlates pretty well with the temperature anomaly.' He produced a plot of the two showing how closely they correlated and mockingly argued from this apparent close relationship that 'the temperature anomaly has a better correlation with the observed number of dead stars than with dead polar bears, tree rings, CO_2 or number of pirates. This is proof that global warming is causing more stars to explode. It's worse than we thought. We are killing the universe. We need more funding.'[38]

Humour aside, in an attempt to deal with declining temperatures as CO_2 increased, climate scientists had to determine how manmade global warming could be reconciled with the exceptionally cold winters and apparent decline in world temperatures. They had to work harder in order to convince an increasingly sceptical public[39] that manmade CO_2 emissions are responsible for most if not all of the global warming experienced during the twentieth century. Scientists need to convince the public that declining temperatures for the past decade are irrelevant and that the steep decline from 1940 to 1975 was an anomaly.

Some scientists have gone to extraordinary lengths to discount any hint that such events as the Medieval Warm Period occurred, even erasing from the temperature record all proxy data that suggest otherwise, as we will see in Chapter 7. In a controversial email sent to the geophysicist David Deming of the University of Oklahoma in 1995, one scientist brazenly wrote, 'We have to get rid of the Medieval Warm Period.' Deming never named the sender, but various authors and commentators suggest it was Jonathan Overpeck, a lead author of the IPCC. Overpeck later featured in one of the Climategate emails where he apparently wanted to deal a 'mortal blow' to the Medieval Warm Period and other 'warm period myths',[40] so it is reasonable to suppose he was the author of the email to Deming.

Deming had earlier written an article for the journal *Science* detailing his reconstruction of 150 years of North American temperature data from borehole cores.[41] But because the article suggested temperatures over that period had increased, some climate scientists mistakenly thought he supported the AGW hypothesis and was therefore in agreement with the politically correct view endorsed by the IPCC. In 2006, Deming explained in a statement to the US Senate Committee on Environment and Public Works:

> In 1995, I published a short paper in the academic journal *Science*. In that study, I reviewed how borehole temperature data recorded a warming of about one degree Celsius in North America over the last 100 to 150 years. The week the article appeared, I was contacted by a reporter for National Public Radio. He offered to interview me, but only if I would state that the warming was due to human activity. When I refused to do so, he hung up on me.
>
> I had another interesting experience around the time my paper in Science was published. I received an astonishing email from a major researcher in the area of climate change. He said, 'We have to get rid of the Medieval Warm Period.'
>
> The Medieval Warm Period (MWP) was a time of unusually warm weather that began around 1000 AD and persisted until a cold period known as the 'Little Ice Age' took hold in the 14th century. Warmer climate brought a remarkable flowering of prosperity, knowledge, and art to Europe during the High Middle Ages.
>
> The existence of the MWP had been recognized in the scientific literature for decades. But now it was a major embarrassment to those maintaining that the 20th century warming was truly anomalous. It had to be 'gotten rid of.'
>
> In 1769, Joseph Priestley warned that scientists overly attached to a favorite [sic] hypothesis would not hesitate

to 'warp the whole course of nature.' In 1999, Michael Mann and his colleagues published a reconstruction of past temperature in which the MWP simply vanished. This unique estimate became known as the 'hockey stick,' because of the shape of the temperature graph.[42]

Then, according to a *Mail OnLine* article by Jonathan Petre, Professor Phil Jones, head of the University of East Anglia's Climate Research Unit (CRU) and a leading IPCC researcher, made a startling admission by conceding 'the possibility that the world was warmer in medieval times than now – suggesting global warming may not be a manmade phenomenon'. Petre adds, 'And he [Jones] said that for the past fifteen years there has been no "statistically significant" warming'.[43]

Despite global temperatures remaining static at most, and even by some estimates declining, after the 1998 peak, atmospheric CO_2 has continued its steady gradual increase according to Mauna Loa

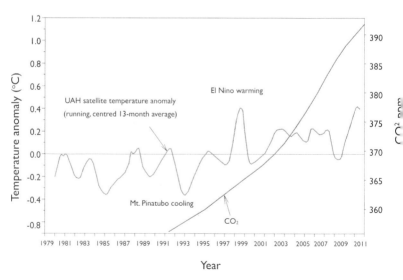

Figure 9. Global temperatures 1980–2011 as measured by satellite (approximate UAH lower troposphere) against CO_2 measured from Mauna Loa. Note Mt. Pinatubo cooling followed by El Niño warming. Temperature trend is unrelated to CO_2 trend.[44]

data, suggesting once again that global temperatures are controlled by other factors. These events of divergent temperature and atmospheric CO_2 clearly undermine the AGW hypothesis (Figure 9) because they fail to satisfy the assumption that increasing CO_2 necessarily forces increasing temperatures.

It is clear from both recent and ancient history that global temperature is not a function of CO_2, but independent of it. Yet according to Gore, Hansen, CRU, the IPCC and many other AGW alarmist scientists, atmospheric CO_2 is a dangerous climate-forcing agent which controls and *drives* temperature by being amplified by atmospheric water vapour. If this were the case, CO_2's steady increase would surely force temperatures in the same direction. Clearly it does not.

One can only conclude that the earth's climate system is not, and cannot, be driven by changes in atmospheric CO_2 because the CO_2 – temperature profile is back-to-front. The earth's entire glacial-interglacial history has been shaped by natural forces while mankind's industrial imprint on the system is minuscule by comparison and has emerged only recently on the geological time-line. It is specious therefore to claim that since the Industrial Revolution in general, but particularly during the twentieth century, CO_2 has become the climate's principal driving force, overpowering all natural influences.

4. Positive or Negative?

Today, everybody remembers Galileo. How many can name
the bishops and professors who refused to look through his
telescope?

James Hogan

What men want is not knowledge but certainty.

Bertrand Russell

The climate science community and the IPCC work on the
assumption that the climate system is highly sensitive to small
forcings and that an atmospheric positive feedback system amplifies
the very slight warming effect of CO_2. The validity of this
assumption is crucial to the AGW hypothesis. Without it the
theory that increasing industrial CO_2 emissions will lead to
catastrophic warming falls apart. In fact, on its own CO_2 is
inadequate as a climate driver (forcing agent). There is simply not
enough of it in the atmosphere to do much one way or another, as
Tyndall demonstrated in 1886. Recently, Roy Spencer pointed out
that 'Feedback is the big-picture, bottom-line, end-of-the-day issue
that trumps all others in the global warming debate.'[1] And if the
feedbacks are negative, not positive, then as a theory AGW is
going nowhere.

CO_2 occupies a paltry 0.0385–0.0390 per cent of the
atmosphere, of which humankind's contribution is about one third.
This means that our *total* industrial CO_2 emissions today represent
approximately 0.012 per cent of the atmosphere, or somewhere
around one *milli*-per cent (see Figure 10). To put this in perspective,

the meteorologist Joseph d'Aleo explains, 'If the atmosphere was a 100 storey building, our annual anthropogenic CO_2 contribution today would be equivalent to the linoleum on the first floor.' Similarly, Reid Bryson of the University of Wisconsin famously remarked, 'You can go outside and spit and have the same effect as doubling carbon dioxide.'

CO_2 in the atmosphere today represents just 0.001 per cent of all CO_2 at the surface of the earth.[2] Most of the earth's carbon has been locked up, stored in rocks and corals for hundreds of millions of years, sequestered from the primordial atmosphere whose CO_2 content was many thousands of times higher than it is today. Over these aeons, CO_2 has gradually but surely trended downward. Today it is no more than a minor trace gas, a vestige of ancient geological history.

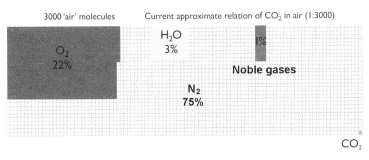

Figure 10. The main constituent gases in the atmosphere, including the tiny proportion represented by CO_2, the dot in the lower right-hand corner, of which only one in three is due to industrial emissions. ($O_2 \approx 630$ molecules; $N_2 \approx 2,250$ molecules; $H_2O \approx 90$ molecules; Noble gases ≈ 30 molecules; $CO_2 \approx 1$ molecule in 3,000). Approximate percentages shown.[3]

That much is conceded by scientists trumpeting the dangers of global warming through industrial emissions of CO_2. Even Al Gore admits that, by itself, CO_2 is incapable of forcing global climate in any direction. Therefore, in order to force the climate system, it requires an 'amplifier' to supply positive feedback. This is essential if there is any merit in the AGW hypothesis.

The only serious candidate is water vapour, yet all twenty-three computer models endorsed and used by the IPCC assume clouds *also* provide positive feedback in the climate system. This has been shown to be wrong by Roy Spencer and John Christy, both climate scientists at the University of Alabama, Huntsville. In any event, water vapour provides around 95–8 per cent of the greenhouse effect which keeps the earth's temperature above an icy −18°C (255° Kelvin) or so, the temperature that might otherwise result if nearly all of the sun's radiant energy were radiated back as infrared energy and lost to space in the absence of an atmosphere. Without the greenhouse effect, life on earth would be impossible. And without water vapour, CO_2 as a climate-forcing agent is useless. However, there is a limit to its effectiveness, as pointed out in Chapter 2, where normal atmospheric convection prevents extremes of temperature at the surface.

All current climate models employed by the IPCC work on the premise that increased atmospheric CO_2 also increases the moisture content of the air by the very slight initial warming it provides. This slightly higher moisture content increases as temperature increases because warm air holds more moisture than cold air. While water vapour acts as the main greenhouse gas, it further warms the atmosphere which releases more CO_2, mainly from the oceans, but added to by our industrial emissions.

The IPPC assumes also that this warming process results in less cloud cover since unusually warm years are observed to have less cloud. This allows in more sunlight, thus adding to the process already begun and a positive feedback follows – or at least that is the premise on which all the IPCC's feedback models are based (see endnote for ancient precedents).[4] The question is, once such a positive feedback is under way, what stops it from going out of control and descending into runaway global warming? The fact this has never happened should be reason enough for doubt.

Nevertheless, the idea that manmade CO_2 emissions are now driving the climate is presented as a *fait accompli*, akin to Holy Writ. Therefore, positive feedback from water vapour is 'needed' to overcome the saturation limit of CO_2 in the atmosphere because the 'greenhouse' temperature response of CO_2 is logarithmic, not linear. But the IPCC completely misinterprets how clouds influence the system and believes cloud feedbacks are also positive for the reasons outlined above, so the assumption is made that the *increased warming caused the decrease in cloud cover*, not the other way around.[5]

Even so, the behaviour of water vapour and clouds in the atmosphere is far from fully understood, something the IPCC concedes in its 2007 report. The IPCC further admits that measuring such feedbacks in the climate system is currently impossible because no known method exists,[6] and so they cannot be directly verified. This suggests that all climate forecasts and policy decisions based on the IPCC's General Circulation Models (GCMs) must be unreliable and somewhat arbitrary. Yet the IPCC continues to accord clouds a positive feedback role in their GCMs. These models are also unreliable in terms of describing the latitude and altitude distribution of water vapour, which is far from uniform.[7] CO_2 is also unevenly distributed. Both water vapour and CO_2 in the atmosphere are somewhat 'lumpy' and very changeable.

By their very nature, clouds present very complex problems to climate modellers. But in the early years of the IPCC their behaviour was simplified by assuming they *always* provided a net positive feedback, albeit of varying degrees of sensitivity.

Tom Harris, Executive Director of the International Climate Science Coalition, in his presentation to the United Nations Climate Change Conference in Copenhagen 2009 explained:

> Clouds were thought to be a net positive feedback to the climate system . . . because water vapour is obviously a major greenhouse gas. But over the years, they started to understand that in fact clouds reflect energy into space at a far greater rate than they trap it . . . so the more recent models show it as a net negative. It's a negative feedback. The more clouds there are, the cooler it gets. *Clouds have many times*

> *more impact on the climate than all human activities*
> *combined* [emphasis added].

However, the IPCC ignores these later models because they do not fit the current paradigm that human CO_2 emissions force the climate system, overpowering all other natural influences that might take it in the other direction. Yet, there are as many indications that the actual feedbacks within the climate system are predominantly negative, so it is difficult to understand why the IPCC endorses only positive feedback models.[8]

Spencer argues that the climate science community misunderstands what is actually going on in terms of cloud feedbacks because they have confused cause and effect.[9] He writes, the experts 'have convinced themselves that only a temperature change can cause a cloud cover change, and not the other way around. The issue is one of causation. They have not accounted for cloud changes causing temperature changes,' and adds, they 'have simply mixed up cause and effect when observing how clouds and temperature vary'.[10] He points out that, since warmer years have less cloud cover, there has always been a tendency to assume less cloud cover is the *result* of warming and not the cause of it, that the warming came first. This mistake 'has led to the "scientific consensus" that cloud feedbacks in the real climate system are probably positive, although by an uncertain amount'. This is why later GCMs suggesting a negative feedback are dismissed as worthless. Spencer concludes, 'This is important because if decreasing cloud cover caused warming, and this has been mistakenly interpreted as warming causing a decrease in cloud cover, then *positive feedback will have been inferred even if the true feedback in the climate system is negative*.'[11] When the fact that clouds are easily capable of causing temperature change is taken into account, it is clear that cloud feedbacks are strongly negative and that this negative feedback 'more than cancels out the positive feedback from water vapour'.[12]

That such a basic fact has been overlooked by the majority of climate scientists and the IPCC is astounding. Yet this blunder, as Spencer calls it, has resulted in a comedy of climate science errors, giving rise to one of the biggest scientific shams in history: the 'catastrophic anthropogenic global warming' hypothesis (CAGW), on which an entire industry has been built.

In the absence of a reliable system of direct feedback measurement, it is tempting to ignore the problem of uncertainty and fall back on GCM outputs because they at least can be tailored with a multitude of fudge-factors and assumptions to fill in the blanks. They can also be tailored to provide the 'expected' outcome, which may itself be weighted with a political motive because of government funding for the research.

The evolutionary biologist Richard Dawkins pointed out this failing when he explained, 'The power of a scientific theory may be measured as a ratio: the number of facts that it explains divided by the number of assumptions it needs to postulate in order to do the explaining. A theory that assumes most of what it is trying to explain is a bad theory.'[13] Although Dawkins was discussing Darwin's theory of evolution, which he considers an example of a good theory, his observation of what constitutes a *bad* theory applies well to CAGW because, in order to make any sense of the real world, climate modellers depend heavily on assumptions.

In view of their complexity and inherent uncertainties, climate models also give rise to false expectations and a mistaken impression of accuracy. According to Patrick Frank, the IPCC's climate models are so useless they 'cannot discern an ice age from a hothouse from five years away, much less 100 years away. So far as GCMs are concerned, Earth may be a winter wonderland by 2100 or a tropical paradise. No one knows.'[14] This is because uncertainties accumulate over time, becoming ridiculously large in just a few years, so that even a '99 per cent accurate GCM couldn't discern a new Little Ice

Age from a major tropical advance from even 20 years out.'[15] Their predictive ability is no better than a random guess, according to Frank,[16] little better than reading tea leaves or animal entrails. Indeed, current climate models are just as inadequate at interpreting *past* climate when all the facts are known. According to the German academics Sebastian Lüning, Fritz Vahrenholt and Pierre Gosselin, 'One of the main points of criticism of the CO_2-dominated climate models is that they fail to reproduce the temperature fluctuations over the last 10,000 years.'[17] The IPCC modellers discount such obvious factors as the sun and focus on CO_2 and positive feedbacks, which render them useless as predictive tools. 'The obvious discrepancy between modelled theory and measured reality has been brought up time and again,' writes Lüning.[18]

Here Lüning and colleagues were discussing the work of a research team led by Gerrit Lohmann of the Alfred Wegener Institute, Bremerhaven, which unexpectedly showed that '[climate] models do not even come close to properly reproducing the reconstructed temperatures of the past'.[19] This outcome came as a surprise to Lohmann's research team who seem to have assumed the IPCC models were valid and would be verified by their research. For some reason, they appear to have misinterpreted the cause of the discrepancy and put it down to having *underestimated* the sensitivity of the climate to CO_2-forcing in the models, implying that more positive feedback estimates would correct for it. This is an astonishing conclusion considering the many reasons to doubt such positive feedbacks in the climate system. Instead of suspecting the models themselves, they argue that the issue is really just a question of sensitivity adjustment, reminiscent of the early American and Soviet Venus landers' discovery of unexpectedly high surface temperatures being put down to 'instrument error'. The real-world data hinting at the opposite conclusion is trumped by a robust confidence in the IPCC's CO_2-centric models, none of which has proved capable of producing accurate forecasts or indeed hind-casts a few years in either direction. They are seen as infallible despite these transparent failures.

Lüning explains why the Lohmann team missed the crux of the problem:

> The thought that the climate model might be fundamentally faulty regarding the weighting of individual climate factors does not even occur to Lohmann. There's a lot that indicates that some important factors have been completely underestimated (e.g. sun) and other climate factors have been grossly overestimated (e.g. CO_2). Indeed the word 'solar' is not mentioned once in the entire paper.[20]

They argue that, despite the inability of current IPCC models to hind-cast climate, let alone their lamentable reputation at *fore*casting future climate, Lohmann and colleagues stand firmly behind them and assume that the problem is simply a case of having underestimated climate sensitivity. The implication is that once this has been corrected for, the IPCC models will be able to provide accurate hind-casts. Meanwhile, the sun and other important factors still play little or no role. Furthermore, a 2011 study carried out by R. Fildes and N. Kourentzes and published in *Journal of Forecasting* in which current climate models were compared and tested for their forecasting ability found they performed far worse than what might be expected from an uninformed guess.

Yet it is on the strength of these models that governments make policy decisions affecting the lives of millions. These problems were well understood by Pierre Gallois, a French geo-politician, who observed: 'If you put tomfoolery into a computer, nothing comes out of it but tomfoolery. But this tomfoolery, having passed through a very expensive machine, is somehow ennobled and no one dares criticize it.'

Even so, some researchers claim they can 'prove' the accuracy of IPCC climate model projections simply by employing another model projection using the same assumptions. If this sounds like circular reasoning, it is. According to Richard A. Lovette, writing for the journal *Nature*, 'New Zealand's mountain ranges *could* lose up to 85 per cent of their glaciers by 2100'[21] and furthermore, scientists have '*projected* that most of the world's smaller glaciers will be gone by 2100'. Lovette says this research, using modelling projections carried out by American and Canadian scientists, confirms the IPCC's own *estimate* that by 2100 'complete or partial melting of smaller glaciers will contribute about the same amount to sea-level rise as melt water from the giant ice sheets of Antarctica and Greenland'.[22] So the researchers used one projection, based on a series of assumptions, to 'confirm' another projection, based on the same assumptions.

On the strength of this research, Steve Running, an IPCC ecologist at the University of Montana, concludes that the IPCC's estimate of the sea level rise to be expected from glacier melt was 'about right'.[23] 'About right' because another estimate agrees with it? How does one guess confirm another guess? We might also wonder how the scientists would 'confirm' their second set of projections to 'confirm' the first ones used by the IPCC. Perhaps yet another model will project yet another 'confirmation'. But then that projection would also need to be 'confirmed' with yet another model projection, which itself would need to be 'confirmed' with yet another . . . As one blogger succinctly put it, 'So the IPCC prediction[s] are in complete agreement with the IPCC predictions',[24] which is interpreted as proof the IPCC got it right. Apparently real-world data are irrelevant anyway because, according to Chris Folland of the Hadley Centre for Climate Prediction and Research, 'We are not basing our recommendations on the data. We're basing them on the climate models.' Who needs actual data when you have models to provide the answer you want? Similarly, the Oxford University climate modeller David Frame admits, 'The models are convenient fictions that provide something very useful.'[25] Just what they provide that is useful is anybody's guess.

The IPCC has of course turned a blind eye to the shortcomings in its model accuracy, yet no one seems to have challenged it on the issue. The fact that feedbacks are crucial to climate projections makes them even more important to future policy debates which are based on them. 'So, why has it been so difficult to measure feedbacks in the climate system?' Spencer asks, 'This question is not answered in the IPCC reports because, as far as I can tell, no one has bothered to dig into the reasons'.[26] The reason why no one has bothered – or dared – to challenge the IPCC is that to do so is to challenge the political authority behind the scenes. And to threaten or challenge the politics is to threaten the funding that drives the climate modelling 'industry' in the first place.

Today's much vaunted climate models tend to be CO_2-centric and fail to predict or even hind-cast the earth's climate with any accuracy. Yet the IPCC holds to them as though they represent irrefutable evidence for their 'consensus'. There is nothing new in this expedient of adding arbitrary 'fixes' to force real-world data to represent a particular paradigm whose survival is paramount because many reputations and careers rely on it. It is the time-honoured practice of the ruling 'scholastic' bureaucracy – from the early Church to the modern scientific establishment – to encase the dominant scientific paradigm in the armour plate of conviction. They are impervious to contradictory empirical evidence delivered by 'heretics', no matter how compelling or accurate their views may be. The establishment invariably wins this contest because they have the power to silence the heretic with the threat of unpleasant consequences – ranging from the hot poker and the gibbet in past ages to losing one's job and career today.

The problem the establishment faces is that, over time, the ad hoc model becomes so cumbersome it defeats its own purpose and has to be abandoned, regardless of how elegant or expensive, or indeed how politically aligned, it might be. But this shift in thinking may take decades and is usually forced on the establishment by a troublesome heretic wielding an ugly fact that will not go away, just as Copernicus and Kepler did.

The imperative on today's climate modellers to produce politically acceptable and timely results far outweighs the requirement that they be accurate representations of nature. William Connolley, an IPCC climate modeller, admits this in his blog 'The IPCC: Dissolve it or Not?' He argues that climate modellers are under political pressure to overlook the issues because other more compelling forces are at play. He complains,

> At the moment, getting your model run into the IPCC report is a badge of having Made It, which is why something like a quarter of the models in the AR4 [Fourth Assessment Report] are a bit crap, and some are awful . . . Too many modelling schedules are then driven by getting into the next report. Too many peoples [sic] papers are aimed at being the right degree of sexiness to fit in.[27]

This is understandable if you consider the British climatologist John Mitchell's argument that 'People underestimate the power of models. Observational evidence is not very useful', he says. Mitchell then admits that, 'Our approach is not entirely empirical.'[28] This is a startling admission. Indeed, it admits to the intention of ignoring any and all observational evidence, regardless of its merit, that might contradict them. The only way this could happen is if politics, money, or both, corrupt and divert scientists from their true purpose: the honest and open pursuit of knowledge by evidence-based science, the 'scientific method'.

Computer modelling, then, is like a comfort blanket for the IPCC in times of adversity – the adversity of nature's 'failure to comply' with political expectations. But the behaviour of cloud and water vapour on climate is far too chaotic and complex to be reduced to a handful of manageable factors useful for computer modelling. There is too much gain in the system where an infinity of interconnected, interdependent events, involving such variables as cloud behaviour, air temperature, atmospheric dust, land and ocean effects, humidity, altitude, latitude, air density, plus the effects of other constituent gases among myriad other quantities and variables,[29] quickly assume unwieldy proportions and cannot be modelled or predicted to any useful degree.

Attempting to establish accurate climate forecasting information many decades into the future based on such models is nothing short of a fool's errand, little different from Ptolemy using his convoluted system to predict the position of the moon and planets accurately decades into the future. Indeed, during the 1970s ice age scare when the same argument was going on, but in reverse, scientists realized that the climate system is too complex to be fully understood with such a huge number of variables to be taken into account. David M. Gates, then Professor of Botany at the University of Michigan, pointed out that 'with a giant hydrodynamic, thermodynamic machine as complex as the earth's ecosystem of ground and atmosphere' proving cause and effect with atmospheric CO_2 is extremely difficult.[30] This problem remains, despite the huge advances in computing power since then.

IPCC's inability to forecast accurately was made clear in its failure to predict the downturn in global temperatures following the 1998 El Niño spike. In a revealing email to Michael Mann, creator of the controversial 'hockey stick' graph, IPCC lead author Kevin Trenberth admitted, 'The fact is that we can't account for the lack of warming at the moment and it is a travesty that we can't.'[31] Yet all the clues are there. John Barnes, a researcher working on atmospheric aerosols at the Mauna Loa laboratory, in another revealing comment, wonders why, despite steadily accumulating greenhouse gases, global temperatures *stalled* for the past decade. 'There's a lot of scatter to it [global temperature]. But the [climate] models go up. And that has to be explained. Why didn't we warm up?'[32] The answer is simple: CO_2 emissions have nothing to do with climate and the climate models are wrong.

This was shown in a 2006 paper by atmospheric physicist Ferenc Miskolczi who discovered that a self-regulating mechanism acts on the planet's greenhouse, putting an upper limit on its effectiveness, which climate models obviously fail to take into account. Miskolczi showed that external forcing, like increased CO_2 and other greenhouse gases including methane, are counteracted by the atmosphere's own dynamic response to them. So it is impossible to force global climate in any direction simply by changing the amount of CO_2 that enters the atmosphere artificially. His paper was not well received by his employer, NASA contractor Analytical Services and Materials, who told him to withdraw it. NASA refused to allow Miskolczi to publish it. 'They just sat on it', he says. By late 2006, Miskolczi resigned after months of trying to get his paper published. He complained in his resignation letter that NASA were hindering publication of research that has 'far-reaching consequences in the general atmospheric radiative transfer', meaning research in the greenhouse effect that challenges manmade global warming. Miskolczi writes, 'My idea of freedom of science cannot coexist with the way NASA handles new climate-change-related scientific results.'[33]

But Miskolczi's paper did have far-reaching consequences elsewhere. Another Hungarian physicist, Dr. Miklos Zagoni, 'was ousted last year as senior climate advisor of the Budapest Ministry of Environment and Water after publicly supporting Miskolczi's research' writes Kirk Myers in *The Examiner*. Myers says that Zagoni had 'been a staunch advocate of the AGW theory. But his views shifted after studying Miskolczi's research.' Zagoni explained that, 'First the government tried to frighten me, and then when that did not work, they kicked me out from my job. I lost my job because of my scientific convictions. I wanted to talk publicly about Dr. Miskolczi's results, but in the pre-Copenhagen days it was not tolerated by my government superiors.'

Nevertheless, because of the vast complexities within the biosphere, the problems associated with modelling are not dissimilar to air turbulence which is also considered far too chaotic to be modelled accurately. How, then, could a living, breathing atmosphere characterized by such complexities on a colossal scale be similarly approximated? The physicist Richard Feynman once pointed out that 'turbulence remains one of the unsolved problems in classical physics'. This applies equally to the climate system because of its dynamic complexity, its vast number of interconnected variables, few of which are taken into account. There is too much going on and too much randomness to predict outcomes too far into the future as the errors mount exponentially.

According to Henk Tennekes, former Director of Koninklijk Nederlands Meteorologisch Instituut (KNMI, the Dutch Meteorological Institute), 'The models which aim to predict the climate are totally useless' because they fail to take into account so many aspects of the biosphere, such as the oceans. 'Why does the IPCC ignore the oceans?' he asks.[34] And for questioning the 'consensus' view of manmade global warming by criticizing the IPCC's model accuracy, Tennekes was advised to clear his desk. He adds, 'First you must believe in something. Only then you are allowed to participate in their discussions', by which he meant the domination of climate research by a 'small clique that tolerates no contradiction, and equates dissenters to Holocaust deniers'.

Freeman Dyson, a theoretical physicist at Princeton University, pointed out the failure of models which 'do a very poor job of describing the clouds, the dust, the chemistry, and the biology of fields and farms and forests',[35] all of which have an influence on climate. The IPCC's GCMs also fail adequately to take into account the changing behaviour of the sun and consistently 'underestimate the variability and changes from solar-induced climate signals' – hence their influence on the earth's climate system.[36] The chaotic and unpredictable interactions of all the elements within the climate system preclude even approximation by computer modelling and generate very coarse, broad and uncertain outputs that have no correspondence with reality. Yet the IPCC persists in ignoring such problems, but based on its results recommends drastic restrictions on industrial output.

All of the IPCC climate models assume that positive feedbacks predominate, yet the strong negative feedbacks in the climate system are clear: warming causes evaporation from the oceans, which produces clouds; increased cloud cover increases the earth's albedo and this in turn reduces the amount of solar radiation reaching the oceans, which then cool. This feedback loop was observed during the Tropical Ocean Global Atmosphere Coupled Ocean Atmosphere Response Experiment (TOGA COARE) in 1992, which, according to Willem de Lange of the University of Waikato, 'found that rainfall would cool the ocean surface, so increased evaporation producing rain is another feedback loop'.[37] De Lange further explains,

> The observed climate change is consistent with variations in albedo and associated ocean warming and cooling, suggesting that it is . . . a natural cycle. This pattern of behaviour is evident in palaeoclimate data for most of the last 10,000 years. None of this is simulated in climate models, which instead focus on the twentieth century increase in CO_2, CH4 and a few other greenhouse gases and infer from a correlation with global temperature that the greenhouse effect is driving temperature.[38]

Richard S. Lindzen, Alfred P. Sloan Professor of Meteorology at Massachusetts Institute of Technology, argues that the IPCC's current climate models are 'disturbingly arbitrary' in the way they handle clouds and water vapour, partly because 'the underlying physics is simply not known'. He further argues that there are errors in the models themselves and that there is 'compelling evidence for all the known feedback factors actually to be *negative*' (emphasis added).[39] Furthermore, in a peer-reviewed paper Lindzen and Yong-Sang Choi showed the earth's climate system to be far less sensitive to changes in temperature from such forcings as CO_2 than current IPCC model predictions suggest.[40] According to Spencer,

> [Lindzen and Choi] showed that satellite-observed
> radiation loss by the Earth increased dramatically
> with warming . . . In stark contrast, all of the
> computerized climate models they examined did just
> the opposite, with the atmosphere trapping more
> radiation with warming rather than releasing more
> . . . The implication of their results was clear: most if
> not all climate models that predict global warming
> are far too sensitive, and thus produce far too much
> warming and associated climate change in response
> to humanity's carbon dioxide emissions.[41]

This is in stark contrast to the conclusion reached by the Lohmann research team, who argued that model sensitivities were too *low* and needed to be increased! Despite the errors in the models and the acknowledged uncertainties of cloud and water vapour feedbacks, all current IPCC model projections consistently overestimate warming and by a substantial margin. The IPCC then publishes these results as authoritative assessments of future climate. Neither doubt in their veracity nor scepticism in the science is tolerated, regardless of the problems and uncertainties that are known to exist and even acknowledged by the IPCC.

The IPCC, also in its Third Assessment Report, suggests projected temperature increases due to a doubling of atmospheric CO_2 ranging from 1.4°C to 5.8°C and comprising 245 separate predictions.[42] With such broad-ranging results, anything is possible. According to the IPCC, everything within this range is equally likely. But this raises the question, what is the point of investing billions of dollars in climate models if the projected temperature range they provide has an uncertainty envelope as wide as 4.4°C? This is a margin of error more than six times the IPCC-endorsed temperature increase since 1900 of a trifling 0.7°C, which is apparently compelling enough for politicians to focus on and then recommend a drastic cutback in greenhouse gas emissions to prevent it increasing further.

We are talking here of less than one degree Celsius over an entire century. In reality this is so slight it is not only lost in the background 'noise', but almost impossible to discern. One might experience it by walking from the kitchen to the lounge. And yet the IPCC suggests that an increase of 0.7°C over a century is extreme, while publishing climate projections with error margins orders of magnitude greater as though they are of no consequence. As Lindzen comments,

> future generations will wonder in bemused amazement that the early 21st century's developed world went into hysterical panic over a globally averaged temperature increase of a few tenths of a degree, and, on the basis of gross exaggerations of highly uncertain computer projections combined into implausible chains of inference, proceeded to contemplate a roll-back of the industrial age.[43]

To make matters worse, climatologist Patrick J. Michaels points out that the IPCC provides no guidance as to which of its model projections is more or less likely as a reliable climate scenario on which to base future economic policy decisions. According to Stephen Schneider, formerly of Stanford University, the IPCC failed to do so because they wanted to avoid arguments. Therefore, says Michaels, they leave it to the policy advisers to select whatever scenario takes their fancy. Interestingly, the IPCC also fails to mention that the actual average of all 245 temperature forecasts is 2.2°C, whereas normal distributions based on a bell-shaped curve produce an arithmetic mean of 3.6°C. On this point Michaels remarks, 'The IPCC has known this all along, yet they've let a hysterical environmental and popular press run with apocalyptic scenarios touting the huge 5.8°C warming.'[44]

In 2001, Richard Lindzen, Ming-Dah Chou and Arthur Hou[45] published a provocative paper in which they poured more cold water on the positive feedback theory. Their research indicated the existence of a self-regulating mechanism in the atmosphere over the tropics, which they called the 'Infrared Iris'. Essentially, this maintains stability of the earth's temperature regardless of atmospheric CO_2 content. Lindzen *et al* showed that as tropical temperatures *increase*, two things occur: low-level water clouds increase in coverage while total coverage of high-altitude ice clouds *decreases* more rapidly and to a greater extent. This tends to regulate tropical temperatures because ice clouds on their own have a net warming effect by trapping more long-wave radiation than is reflected by incoming short-wave radiation. Water clouds have an opposite, cooling effect by reflecting more short-wave solar radiation than is trapped by long-wave radiation from the earth's surface. Similarly, lower temperatures in the tropics lead to less water cloud coverage, allowing more solar radiation to reach the earth's surface, and at the same time more high-altitude ice clouds, resulting in a net radiation increase.[46] They found that by these means the system is self-regulating.

Since its publication, the Iris hypothesis has gained support from other researchers, including the climate scientists Spencer and Christy, who also found an increase in low-altitude water cloud coverage due to warming, but only an *initial* decrease in high-altitude ice cloud coverage.[47] Despite this slight discrepancy over ice cloud formation, it seems clear that the Iris effect does indeed provide a net negative feedback to warming, thus adding to atmospheric stability.[48]

And therein lies the crux of the matter: if, as the IPCC assumes, increased CO_2 leads inevitably to increased water vapour due to its very slight initial warming effect, and this in turn leads to more CO_2, followed by further increases in water vapour and temperature, the atmosphere would quickly become unstable and we would reach a point of thermal runaway – 'runaway climate change' – coupled with a saturated atmosphere. That this has never happened in the history of the earth – when on many occasions atmospheric CO_2 has been many times higher – should give the IPCC and global warming alarmists pause for thought. Even Gore admits that the earth's geological past frequently experienced periods of higher CO_2 and higher temperatures than today *without* resulting in such an outcome.

5. The Brink of Armageddon

> No one should approach the temple of science with the
> soul of a money changer.
>
> *Thomas Browne*

The catastrophic anthropogenic global warming (CAGW)
hypothesis depends on two crucial assumptions: first, that the
warming effect of atmospheric CO_2 necessarily increases with
increasing concentration; and second, that a 'tipping point' will
ultimately be reached because of amplification by water vapour.
The idea is that any subsequent reduction in CO_2 to reverse the
latter will have little or no effect and runaway climate change will
follow. The tipping point is based on an assumed positive feedback
factor greater than one where it is believed the climate will
necessarily spin out of control. However, such positive feedbacks
are practically non-existent in nature, especially with regard to the
earth's climate system.

It is the question of the alleged trigger for this event that
appears to have been overlooked in the global warming debate.
The term 'tipping point' is frequently used by scientists, politicians
and environmentalists to describe our inescapable climate future,
should we fail to reduce our greenhouse gas emissions, especially
CO_2. The very idea of a point of no return inspires fear, when the
atmosphere goes into meltdown and spins out of control because
someone, somewhere emitted the final modicum of CO_2. It sets a
speculative deadline to our industrial activities beyond which lies
catastrophe unless we curb our interest in technological progress
and the lifestyle it generates. Or so the theory goes.

The alarmist lobby of scientists and politicians, spurred on by the media and the environmental movement, who between them fan the flames of alarm, frequently employ this frightening mental image to encourage public acceptance of its inevitability. A grim future of climate chaos awaits us unless we also accept their unpalatable remedies to prevent it. The concept is a marketing dream because it is easy to sell to an impressionable public who, they must assume, will know no different, yet who will be impressed by the very idea. And quite naturally, no one wants the planet to end up like Carl Sagan's Venus, whose extreme surface temperature he put down to a runaway greenhouse effect as we saw in Chapter 2, so we capitulate with this powerful image in our minds. The terms 'runaway climate change' and 'tipping point' graphically set the scene for a hellish future, guaranteed to materialize unless we amend our bad behaviour by reducing carbon 'pollution' to 'safe' levels, theoretically determined by the IPCC and Hansen as 350 ppm of the atmosphere. However, since atmospheric CO_2 has frequently been *many* times higher than this in the past with no deleterious consequences for life on earth, Hansen's figure cannot be based on historical events. It is instead merely conjecture. 'The issue is that no one does know what a safe level of CO_2 is' admitted one NIWA scientist.[1] Yet Hansen's supposed 'safe level' is not the so-called tipping point, which is assumed to occur at some unspecified time in the future if levels continue to rise.

Indeed, climate alarmists, scientists and politicians between them have issued a dizzying variety of future tipping points, all of them different in urgency, yet all based on the idea that increasing atmospheric CO_2 will inevitably lead to disaster.[2] According to the *Independent*,[3] scientists expect a tipping point to occur by the year 2200. However, Prince Charles decided we have only ninety-six months, a mere eight years, to avert 'irretrievable climate and ecosystem collapse, and all that goes with it'.[4] More pressingly, in 2009, Prime Minister Gordon Brown declared 'negotiators had fifty days to save the world'.[5] Not to be outdone, the environmentalist and Canadian Green Party leader Elizabeth May decided the situation was far worse than anyone thought – 'we have [only] hours to prevent climate disaster'.[6] Not months, not years, just hours. Precious little time at all to save the world from the horrors of CO_2. The World Wildlife Fund was more sanguine and declared we had five years to prevent climate catastrophe,[7] a figure based perhaps on Gore's authoritative assertion made in 2006 that we had ten years left to save the planet.

However, according to James Lovelock, whose Gaia hypothesis proposes that the planet functions as a single, self-regulating organism, they were all wrong. 'Who [really] knows?' he asked. 'Everybody might be wrong. I may be wrong. Climate change may not happen as fast as we thought, and we may have 1,000 years [left] to sort it out.'[8] Yet in 2006, Lovelock was so pessimistic about the future he predicted that 'before this century is over, billions of us will die and the few breeding pairs of people that survive will be in the Arctic where the climate remains tolerable'.[9] So the warnings of approaching disaster range from a few hours to an entire millennium. Take your pick. Of course, according to Hansen it all hinges on the arbitrary 'safe' level of 350 ppm anyway, after which – and no one can say when – things apparently start to deteriorate at an alarming rate until the earth resembles Venus. The problem is that everyone, including Hansen, is guessing.

Nevertheless no one seems to have questioned the validity of the idea in the first place. Why has it not been fully defined and quantified by the scientists promoting the manmade global warming hypothesis? After all, they boast of the means to forecast future climate based on known levels of atmospheric CO_2 and known temperature trends, and the science tying it all together is supposedly settled. Indeed, it is on this basis that the IPCC is able to recommend to governments worldwide very specific reductions in CO_2 within very specific time-frames. So why can they not also quantify and forecast the tipping point which they say will inevitably result if we fail? It is not an unreasonable expectation considering the aggressive confidence of the IPCC in its projections of future climate. Admittedly, the IPCC and its supporting scientists are careful to refer to these projections as 'scenarios' not 'forecasts', as though they should not be taken too seriously. But this term is really a subtle disclaimer in case the projections prove to be wildly inaccurate due to their dependence on computer modelling and the multitude of assumptions and fudge-factors that accompany it.

Supposedly, current temperature and atmospheric CO_2 levels are known with some precision, and similarly their gradients according to the CO_2 monitoring station at Mauna Loa and the various temperature monitoring authorities like the Hadley Climate Research Unit, the National Oceanic and Atmospheric Administration (NOAA) and the Goddard Institute for Space Studies (GISS) which monitors sea surface temperatures. Why, then, has no one stated with equal certainty at what level (in ppm) of CO_2 the tipping point will occur? Why has no one using the term been confident enough to forecast a specific future date or year, referenced to specific levels of CO_2 and temperature?

No one is willing or able to predict such a tipping point because the theory is fundamentally flawed. It would take a foolhardy or brave scientist. Reluctance to do so is a clear vote of no confidence in the IPCC's computer-generated projections. The idea of runaway climate change is based on the common misapprehension that the forcing influence of atmospheric CO_2 is linear and has no upper limit. It is a tacit assumption that temperatures increase incrementally with corresponding increases in CO_2, as though the two are in linear lockstep and that eventually the system will reach a 'flashpoint' and send the entire biosphere into uncontrollable meltdown.

This basic proposition, fed to academia, the media and the general public, is neither explored nor corrected by scientists working for the IPCC, even though they know the relationship between temperature and CO_2 is *not* linear, but a reverse logarithm (Figure 11). They are aware of this and they understand that atmospheric CO_2 is governed by the principle of diminishing returns – the more that is added, the *less* incremental warming

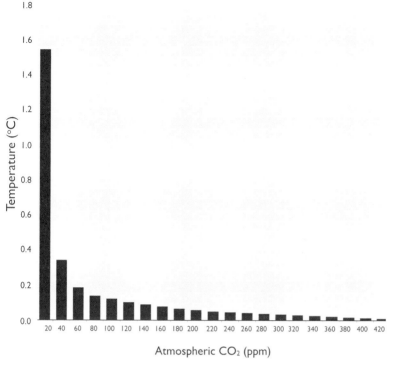

Figure 11. Reverse logarithmic relationship between temperature and atmospheric CO_2, where the first 20 ppm have the greatest effect and every subsequent 20 ppm increase has less and less effect. Climate sensitivity thus decreases with increasing CO_2 concentration, tapering off to infinitesimally small temperature increases. Redrawn from original.[10]

effect it has. The first 20 ppm have a greater impact on temperature than the next 400 ppm.

CO_2 quickly reaches its saturation point in the atmosphere and at 385–390 ppm it is already a spent force. Any further increase will do next to nothing to global temperatures, despite the dire warnings issued by the IPCC of 'runaway climate change' if levels are not reduced to Hansen's theoretical, but essentially arbitrary, 'safe limit' of 350 ppm. According to current estimates, the annual rate of increase of CO_2 over the last thirty years has averaged approximately 1.7 ppm, an insignificant figure in terms of increments to the atmosphere's constituent gases. By 2030, atmospheric CO_2 is expected to rise by another 40 ppm or so, to around 420 ppm, with a corresponding increase in temperature of 0.04°C.[11] Hardly detectable, let alone catastrophic.

The annual increase in both CO_2 and the theoretical corresponding effects on temperature are so small they are well below the margins of error in all IPCC projections – that is, the expected error margins are orders of magnitude greater than the actual resultant temperature anomaly.

CO_2 literally runs out of steam well before temperatures can rise to anywhere near the levels projected by the IPCC simply because there *is* an upper limit to its effectiveness as a climate-forcing agent. It is for this very reason that conditions on Venus are not the result of carbon dioxide in its atmosphere.

The popular belief that atmospheric CO_2, increasing interminably, is capable of forcing climate to such an extent originates with Svante Arrhenius. In an 1896 paper, he calculated a 5°–6°C temperature rise for a doubling of CO_2 above pre-industrial levels. This is often quoted by proponents of the AGW theory to support their argument that 'the science is settled'. The implication is that since Arrhenius worked it out more than a century ago, and his work is endorsed by the IPCC, it is beyond debate because everyone 'knows' it to be a 'fact'.

There is, however, more to this story that is not readily admitted. Arrhenius reworked his calculations in 1906 and reduced the degree of warming by a doubling of CO_2 to only 1.6°C. He wrote, 'I calculate in a similar way, that a decrease in the concentration of carbonic acid by half or a doubling would be equivalent to changes of temperature of −1.5°C or +1.6°C respectively.' His revised figure is generally ignored by the warming alarmists because it reduces the effect of CO_2 while the earlier figure supports the notion of catastrophic manmade global warming.

More recent calculations have revised this theoretical temperature increase downward even further, so that a doubling of CO_2 above pre-industrial levels should result in slightly less than 1°C increase, while some calculations suggest as little as 0.5°C.

And if CO_2 is doubled again, from 560 ppm, the resultant temperature increase will be less again because of the logarithmic relationship. It is clear, then, that CO_2 quickly reaches its upper limit in terms of climate forcing.

According to Timothy Ball, Professor of Geology at the University of Winnipeg,

> Even if CO_2 concentration doubles or triples [above the current level of 385 ppm], the effect on temperature would be minimal. The relationship between temperature and CO_2 is like painting a window black to block sunlight. The first coat blocks most of the light. Second and third coats reduce very little more. Current CO_2 levels are like the first coat of black paint. Computer climate models get around this by assuming that a highly questionable hypothesis is correct, namely that small increases in temperature due to large CO_2 rises cause more evaporation and the subsequently higher concentration of water vapour (the major greenhouse gas) in the atmosphere will cause further temperature rise. More likely, the resultant increased cloud cover will drive temperatures down.[12]

So much for Hansen's 'safe limit' of 350 ppm. Atmospheric CO_2 is 'safe' well beyond 1,000 ppm, as any commercial greenhouse operator can testify. Sherwood B. Idso adds:

> While admittedly incomplete and highly approximate general circulation models of the atmosphere predict that a 300–600 ppm doubling of the air's CO2 content will raise mean global air temperature a few degrees Celsius, natural experiments based upon real-world observations suggest that a global *warming of no more than a few tenths of a degree could result from such a CO2 increase* [emphasis added].[13]

The IPCC's climate projections, based on computer models, are out by orders of magnitude in terms of accuracy and correspondence with the real world. Idso argues that modern climate models fail to take into account natural 'planetary cooling forces that are intensified by increases in temperature and which therefore tend to dampen any impetus for warming'. Furthermore, most of these cooling forces 'can be amplified by increases in biological processes that are [themselves] directly enhanced by the aerial fertilization effect of atmospheric CO_2 enrichment'.[14] In other words, the very slight warming effect of increasing atmospheric CO_2 leads to corresponding increases in biological (mostly plant) activity, which in turn tends to dampen further warming. As atmospheric CO_2 rises, plant growth accelerates and CO_2 is consumed in the process. Another negative feedback.

Carbon dioxide is vital for plant life. Increased atmospheric CO_2 inevitably leads to enhanced growth in terms of biological mass and plant number, where experience shows that 1,000 ppm is considered optimal. This is more than twice the concentration currently in the atmosphere. At the same time, the requirement for water decreases as growth activity increases in efficiency. Commercial greenhouses routinely operate with their internal atmospheres at around 1,000 ppm without descending into uncontrollable meltdown due to a so-called 'tipping point' occurring.

Despite this evidence that carbon dioxide is beneficial and the complete *lack* of evidence that it is dangerous, the IPCC and prominent climate alarmists base their argument on one underlying assumption, that increasing atmospheric CO_2 inevitably leads to catastrophic global warming. On the contrary, the earth's atmosphere today is *starved* of CO_2 because it is well below the optimum level for plant life; indeed, much below the current level of 385 ppm, plant life begins to fail.[15] Atmospheric CO_2 today is the lowest it has been in 300 million years.[16]

David Bellamy, the well-known botanist and environmental campaigner, argued provocatively in the *Daily Mail* that not only is increased CO_2 not a danger, it is positively beneficial to life on earth:

Increase the amount of carbon dioxide in the atmosphere, double it even, and this would produce a rise in plant productivity. Call me a biased old plant lover but that doesn't sound like much of a killer gas to me. Hooray for global warming is what I say, and so do a lot of my fellow scientists.[17]

Bellamy says that for this contrary view he was shunned by the BBC, who axed his popular television programme.[18]

Burt Rutan, the aviation and space pioneer, agrees with Bellamy. 'Those who call themselves "green planet advocates" should be arguing for a CO_2-fertilized atmosphere, not a CO_2-starved atmosphere. Diversity increased when the planet was warm and had high CO_2 atmospheric content.'[19] William Happer, a Princeton physicist, concurs:

As far as green plants are concerned, CO2 is not a pollutant, but part of their daily bread – like water, sunlight, nitrogen, and other essential elements. Most green plants evolved at CO2 levels of several thousand ppm, many times higher than now. Plants grow better and have better flowers and fruit at higher levels. Commercial greenhouse operators recognize this when they artificially increase the concentrations inside their greenhouses to over 1,000 ppm.[20]

Current climate models fail to take into account the beneficial effects of increased CO_2 on plant life, which lead to negative feedbacks – another thing not factored into IPCC models. According to the British writer Lewis Page, 'A group of top NASA boffins says that current climate models predicting global warming are far too gloomy, and have failed to properly account for an important cooling factor which will come into play as CO_2 levels rise.'[21]

The IPCC and its supporting scientists know that the relationship between CO_2 and temperature is logarithmic, not linear, and that CO_2 in the air quickly reaches saturation in terms of its very slight warming effect. Nevertheless, these same scientists do not hesitate to use the phrase 'runaway climate change' as though the planet was heading for an atmospheric Armageddon despite increases in CO_2 being so insignificant. This theory implies that earth's climate has been fixed for millions of years and governed by a well-regulated, clockwork universe in which nothing changed until humankind threw a spanner in the works by emitting a modicum of CO_2 into the atmosphere, sending the climate into an uncontrollable heat spiral. Considering the age of the planet and humankind's insignificantly short occupation of it, this is not very likely.

It appears that the IPCC is deliberately exploiting the media and the public, allowing the concept to linger in the public domain, unexplained and completely unchallenged. According to Paul Georgia in Environment and Climate News, Lindzen raised this issue at a briefing to the US Senate Environment Committee just prior to the release of the IPCC's Third Assessment Report. Among other problems, Lindzen criticized the IPCC because

> It uses summaries to misrepresent what scientists say. It uses language that means different things to scientists and laymen. It exploits public ignorance over quantitative matters. It exploits what scientists can agree on, while ignoring disagreements, to support the global warming agenda. And it exaggerates scientific accuracy and certainty and the authority of undistinguished scientists.[22]

Thus, 'runaway climate change' is little more than a catchphrase lacking scientific merit, a slogan designed to frighten the public into conformity, to encourage resigned acceptance of the flawed hypothesis that human beings are causing catastrophic global warming through the emissions of CO_2. It is a legacy of Sagan's 1970s Venus greenhouse theory which was really employed to deal with Velikovsky.

6. Nothing New under the Sun

> Earthquakes may be brought about because wind is caught
> up in the earth, so the earth is dislocated in small masses
> and is continually shaken, and that causes it to sway.
>
> *Epicurus*

Epicurus understood more about how the earth behaves than the
IPCC does two millennia later.

Human impact on the earth is trifling in comparison to the
extremes of change, the violence and fury that nature inflicts upon
it. The earth's continuing evolution means that change is the
norm, not the exception. The atmosphere is in a constant state of
turmoil, in addition to other natural forces always at work. We are
at the mercy of the sun's vast energy output and the sun itself is
constantly changing. Only a frozen lifeless planet undergoes little
or no change. The earth has not been without colossal upheavals
on a *global* scale even well within humankind's brief occupancy.

To believe change is abnormal is to be ignorant of the earth's
history, but perhaps understandably, as the idea that humankind's
influence is negligible may seem counter-intuitive considering the
paradigm today that our footprint on the earth is significant and
that it has supplanted all other factors influencing climate. The
modern view is that our industrial CO_2 emissions are a scourge,
easily capable of overpowering natural forces and driving the earth's
climate system to extremes.

Yet the last 4.5 billion years of the earth's history have been
anything but stable. The earth has been subjected to everything
from cataclysmic global upheavals to gradual, incremental

evolutionary development. Ice ages lasting millennia, followed by interglacial periods of relative warmth, have also shaped the planet. The balmy interglacial periods were themselves briefly interrupted by *mini*-ice ages lasting a few hundred years or less, the last of which ended in the middle of the nineteenth century, from which the earth has been emerging ever since. And yet many times in the earth's history, global temperatures *and* atmospheric CO_2 have been far higher than today without any ill effects.

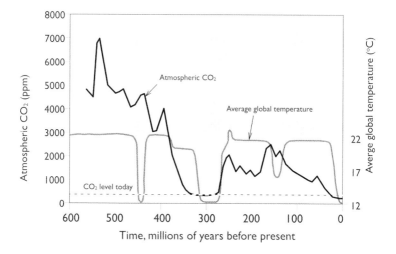

Figure 12. Approximate global temperature and atmospheric CO_2 over geological time. Note that 315–270 million years ago is the only period in the last 600 million years when both atmospheric CO_2 and temperatures were as low as they are today. Drawn by author from original.[1]

On many occasions, as the ice sheets retreated and forests expanded up the alpine slopes to higher altitudes and higher latitudes,[2] life became abundant and vital until the next ice age imposed its icy grip for millennia. Places like Greenland, as its name implies, changed from almost complete ice cover to plush green vegetation, especially in its southern latitudes, and back again.[3] The earth has always been changing and always will, while humankind's presence is a mere blip, an insignificant signal lost in the background noise to which nature is utterly indifferent, a fact shown conclusively in a peer-reviewed paper[4] by Nicola Scafetta of Duke University, North Carolina.

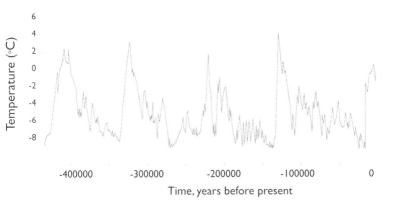

Figure 13. The earth's temperature history for the last ~450,000 years as determined from oxygen isotope $\delta^{18}O$ in ice cores taken at Vostok, Antarctica.[5]

Along the way, events of extreme violence intervened to shake the globe. Meteorite impacts and close encounters with large celestial objects such as comets wiped out entire species; volcanic eruptions devastated vast areas; super-floods swept all before them as ice sheets retreated and their melt waters, held back by natural dams, were released into the valleys and plains.[6] And humankind played no part in it, but rather has been a victim of nature's fury and capriciousness.

But today, there is a tendency to play down such massive, sudden and violent changes in the earth's geological past despite overwhelming evidence that they really did happen, even within the memory of man, and in all probability will happen again. There is a political expedient to ignore this evidence, even deny that some of these events occurred and that they had momentous impacts on global climate. Today's politically charged paradigm is that *humankind* now controls the climate, not nature.

This is the IPCC's conclusion, but it is difficult to justify when natural changes can easily be demonstrated from ice core evidence and other proxies, including the geological remains of past massive trauma. Instead, the evidence for earlier climatic extremes is in some cases completely expunged from the record.[7]

The fact of the Medieval Warm Period (MWP), a time of prosperity when the great cathedrals were built in Europe and Eric the Red colonised Greenland, became politically incorrect and thus failed to get a mention in the IPCC's 2001 Third Assessment Report. And, along with the MWP, the Little Ice Age (LIA) too lost its place in history.

Since Velikovsky's time, there has been a grudging acceptance by orthodox science that catastrophes have occurred, even that asteroid impacts may have contributed to the extinction of various species. But these events are still mostly considered isolated and local in scope, necessarily in the distant past and long before humankind's appearance. They are seen as anomalies, exceptions to the rule, and those events that contradict the IPCC's conclusions of man's climate culpability today are dismissed as fictions.

Ironically, the grudging and discriminatory acceptance of past catastrophe was forced on a reluctant establishment over the past few decades by a mountain of physical evidence pointing to large-scale cataclysms of unimaginable violence which devastated the entire globe, but again put in the very remote past *despite* indications that such events occurred well within recorded ancient history. Yet the idea is still encouraged that the planet holds a special place in the universe, a safe haven from celestial violence, its peace only recently disturbed by man. We are further taught that all fossils and fossilized footprints are necessarily millions of years old; that the violent events that destroyed their owners were isolated and local, of short duration, and were few and far between. And the planet always reverted to millions more years of tranquillity within narrow limits of behaviour acceptable to the orthodox scientific establishment, with everything in its place. Or so the story goes.

It was the departure from this naïve concept that brought so much fury from the scientific establishment onto Velikovsky for exposing it as a myth. He was dismissed as a charlatan for suggesting the earth has undergone repeated global catastrophic changes within recorded history, amassing an impressive array of evidence to back up his claim. And yet the same year that Velikovsky's *Worlds in Collision* came out describing these events, astronomers were already quietly claiming elements of his ideas as their own. The astronomer Fred Whipple, who had earlier joined the crusade against Velikovsky, published in the very same year his 'new' theory that a collision had occurred between a comet and an asteroid only 1,500 years ago. Yet Velikovsky was mocked by Whipple and others for suggesting a near collision had occurred between earth and a comet (later identified as the planet Venus) 3,500 years ago, bringing a catastrophic end to many civilizations of the old world simultaneously, including the Egyptian Middle Kingdom and the Minoan Empire. Civilizations around the world recorded the same upheavals in similar ways and reported seeing a comet which they consistently described in terms we now associate with planet Venus. During these upheavals, the face of the earth dramatically and violently changed.

Ironically, also in that same year of 1950, renowned Japanese astronomer Tsuneo Saheki proved the vulnerability of the planets in the solar system to catastrophic events. According to John J. O'Neill of the *New York Herald Tribune*, Saheki observed a 'brilliant explosive flash lasting several minutes'[8] on Mars, followed by a huge yellowish-grey mushroom cloud forming above the surface of the planet over its southern limb. The cloud extended over 1,500km horizontally and 100km high and was put down to a collision between Mars and a planetoid by astronomer and astrophysicist E. J. Öpik in the *Irish Astronomical Journal*[9]. However, because the catastrophic collision observed by Saheki was uncomfortably close in both time and location and in any case considered unlikely, more orthodox commentators dismissed it as merely a local volcanic eruption while others suggested it was an atomic explosion by the 'inhabitants of Mars'. Saheki himself ruled out a volcanic eruption because it was far too large and bright, as did astronomers at Osaka observatory, while Alexander-Alexandrovich Mikhailov of the Pulkovo observatory in Saint Petersburg described it as an explosion of colossal power, more akin to a nuclear explosion. They were stumped and floundering for realistic explanations that would not defy the orthodox dogma.

But then it happened again. The more recent spectacular collision between Jupiter and comet Shoemaker-Levi in 1994 once more brought home to scientists the reality and likelihood of Velikovskian-type events close to planet earth which is itself clearly not immune. These recent sightings make the possibility of massive collisions an uncomfortable reality because they occurred right in earth's backyard which has traditionally been considered 'safe', while such events have always been placed in the remote past, well before the advent of man. Saheki's Mars event and Shoemaker-Levi's impact on Jupiter make a mockery of this naïveté and they conflict rather glaringly with the psychologically more appealing, but less realistic view that earth's history has been one of peaceful, gradual evolution, uninterrupted by global trauma until *Homo sapiens* arrived and spoilt it all.

Today, the idea is common that the generally peaceful life of the planet, albeit interrupted by random acts of localised violence in the remote past, lasted four and a half billion years before humankind began despoiling the landscape by exploiting the earth's abundance; whose industry and appetite for energy began vandalizing the environment, as though human beings were not an integral and natural part of it: discovering how to make fire, developing agriculture and animal husbandry and felling trees to build huts and keep the fires alight, and later to build ships which extended humankind's range and influence. Humankind went forth and multiplied, discovered iron ore, made pottery and glass, windmills and bread; burnt wood, then coal and oil, and developed commerce and industry and discovered nuclear energy. They started travelling to more distant places – even to the moon – by virtue of mechanical genius and a sense of adventure.

Yet despite our iniquity, we had more food and security, wealth and abundance, and lived longer. We had music and art and mathematics, science and technology; we had knowledge of grand things big and small. Yet there are those among us who hold these achievements to be pernicious. There are those who think of humankind as a noxious invader.

Pentti Linkola, a Finnish eco-philosopher, prescribes the end of Western civilization to save Gaia, the living earth, 'Everything we have developed over the last 100 years should be destroyed.' Linkola then suggests that 'World War III would be a happy occasion for the planet,' implying that the only way to 'save' it is for complete de-industrialization and the eradication of human beings.[10]

The Voluntary Human Extinction Movement (VHEMT) is a loose network of some 250 people dedicated to saving Gaia through human extinction. This strange alliance of unhappy curmudgeons recommends 'phasing out the human race by voluntarily ceasing to breed [which] will allow Earth's biosphere to return to good health'. In the meantime, 'Crowded conditions and resource shortages will improve as we become less dense.'

Other, somewhat less extreme environmental activists advocate the suspension of democracy in order to impose a totalitarian 'green' ideology on the West, run on the philosophy of Plato.[11] Among them, Clive Hamilton, former Australian Green Party candidate, advises that democracy be suspended for the good of the planet if we are to avoid a temperature rise of 3°C, let alone the 'horrible' thought of 4°C–5°C, and that 'There is a need – more pressing by the day – to question the value of the economic, political and personal liberty that has been won.'[12] Just how the planet's temperature will fall by replacing democracy and personal liberty with an arbitrary totalitarian regime is anybody's guess, but the physics linking them all must be incredibly interesting if not wholly bizarre. Hamilton argues that 'We can only avoid catastrophe – including millions dying in the Third World – if we radically change the way we in the rich countries go about our daily lives. *Above all,*' he says, '*we must abandon our comfortable belief in progress*' (emphasis added).[13]

According to these extremists, democracy and economic and technological progress are incompatible with the needs of the planet. Gaia, it seems, abhors capitalism and democracy.

While these bizarre ideas range from the extreme to the utterly absurd, it is now a popular concept – again endorsed by the politically correct scientific establishment – that, despite past human exploitation of an otherwise benign planet, it was a minor infringement compared to what humans did next. The Industrial Revolution is held to be the turning point, the beginning of the end, the start of environmental and climatic decline from which we are unlikely to recover. Of course, the subsequent progress wrought by industrial technology in the late nineteenth and twentieth centuries allowed us to emit an insignificant amount, a mere sniff, of CO_2 into the atmosphere, a paltry few *thousandths* of a per cent by volume of a perfectly natural minor atmospheric gas whose presence has allowed life to flourish. That, apparently, is our sin. Carbon dioxide is considered a pollutant. Our industrial activities are supposedly now sending the biosphere into a potential death spiral, the like of which the planet has never before experienced. It is further assumed, and now taught, that atmospheric CO_2 at today's level of 385–90 ppm is unnatural, unprecedented, in at least the last million years of the earth's history.

Today's 'unnaturally high' CO_2 levels and 'soaring' temperatures are supposedly abnormal and catastrophically bad for the planet. According to the AGW alarmists, the earth cannot cope with temperature increases of much more than 0.7°C per century, a figure that has sent the highly politicized scientific establishment and the equally politicized IPCC into paroxysms of dread, moving them to forecast imminent climate doom. And yet temperatures are known to have changed twenty times faster 25,000–30,000 years ago when 12°C–15°C per century was not unusual,[14] while CO_2 concentrations are also known to have been orders of magnitude higher in prehistoric times than they are today.

According to research carried out in 2008 by the French National Centre of Scientific Research (CNRS), a major climate shift around 15,000 years ago resulted in a global average temperature drop of 10°C in one or two years,[15] while the Younger Dryas-to-Holocene step-wise change around 11,500 years ago saw equally large temperature rises in just a few decades or less.[16] According to a recent study of Greenland's ancient ice by an international team of scientists led by Stephen Barker of Cardiff University, 'abrupt climate change has been a systemic feature of Earth's climate for hundreds of thousands of years'.[17] Greenland's ice cores 'provided the first clue that Earth's climate is capable of very rapid transitions'.[18] David Deming, in an interview with the meteorologist Brian Sussman, said, 'after the last ice age the temperature of Greenland increased by perhaps as much as 50 degrees in a period of perhaps ten years'.[19] Although his statement was, quite understandably, given in very general terms for the interview, the point Deming was making is that there is nothing unusual for huge temperature variations to occur over very short time-frames.

Why, then, all the fuss over 0.7°C per century and 385–90 ppm of atmospheric CO_2? Naturally, the alarmists overlook the fact that most of that 0.7°C rise during the twentieth century occurred well *before* the post-Second World War economic boom and hence before increased industrial CO_2 could have made any difference. They are necessarily quiet on this issue because the AGW hypothesis implies that the effect of increased temperatures *before* the end of the war must have occurred before its own cause: industrial CO_2 emissions *after* the war. This is as absurd a proposition as that dealing with the 800-year lag between atmospheric CO_2 and global temperatures.

It can be shown that most of the temperature rise of the twentieth century can be explained by natural climate cycles, of which there are many.[20] There is no need, other than for political or other vested interests, to point the finger at industrial emissions in order to account for it. Nature is quite capable of forcing climate change on its own, as it has done throughout the entire history of the planet.

The Australasian researchers Chris de Freitas, Robert Carter and John McLean, in a 2009 peer-reviewed paper, show that most of the warming and cooling during the late twentieth century was indeed the result of natural forces and that the Southern Oscillation (SO) is the key to these climatic events, its cycles preceding corresponding changes in global mean temperature by between six and nine months. The SO cycles back and forth naturally between El Niño and La Niña conditions in the Pacific Ocean, resulting in either warm or cool phases globally lasting years. The researchers show that the SO is a dominant and consistent influence on mean global temperature.

'Shifts in temperature are consistent with shifts in the SOI [Southern Oscillation Index] that occur about seven months earlier.' This means that global temperatures are greatly influenced by the Southern Oscillation and consistently follow it by around seven months, which suggests that the SOI is the primary agent acting on the earth's climate, not atmospheric CO_2. The SOI is by far the strongest indicator of global mean temperature unless it is modified by volcanic activity which, according to John Daly,[21] de Freitas and others, tends to lower temperatures due to the injection of aerosols and particulates into the upper atmosphere. This appears to have occurred during the eruption of El Chichon in Mexico in 1982, and Mt Pinatubo in the Philippines in 1991, both events modifying the strong SOI signal at the time, resulting in lower global temperatures than would otherwise have occurred.[22] However, some commentators dispute the magnitude of the cooling effect and argue that volcanic eruptions have far less of an effect on global temperatures than is generally believed because of the rapid counteracting response of the climate system to such forcing agents.[23]

Other research carried out by Indermühle, Panagi and Flower in 1999 shows that on geological time-scales there are periods where high temperatures coincide with low atmospheric CO_2, when the two are out of phase and heading in opposite directions, and vice versa.[24] Indeed, according to a 1999 paper by Hubertus Fischer, Martin Wahlen, Jesse Smith, Derek Mastroianni and Bruce Deck, 'Despite strongly *decreasing* temperatures, high carbon dioxide concentrations can be sustained for thousands of years during glaciations' (emphasis added), so that dramatic temperature swings may occur independently of atmospheric CO_2.[25] We discovered this in Chapter 3 (see Figure 6).

Clearly then, in comparison to the geological record, today's climate cycles and conditions are quite benign and relatively stable,[26] despite so much alarmist hyperbole from the IPCC and its apologists that it's the other way around. The physicist Ivar Giaever recently highlighted the absurdity of the alarmist's claim that today's temperatures are unnaturally high when he wrote, 'The claim . . . is that the temperature has changed from ~288.0 to ~288.8 degree Kelvin in about 150 years, which (if true) means to me is that the temperature has been amazingly stable, and both human health and happiness have definitely improved in this "warming" period.'[27] Giaever resigned as a Fellow of the American Physical Society 'in disgust over the group's promotion of manmade global warming fears'. He is not alone. In October 2010, another prominent physicist, Hal Lewis, resigned from the APS for similar reasons and in protest over that body's political stance on AGW alarmism. Lewis wrote to Curtis G. Callan Jr., of Princeton University and APS President, lamenting 'the global warming scam, with the (literally) trillions of dollars driving it, that has corrupted so many scientists, and has carried APS before it like a rogue wave. It is the greatest and most successful pseudo-scientific fraud I have seen in my long life as a physicist.' (See Appendix I for the full text.)

Nevertheless, on the strength of today's temperatures and CO_2 concentrations, it is fashionable to think of humankind as a blight on the landscape, a vandal whose presence is inimical to the earth which may take a thousand years to recover. According to the Australian Climate Commissioner Tim Flannery, even 'If we cut emissions today, global temperatures are not likely to drop for about a thousand years.'[28] One might imagine from this that the earth is part of a regulated universe of perfect stability, locked forever in happy stasis, the climate rigidly determined within impossibly strict bounds where nothing changes without human interference.

However, Ross Garnaut, climate adviser to the Australian government, apparently believes the planet can be 'saved' if only we give up our 'carbon habit'. The 'climate risk is set to worsen,' he told reporters, referring to the Brisbane floods and Cyclone Yasi which devastated the area in December 2010 and January 2011. Garnaut warns of more climate chaos to come unless Australians drastically cut their greenhouse gas emissions, as though these were the direct cause.

Climate change is apparently abnormal and global warming necessarily bad, so bad in fact that John Stokes, writing in *The Canadian*, fretted that 'Over 4.5 billion people could die from global warming-related causes by 2012'[29] due to the release of massive amounts of methane from melting permafrost. Clearly, there is an issue with this 'blatant idiocy', as Anthony Watts describes it,[30] because Stokes's prediction implied nearly one billion deaths a year for five years caused by a temperature change that is less than that experienced by most people in the space of twenty-four hours. Furthermore, according to an article in *Science Daily*, 'The most comprehensive modelling yet carried out on the likelihood of how much hotter the Earth's climate will get in this century shows that without rapid and massive action, the problem will be about twice as severe as previously estimated six years ago'[31] and that even this assessment may be optimistic.

Apparently things are now so out of hand that 'There's really no such thing as natural weather anymore', at least according to the climate scientist Donald Wuebbles of the University of Illinois. He writes, 'Anything that takes place today in the weather system has been affected by the changes we've made to the climate system. That's just the background situation and it's good for people to know that.'[32] Natural weather is a thing of the past because humankind overpowered it with a filthy carbon habit. According to the alarmists, everything that happens from now on is entirely unnatural because humankind has superseded nature. What incredible hubris, yet this is the state of climate science today.

The floods and cyclones that occurred in Brisbane are supposedly new and unnatural, events unknown before the Industrial Revolution. One might be forgiven for believing the other 177 cyclones that devastated the Queensland area since records began in 1864[33] were imagined, while the even larger Brisbane floods in the nineteenth century[34] were entirely fictitious. Ironically, the massive 1974 Brisbane flood occurred during the 1970s *ice age* scare. This begs the question, if manmade global warming caused the 2010–11 Brisbane floods, how could global cooling have caused an even bigger flood in the 1970s? But these earlier events are conveniently overlooked because they do not fit the current paradigm of manmade warming causing climate change and all extreme weather. Any divergence from this belief is considered heresy.[35]

During the 1970s ice age panic, extreme weather events were thought to be the likely consequence of global *cooling*. In 1976, Lowell Ponte wrote, 'The optimism has shrivelled in the first chill of the cooling. Since the 1940s winters have become subtly longer, rains less dependable, storms more frequent throughout the world.'[36] How can extreme weather events be the result of both global cooling *and* global warming? Someone must be wrong.[37] Yet there is strong evidence that increased storminess is more likely during *cool* periods than during warm periods, the very opposite of what global warming alarmists today assume to be the case. Extreme weather has been recorded by scholars and other commentators for thousands of years, with detailed accounts from as early as 1 AD (and some less certain anecdotes from as early as 1800 BC);[38] they were obviously grave enough to have been seen as noteworthy by the ancients. *A Chronological Listing of Early Weather Events* includes 'the freezing of the Black Sea in 762 AD, the heavy rainstorms in Great Britain in 553 AD, 918 AD, 1222 AD, 1233 AD,

1330 AD, 1338 AD, and 1348 AD, and the winters in which the River Thames froze in London'. But of course, none of this could really have happened because today's global warming alarmists are certain such events are new to the planet and caused by a small amount of CO_2 leaking into the atmosphere where, apparently, it doesn't belong.

The same is being said of an 'unprecedented' sea level rise of one millimetre or so per year[39] being caused by our CO_2 emissions heating the planet, as though sea levels also have remained static for millennia until the end of the twentieth century. Yet the evidence for past huge and dramatic change is plentiful. In 1926, geologist Reginald Daly of Harvard University brought together coastal evidence from around the world indicating that sea levels appear to have suddenly dropped by some *twenty feet* only 3,500 years ago (incidentally further supporting Velikovsky's theory of catastrophic disturbances in the solar system in the second millennium BC). Later, Philip H. Kuenen of Leyden University came to the same conclusion, that sea levels in diverse places around the world had dropped between twenty and thirty feet around 3,000 to 3,500 years ago. Kuenen said that a number of other investigators had found the same thing 'so that this recent shift [in sea levels] is now well established'.[40] Clearly, this 'well established' fact has since been forgotten.

In reality, however, there is reason to suppose that the occurrence of extreme weather events, especially severe floods, has actually *declined* over the past few decades,[41] but increased reporting of these events - because communications technology today is so widely available and inexpensive – leads to the opposite perception. Today very little of consequence escapes the notice of people who have access to mass communications. Everything is shared very quickly, and this gives rise to the impression that these events are occurring more frequently.[42] The same holds for the perception that extreme weather events are more common because of increased damage reports and increased cost of damage. But this is a function of increased population with more buildings and more widespread infrastructure, not more storm activity. There's simply more to destroy which is misinterpreted as more storms doing the destroying, only because the metric is in cost of damage, which naturally increases with time.

Similarly, some global warming advocates are wringing their hands over heat waves as though these too are relatively new. According to John Roach, writing in *National Geographic News*, scientists claim that global warming is likely causing more heatwaves.[43] Joe Romm of the Center for American Progress and the American climate activist and environmentalist Bill McKibben, among others,[44] agree and seem unable to find any other explanation for such events than human-induced climate change brought about by anthropogenic global warming. They need only look to the heavens and observe the sun to find a more likely causative agent. Thus, the 2010 Russian heatwave was necessarily caused by our carbon emissions because planet earth has never experienced one before. But this also begs the question, what caused the 1911 heatwave in the United States which killed 652 people?

Strangely, AGW alarmists also argue that manmade global warming causes extreme cold. Having hijacked both ends of the argument, they insist that the record winter blizzards experienced in Europe and the United States since 2002 were all the result of human-induced climate change. Yet, the Canadian environment scientist Madhav L. Khandekar points out, 'The observed changes in the earth's climate seem to suggest that winters have become colder and possibly longer in the last ten years. Since the new millennium, there have been four winter seasons in the northern hemisphere which can be assessed as significantly colder and longer as well',[45] a fact put down to *human*, not natural, influences by global warming alarmists.

Thus, when temperatures decline severely, global warming is played down while 'climate change' or 'climate disruption' is emphasized as the cause. In which case it must be asked, what caused the big freeze at the end of the nineteenth century when

Niagara Falls froze over on more than one occasion due to record low winter temperatures? These extreme weather events around the turn of the century occurred well before CO_2 was emitted in any 'significant' quantity – if one can call today's emissions 'significant' when they amount to a few thousandths of a per cent by volume.

Not content with blaming humankind's CO_2 emissions for all extreme weather events, from blizzards to heatwaves, and floods to droughts, over time the alarmists have focused on other arcane issues they also ascribe to manmade global warming, from potent Afghan poppies, to seismic activity, declining bat populations, deaf fish, fat fish and zoonotic diseases.[46]

Today's AGW alarmists seem to have turned their backs on the earth's geological past and expunged it from the history books.[47] It is as though the Roman Warm Period, the MWP and the Little Ice Age had never happened because everything in nature was apparently stable, balanced and unchanging until the Industrial Revolution and the advent of the twentieth century. But these earlier periods did occur and nature is anything but stable and unchanging, as any geologist would attest.

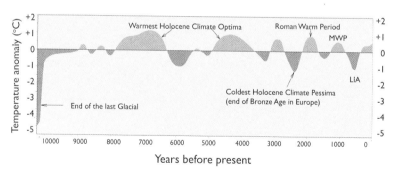

Figure 14. The earth's temperature profile for the last ≈10,000 years showing a prominent Roman Warm Period, Mediaeval Warm Period and Little Ice Age, until the Modern Warm Period today. Redrawn by author.[48]

So the fashionable view is that 'carbon pollution' – whatever that means – is destroying the planet and we need to be taxed because we are too obsessed with our need and desire to burn oil and coal for travel, security and industry. Fortunately, it seems, we can save the planet if we cease all industrial activity and become vegetarians. These drastic measures were recommended by Maurice Strong, adviser to former UN Secretary-General Kofi Annan, and Nicholas Stern, Baron Stern of Brentford. It was Strong's idea that sustainable development could 'be implemented by a deliberate quest of poverty . . . reduced resource consumption . . . and set levels of mortality control'.[49] Echoing Linkola's extreme views, Strong worried, 'We may get to the point where the only way of saving the world will be for industrial civilization to collapse.' And in order to bring about this 'utopian' existence for the benefit of the planet, Strong further advises that

> Current lifestyles and consumption patterns of the affluent middle class – involving high meat intake, use of fossil fuels, appliances, home and work-place air-conditioning, and suburban housing – are not sustainable. A shift is necessary which will require a vast strengthening of the multilateral system, including the United Nations.[50]

How convenient for the United Nations that in order to 'save the planet', their power and influence over our everyday lives, as Strong recommended, have to increase to the point of total control of all resources. Gore proposes similar restrictions on Western lifestyles, suggesting we should use our cars less and install energy-saving light bulbs.[51] Yet, according to some commentators, Gore's own lifestyle is lavish enough to accuse him of hypocrisy.[52] One might take Strong, Gore and others similarly inclined more seriously if they were to lead by example.

Lord Stern is less draconian and merely advises we give up meat consumption to save the planet. His solution to increasing global temperatures and greenhouse gas emissions means that 'People will need to turn vegetarian if the world is to conquer climate change'.[53] The idea that changing one's diet can alter the planet's climate patterns is an astonishing suggestion, primitive in its naivety, akin to the old belief that women and garlic possessed the power to interfere with a ship's compass. Incidentally, that was once the 'consensus' view. Consensus means nothing if the theory is wrong, no matter how powerful and insistent its adherents.

But just when you thought things couldn't get any more bizarre, along comes a serious proposal that humans could be given meat laced with medication 'that triggers extreme nausea, which would then cause a long-lasting aversion to meat eating' – something S. Matthew Liao, Professor of Philosophy and Bioethics at New York University, has called for.[54]

This is no joke. According to Liao, changing the human body in subtle but fundamental ways over time could be a powerful new weapon in the war on climate change. Liao also argues that making humans smaller would help because they would consume less food, resources and energy. He explains that even a slight reduction of 'the average U.S. height by just 15 cm' would result in lower energy and food consumption. But Liao goes further and suggests a reduction in family size, akin to China's one-child family rule, and that a 'fixed allocation of greenhouse gas emissions per family' might protect the planet from the horrors of climate changes.[55]

Clearly, we have come a long way since the days of Fourier and Tyndall.

While the alarmists sing the praises of vegetables and become hysterical over the supposed evils of CO_2 they overlook the reality of the sun. Timothy Ball eloquently described the folly of this attitude in an interview with Martin Durkin for *The Great Global Warming Swindle* documentary. 'The analogy I use,' says Ball, 'is my car's not running very well, so I'm going to ignore the engine, which is the sun, and I'm going to ignore the transmission, which is the water vapour, and I'm going to look at one nut on the right rear wheel which is the human-produced CO_2. The science is that bad.'[56] Nigel Calder too puts things in perspective with his vivid description of the sun: 'The sun is an incredibly violent beast. It's throwing out great explosions and puffs of gas, an endless solar wind that's forever rushing past the earth. We are, in a certain sense, inside the atmosphere of the sun. The intensity of its magnetic field more than doubled during the twentieth century.'[57]

The sun is also highly complex and poorly understood. Will Alexander recently showed that the sun's eleven-year sunspot cycle modulates drought and rainfall patterns in South Africa on a double twenty-one-year cycle. Robert Baker found the same to be the case in Australia and H.N. Bhalme and D.A. Mooley 'published similar conclusions about India's floods and droughts'.[58]

It also appears to hold true for some river levels as Pablo Maus showed when he plotted water levels in the Paraná River in Brazil. Maus found a very close correlation between the flow rate of the Paraná and the sun's eleven-year sunspot cycle,[59] far closer than any imagined correlation between industrial CO_2 emissions and temperature, which is at best only intermittent. Furthermore, slight variations in the sun's apparent diameter also have large effects on its energy output and correspondingly on earth's climate patterns. According to the science writer and astronomer John Gribbin, the sun's diameter changes on a seventy-six-year cycle which modulates its eleven-year sunspot cycle. This in turn shows up in the earth's climatic past by way of variations in tree ring growth, among other natural variables.[60] Gribbin also points out that a study by Ronald Gilliland in 1981 shows that a 'clear relationship with sunspot activity' appears to exist: there are 'fewer sunspots present when the Sun is bigger',[61] and vice versa. Gribbin further suggests that 'If the same anti-correlation can be applied to the longer-term decline in the sun's diameter, it may provide a clue to the dearth of sunspots during the height of the Little Ice Age.' According to Gribbin, during the LIA, the sun's angular diameter was slightly greater than it is today, 'about two-thirds of a second of arc'.[62]

There is clearly a lot going on with the sun that is not well understood but whose influences are nevertheless felt on earth. How could such a complex, powerful and obvious presence be so easily overlooked as though its purpose was merely to provide illumination? How could its role as a potent climate driver be so readily ousted by an unproved hypothesis based on a few *thousandths* of a per cent increase in CO_2, a perfectly natural constituent element of the atmosphere?

The BBC meteorologist Paul Hudson agrees that the sun is habitually ignored because of the politically correct focus on CO_2. Hudson committed heresy by contradicting the BBC's message that global warming is the fault of the human race and that climate change is an unnatural hazard. He says, 'For as long as I have been a meteorologist, the mere suggestion that solar activity could influence climate patterns has been greeted with near derision.'[63] Such heresy within its ranks is an outrage to the BBC, which has been promoting the manmade global warming tear-jerker for decades. But this is not surprising considering the BBC hangs its hat on the Met Office's climate forecasts.

The problem however is that the BBC seems very unsure how accurate the Met Office's forecasts are because of their recent rather poor performance, as environment analyst Roger Harrabin admits to the *Radio Times*: 'The trouble is that we simply don't know how much to trust the Met Office' he complains, and wonders just how often it gets the weather right while comparing its performance with that of the independent forecasters, who seem to have a better track record. But Harrabin is confident that eventually 'we'll all have a better idea of whom to trust. By then the Met Office might have recovered enough confidence to share with us its winter prediction of whether to buy a plane ticket or a toboggan.'[64]

Hudson understands why and suggests that the art of weather forecasting has been relinquished to super-computers and the trend to assume that humankind's impact on climate is far greater than all natural forces combined. In the past, he says, most meteorological studies focused on the sun's apparent brightness as though this were the only variable to be taken into consideration.[65] The almost imperceptible changes in the sun's irradiance (around 0.1 per cent) are considered insufficient to account for climate change on the earth so the AGW alarmists focus exclusively on CO_2 emissions and assume that the sun's many other dynamic factors can be safely ignored. If they can't be seen, they can't possibly exist. In any case, figures obtained by satellite of the Total Solar Irradiance (TSI) are now in question and thought to be artificially low due to absorption by the furthest reaches of the earth's outer atmosphere, *below* which the Solar Radiation and Climate Experiment (SORCE) satellite orbits, at 645 kilometres. 'Unfortunately, a funny thing happened to the TSI on its way to the SORCE satellite' writes Tim Cullen in his recent article on the problem. Cullen points out that the earth's outer atmosphere is 'transforming' TSI before it gets to the satellite's sensors, giving skewed results of solar irradiance measurements which cannot be relied on. Therefore, he says, 'Climatology's energy budget is wrong', the 'Greenhouse Effect is wrong' and 'global warming science is wrong'.[66]

But a host of other solar variables do exist whose combined effects are far more influential on the earth's climate than apparent brightness alone and orders of magnitude more influential than the trivial amount of CO_2 in the atmosphere. Yet it is precisely by observing such solar effects, especially sunspot activity, and their effects on cosmic rays that enables the independent meteorologist and astrophysicist Piers Corbyn to outperform the Met Office, even months in advance.

In December 2010, Boris Johnson pondered how this was possible and asked the question that was 'bugging' him: 'Why did the Met Office forecast a mild winter'[67] when the country was in the grip of record blizzards? The Met Office had forecast that the winter would be slightly warmer than average, for which everyone prepared, while Corbyn forecast the coldest winter in a century, which the authorities ignored. The Met Office's wildly incorrect forecast resulted in the country being caught totally unprepared.

After record snow fell, Johnson complained, 'I can't remember a time when so much snow has lain so thickly on the ground, and we haven't even reached Christmas. And this is the third tough winter in a row. Is it really true that no one saw this coming?'[68] Well the Met Office certainly didn't, despite access to super-computers and the best technology, whereas Corbyn *did* using only a laptop and high-quality data. The Met Office had been blinded by the political dazzle of the AGW myth in which the sun plays little or no role. They cannot see the forest for the trees, whereas Corbyn observes sunspot activity and cosmic ray interactions, among many other sun-earth-moon influences.

Observations of sunspot activity are clearly part of the key to success, not super-computers. As mentioned earlier, it was the astronomer William Herschel who noticed the connection between sunspots and wheat prices two centuries ago, during the LIA period. Why has it been forgotten and routinely ignored by the Met Office? The same holds true for many other meteorological services around the world which have been similarly seduced by pseudo-scientific fads, politics and money. As though to prove the point Herschel made in 1801, Eigil Friis-Christensen of the Danish Space Research Institute plotted sunspot activity for the twentieth century and found a very close correlation that accurately mapped the rise in temperatures to 1940 and the following decline in temperatures until 1975. The correlation was however dismissed by his detractors as coincidence, so Friis-Christensen repeated the test for the last 400 years and found precisely the same, removing any possibility that the link is coincidental.

In 2002 the Israeli astrophysicist Nir Shaviv at the Hebrew University in Jerusalem took the cosmic ray link even further back to around 500 million years and identified a cosmic ray signature in the earth's geological climate patterns.[69] How odd that while the AGW alarmists dismiss Friis-Christensen's very close correlation between sunspot activity and temperature for the twentieth century as 'coincidental', they see the loose and only occasional correlation between CO_2 and temperature over the same period as utterly convincing.

Friis-Christensen and Svensmark found an even closer correlation between cloud cover and cosmic ray flux from deep space. They argued that 'solar activity may be a controlling factor for climate by changing low-level cloud cover'[70] due to cosmic ray interactions within the atmosphere being modulated by the solar wind. Simply put, low solar activity results in more cosmic rays entering the atmosphere from deep space where they 'seed' clouds by forming microscopic water droplets around ionized nuclei. This aerosol formation in turn results in the growth of more low-level clouds and lower corresponding temperatures as the clouds then reflect the sun's incoming radiation back into space. With high solar activity, the opposite occurs.

The theory was panned by orthodox climate science because it diminished the importance of greenhouse gases, particularly CO_2. Svensmark, however, measured the effect by comparing cosmic ray flux (the number of charged particles arriving at a given time) with cloud cover and concluded, in simple terms, that 'Data on cloud cover from satellites, compared with counts of galactic cosmic rays from a ground station, suggested that an increase in cosmic rays makes the world cloudier.'[71]

Svensmark explains 'that cloudiness is more clearly linked with solar-modulated galactic cosmic rays than with other solar phenomena such as sunspots or the emissions of visible light, ultraviolet and X-rays'.[72] According to his observations, cloud changes could be as much as 3–4 per cent and appear to follow the sun's eleven-year sunspot cycle. The link is undeniable, but also highly significant considering that a persistent change in cloudiness of just 1–2 per cent is enough to account for the 0.6–0.7°C temperature increase for the twentieth century, as Spencer noted.[73] The IPCC, on the other hand, attributes this to CO_2 and other minor greenhouse gases. So the sun 'controls' or modifies the constant rain of cosmic rays from deep space. An active sun means

Variations in cosmic ray intensity and cloud cover (1984–94)

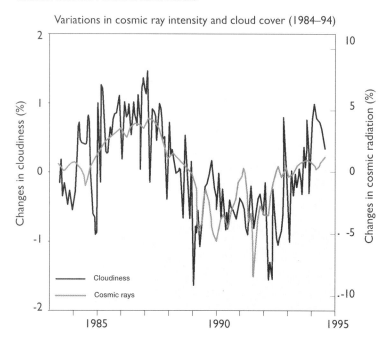

Figure 15. The clear correlation, observed by Svensmark, between cosmic ray flux (grey line) and low-altitude cloud cover (black line), as measured by satellite.[74]

fewer cosmic rays entering the earth's atmosphere to seed clouds, while a quiet sun results in more.

Then an independent study by Laken and colleagues came to the same conclusion: 'small fluctuations in solar activity may be linked to changes in the earth's atmosphere via a relationship between the GCR [galactic cosmic ray] flux and cloud cover; such a connection may amplify small changes in solar activity.'[75] Spencer says this research 'was especially interesting since it showed satellite-observed cloud changes following changes in cosmic ray activity'. He adds, 'the results gave *compelling quantitative evidence of a cosmic ray effect on cloud cover.*'[76]

The correlation is so obvious; it is a travesty that the UK Met Office and other mainstream meteorological institutes allow the politically correct, alleged correlation between CO_2 and temperature (where CO_2 is considered the driving force) to invalidate observed cosmic ray interaction. Furthermore, the recent CLOUD experiments carried out at CERN in Geneva, led by Jasper Kirkby, have now vindicated Svensmark and Friis-Christensen. The results have thrown the mainstream climate science community into a panic and embarrassed the CERN leadership, who appear to have been hoping for a negative result or at least an inconclusive one. Instead they were hit with a bombshell. According to Nigel Calder, the CERN boss thought the CLOUD team's report 'should be politically correct about climate change'[77] and that 'they should on no account endorse the Danish heresy'.[78] Calder says that the forces behind the AGW movement, especially the IPCC, NASA-GISS, Pennsylvania State University and CRU, 'always knew that Svensmark's cosmic ray hypothesis was the principal threat to their sketchy and poorly modelled notions of self-amplifying action of greenhouse gases'.[79]

Calder referred to the results of the CLOUD experiments as a bursting dam because it is now threatening the billions of dollars financing and empowering the AGW machine. This may explain why the physicists working on the CLOUD experiment have allegedly been 'gagged' by their bosses, who 'have asked their colleagues to present the results clearly, but not to interpret them',[80] since that 'would go immediately into the highly political arena of the climate change debate'.[81]

The implication is that for 4.5 billion years, nature was in the driving seat and the earth's climate was at the mercy of the sun alone until human beings took over for the infinitesimally short 150 years or so at the end of that period. All of nature's forces were abruptly consigned to the background, to be followed immediately by manmade chaos and the road to climatic oblivion, all because of a 'measly' increase in CO_2, as the late meteorologist Augie Auer described it. The suggestion is that humanity is on the road to hell in a carbon-based handcart and taking the planet along for the ride. And the sun no longer plays any part in the proceedings.

It is strange how the warmists have lost their sense of proportion in this. On the one hand, they lose sight of how insignificant our CO_2 emissions really are against the backdrop of the earth's atmosphere. As pointed out earlier, our CO_2 emissions amount to a trivial 1 *milli*-per cent, or so of the atmosphere, a figure so small it is impossible to measure with any degree of certainty. On the other hand, they lose sight of how brief human tenure and activity have been in the planet's supposed *4.5 billion*-year history, let alone the few decades – starting in the 1940s – during which industrial emissions are supposed to have overpowered the forces of nature. But let's be generous and assign the full 150 years or so since the Industrial Revolution to when we really started putting CO_2 into the air, a period amounting to 0.000000033 of the planet's entire history. This is not very long on the geological time-scale. The mere blink of an eye. Yet the warmists imply that for all this time the forces of nature reigned supreme, the sun drove the earth's dynamic climate – and with temperatures and CO_2 levels on myriad occasions many times *higher* than today – and then suddenly CO_2 levels and temperatures that are actually *lower* than they have been in the past have given rise to catastrophic global warming.

This theory really is medieval in its silliness. And like Sagan's 'greenhouse' Venus hypothesis it is based on manipulated data, bad science and dubious scientific practices tainted by political interests and the availability of 'soft money'.

7. Smoke and Mirrors

> Get your facts first, and then you can distort them as much
> as you please.
>
> *Mark Twain*

> A conjecture can be dressed up as a dead certainty with
> enough rhetoric and protected against dissent with enough
> threatening language.
>
> *Clive James*[1]

'Unfortunately, the way the IPCC works, they are allowed to make stuff up, then it's their critics [sic] job to prove it is untrue,'[2] writes Ross McKitrick, Professor of Economics at the University of Guelph. Mark Twain undoubtedly would have agreed, charging the IPCC and the climate science community collectively with corrupting science for political or other unscientific purposes. He might have poured scorn on the IPCC for masquerading as a model of scientific excellence when it is dominated by political agendas and hijacked by environmental non-government organizations like Greenpeace and the World Wildlife Fund, as Donna Laframboise revealed in her book *The Delinquent Teenager Who Was Mistaken for the World's Top Climate Expert*. In an interview with Charles Adler, Laframboise also accuses the IPCC of negligence for enlisting young, inexperienced non-experts since the mid-1990s[3] and for allowing brazen activists and graduate students to write reports, using newspaper clippings and press releases as source material.[4] She also demonstrates that only a third of the papers referenced by the IPCC for its Assessment Reports are peer-reviewed. 'We have been misled very systematically for a long time.'[5] But as the IPCC was set up for propaganda and political purposes, a lack of scientific rigour and integrity is hardly surprising.

According to Timothy Ball, every segment of the organization was set up

> for the maximum public relations effect. This meant emphasis on emotional impact, especially by exploiting fear. The first need was to direct and control the science. It was achieved at the 1985 meeting in Villach, Austria chaired by Canadian bureaucrat Gordon McBean with Phil Jones and Tom Wigley from the East Anglia Climate Research Unit in attendance.
>
> The second need was for maximizing the fear factor to force political action.[6]

The science was weak right from the beginning because the agenda at Villach, and later the IPCC itself, was dominated by political interests which exploited scientists to lend a veneer of credibility in order to convince the public of a bogus crisis. The science writer and presenter Joanne Nova argues that even Rajendra Pachauri, chair of the IPCC since 2002, admits the IPCC guesses the numbers. 'Such is the pressure finally beginning to bear on the IPCC that Pachauri has been forced into the ridiculous position of trying to rescue credibility by contradicting most of their past PR campaign. He's taken the extraordinary step of admitting they don't have hard numbers.'[7] However, the rot set in well before the advent of the IPCC with the World Meteorological Organization (WMO) and the United Nations Environment Programme (UNEP) in 1988, and of the many other politically and financially motivated interests that today promote global warming alarmism.

As we saw in the first chapter, the scientific case for AGW went off the rails as early as 1938 with Callendar's selective CO_2 measurements. But even before that, the science was skating on thin ice (pun intended) with Arrhenius's flawed calculations. It was Callendar's efforts, however, that established the long-held assumption that pre-industrial CO_2 levels were relatively stable at around 280–290 ppm and subsequently steadily increased to today's 385–390 ppm, as measured at Mauna Loa, due to the burning of fossil fuels.

Following Callendar, we have seen that Gilbert Plass, Charles Keeling and even Carl Sagan – albeit for different reasons – actively promoted the theory that increased CO_2 resulted in a corresponding increase in global temperature, which supposedly would lead ultimately to climate doom unless emissions are reduced. They did so with nothing more compelling than an occasional, coincidental correlation, from which they concluded that humankind was in the driving seat of the earth's climate, analogous to Ptolemy's view of humans occupying the centre of the universe. We have long since dispensed with Ptolemy's geocentric model, but have adopted an equally spurious CO_2-centric model to describe the planet's climate system.

Today the flag is waved by GISS Director James Hansen, Michael Mann of Pennsylvania State University, Gavin Schmidt (NASA climate modeller), Phil Jones of the University of East Anglia's Climate Research Unit (CRU), Mike Hulme, Tom Wigley, Benjamin Santer, Kevin Trenberth, Keith Briffa (deputy director of CRU and one of the key players in the Climategate affair), Malcolm Hughes, Raymond Bradley, John Holdren, Jonathan Overpeck, Caspar Amman, Michael Oppenheimer, Tom Crowley, William Connolley (Wikipedia revisionist editor, banned for six months from making further edits to contributors' entries after complaints he deleted more than 500 of their articles and rewrote many more – many by respected climate scientists sceptical of manmade global warming),[8] Tim Osborn, Thomas Karl, Andrew Weaver, Eric Steig[9] and, until his untimely death, Stephen Schneider of Stanford University and former Al Gore confidant – not to mention Gore himself. They join a host of scientists, academics and government research bodies around the world, all accused variously of either distorting climate data or exaggerating the effects of CO_2 on temperature. Their combined efforts have helped establish the 'consensus' of opinion as portrayed by the mainstream media that today's climate is 'likely' to have been caused by industrial CO_2 emissions. Yet this consensus is a myth, a charade enthusiastically endorsed and fostered by the IPCC and most Western governments. The Australian climate analyst John McLean explains in his 2009 paper 'The IPCC Can't Count its "Expert Scientists"' that the consensus boils down to just sixty scientists who support the IPCC's claim of catastrophic human-induced global warming.

But the numbers used to endorse the IPCC matter. In a revealing email sent in 1997 to Mike Hulme and Rob Swart, Joseph Alcamo, director of the Center for Environmental Systems Research in Germany, writes:

> Sounds like you guys have been busy doing good things for the cause. I would like to weigh in on two important questions – Distribution for Endorsements – I am very strongly in favor of as wide and rapid a distribution as possible for endorsements. I think the only thing that counts is numbers. The media is going to say, '1000 scientists signed' or '1500 signed'. No one is going to check if it is 600 with PhDs versus 2000 without. They will mention the prominent ones, but that is a different story.
>
> Conclusion – Forget the screening, forget asking them about their last publication (most will ignore you). Get those names![10]

Yet there is no certainty in the belief that human beings are heating the planet catastrophically, despite claims that the scientific case is a 100-year-old fact based on the work of Arrhenius, because all players, including the IPCC, are well aware of the flaws and uncertainties in the science and are careful to avoid terms any stronger than 'likely'.

As Christian Gerondeau, former adviser to the French Prime Minister Jacques Chaban-Delmas and author of the bestselling book CO_2, *un mythe planétaire*, pointed out:

> The use of the adjective 'likely' . . . stems from the IPCC's proceedings. Members are asked to choose terms to express likelihood, e.g. 'very unlikely', 'more likely than not', 'likely', 'very likely', etc. and, depending on the case, to express their judgement on the correctness of the submitted data following a scale from 'very high confidence' to 'very low confidence'.[11]

This fails the criteria of scientific methodology. There is no certainty in the view that present CO_2 emissions are heating the planet catastrophically. It is at best a hunch, a *belief* based on *political* agreement and encouraged with the promise of research grants. Hence the anger and vitriol reserved for anyone who contradicts the message. The 'consensus' is political, not scientific, but it is supported by vast sums of money and anyone who threatens this is immediately the target of intense hostility.

By itself this is a subtle admission that the scientific case is weak, despite vociferous and ardent claims to the contrary. This explains why celebrities are recruited to endorse the theory for the benefit of a scientifically semi-literate public and mainstream media who would hardly know the difference. The theory calls for glitz because it cannot sell itself on its merits. But why would a scientific theory require the endorsement of actors and singers? It would have been laughable for Albert Einstein to employ the services of Charlie Chaplin, Douglas Fairbanks or Billy Murray to promote his Theory of Relativity; inconceivable for atomic theory to have required the services of Bette Davis, James Cagney or Katherine Hepburn to jazz it up for popular consumption. These theories survived scrutiny because the science could be demonstrated. There was no suppression of data, no need to claim with arrogant authority that the science was settled – the very hallmark of a weak argument. The AGW hypothesis, however, needs to be endorsed by Bono, John Travolta and Bob Geldof, among other high-profile celebrities. It even entails ecclesiastical support from Archbishop Desmond Tutu.

Why, if the science is undeniable, does it need celebrities to promote it? If the science were self-evident, the AGW hypothesis would survive without the need for scientists to tamper with the evidence. It would survive without the need to delete incriminating emails and suppress contradictory data. And it would survive without the need to insert spurious data where it does not belong.

This last expedient was apparently employed in a study of West Antarctic temperature trends by a team of scientists led by Eric Steig of the University of Washington which concluded: 'significant warming extends well beyond the Antarctic Peninsula to cover most of West Antarctica, an area of warming much larger than previously reported. West Antarctic warming exceeds 0.1°C per decade over the past fifty years.'[12] Furthermore, the entire Antarctic continent has warmed by around 1°F since 1957. The finding appeared to contradict the argument of the sceptics that Antarctica was bucking the supposed global warming trend and was steadily cooling, as evidenced by increasing sea ice.[13]

However, due to the very sparsely distributed weather stations in the western Antarctic region, the scientists *inserted* data to cover areas where none existed. 'What we did is interpolate carefully instead of just using the back of an envelope,' admitted Steig. 'The team employed a computer program that essentially guessed what the weather station data might have been had the stations existed.'[14] They achieved this by splicing satellite data onto surface station data and assumed the overlap would be an accurate representation of the missing surface stations. 'In other words,' says Melanie Phillips, 'the findings that caused such excitement were based on data that had been *made up*.'[15] But not everyone on Steig's side of the AGW debate was convinced. IPCC's lead author Kevin Trenberth, at the National Center for Atmospheric Research, Colorado was uncomfortable with the expedient and emailed, 'I remain somewhat sceptical . . . It is hard to make data where none exist.'[16] Quite so.

Even worse, the report was plagued by other problems that cast further doubt on Steig's warming prognosis. Steve McIntyre, who analysed the results in detail, uncovered a serious problem with station identity. One station in particular, known as Harry, showed a suspiciously large warming trend while the others showed either cooling or at most very slight warming,[17] one that was hardly discernible from no trend at all. But the Harry station, having been buried in snow for years and then re-sited in 2005,[18] exhibited an unusually large upswing in temperatures, presumably after its sensors were dug out of the snow and exposed to the warmer ambient air.

Meanwhile, the data Steig used, which supposedly came from the Harry site, were 'actually old data from another station on the Ross Ice Shelf known as Gill with new data from Harry added to it, producing the abrupt warming,' writes the columnist Andrew Bolt.[19] Gill, however, has a negative trend so that when its data were spliced onto Harry's, the result is an artificial warming that finds its way into the Antarctic average. 'It's a mess,' says McIntyre.

Not only is evidence fabricated to support the AGW hypothesis, but in one case physical evidence that contradicted it was destroyed by activists because it invalidated the rising sea level alarm in the Maldives. World-renowned sea level expert Nils-Axel Mörner, who had been planning a television documentary casting doubt on rising sea levels there, said in an interview with Gregory Murphy in 2007:

When I came to the Maldives, to our enormous surprise, one morning we were on an island, and I said, 'This is something strange, the storm level has gone down; it has not gone up, it has gone *down*.' And then I started to check the level all around, and I asked the others in the group, 'Do you see anything here on the beach?' And after a while they found it too. And we had investigated, and we were sure, I said we cannot leave the Maldives and go home and say the sea level is not rising, it's not respectful to the people. I have to say it to Maldive television. So we made a very nice program for Maldive television, but it was forbidden by the government! Because they thought that they would lose money.

You know what happened? There came an Australian sea-level team, which was for the IPCC and against me. Then the students pulled down the tree by hand! They destroyed the evidence. What kind of people are those? And we came to launch this film, 'Doomsday Called Off,' right after, and the tree was still green. And I heard from the locals that they had seen the people who had pulled it down.[20]

When the visible evidence contradicts the alarmist message of the IPCC, it is deemed morally justified to destroy it in order to further the alarmist AGW cause. It is absurd that the default conclusion of climate chaos and 'unprecedented' global warming reached by CRU and the IPCC and which lacks scientific rigour results in Western economies being coerced into imposing onerous economic penalties on 'carbon emitters', which will threaten national industries and the prosperity of all citizens.

Everything hinges on unscientific terminology – 'could', 'may', 'might', 'likely' or 'very likely'. Much is 'likely'; anything 'could' or 'might' happen. But what do the data say *before* being adjusted, tweaked or falsified to give the impression that climate doom is just around the corner? Richard Lindzen famously remarked of politically driven global warming alarmism that 'The consensus was reached before the research had even begun.'[21] And the geologist Bob Carter writes, 'at its point of origin and reporting, the IPCC is set up to consider not climate change in general, but only change caused by *human* perturbation of the atmosphere'.[22] This is a damning indictment not only of the IPCC, but also of its compliant scientists and their research institutes and of the politicians who fund them. There was no interest in whether today's climate system is a function of *natural* forces.

The belief that humans are now driving the climate system is so firmly entrenched and buttressed by political and financial interests that sceptics such as Lindzen and many other respected scientists are routinely dismissed as 'deniers', 'cranks' or 'flat-earthers'. Many are also subject to intimidation and pressure tactics to make them comply with the political pronouncements of the IPCC or keep quiet. As the distinguished natural scientist, the late Charles Fleming, presciently observed in 1986, 'Any body of scientists that adopts pressure group tactics is endangering its status as the guardian of principles of scientific philosophy that are worth conserving.'[23] In a revealing interview with Deborah Amos for the PBS *Frontline* series in April 2007, former senator Timothy Wirth, the man who helped James Hansen put the global warming cause to the Senate in 1988, admitted to using subterfuge in order to convince the politicians of the message. Wirth told Amos that they deliberately timed the Senate hearing to take place on what would likely be the hottest day of the year, based on enquiries made with the Weather Bureau who provided a forecast. 'So we scheduled the hearing that day' Wirth says, 'and bingo, it was the hottest day on record in Washington, or close to it.' Amos then asked if the temperature in the hearing room had been altered that day as well, to which Wirth responded, 'What we did is that we went in the night before and opened all the windows . . . so that the air conditioning wasn't working inside the room' which resulted in sweltering temperatures inside for the duration of the hearing.[24]

However, the science behind AGW was broken well before the formation of the IPCC, even before the Thatcher government poisoned the well with political interests in the 1980s. But it was this political intervention that encouraged scientists to manipulate the evidence further to support their political masters, who then rewarded them with lucrative research grants. Thus the foundations of a corrupt, self-sustaining industry, driven by politics and money, were laid. This has been borne out by the Climategate scandals in which thousands of emails were released from the University of East Anglia's CRU into the public domain by a whistleblower or hacker in November 2009 and again in 2011.[25] The emails reveal an organized campaign by alarmist climate scientists around the world, but predominantly by the CRU, to distort data, delete incriminating emails, stifle dissent and discredit scientists openly critical or sceptical of the case for AGW.[26]

In their compelling and authoritative account of the affair, *Climategate: The Crutape Letters*, Steven Mosher and Thomas Fuller write, these scientists 'had almost convinced the world that temperatures had never been higher than they are today, and that they were climbing rapidly'.[27] This was of course an outright lie, but Mosher and Fuller explain that the deceit was achieved

> by hiding how they presented data, and ruthlessly suppressing dissent by ensuring that contrary papers were never published and that editors who didn't follow their party line were forced out of their position. And when Freedom of Information requests threatened to reveal their misbehavior, the emails showed them actively conspiring to delete emails to frustrate legitimate requests for information. Worst of all, one scientist threatened to actually delete climate data rather than turn it over – and that data is still missing.[28]

So much for the scientific method and the peer review process, which they ignore themselves while insisting that all sceptics adhere to the rules. But, as some sceptics have discovered, the peer review process itself has been hijacked by alarmist scientists who threaten and cajole scientific journals likely to publish them, referring to research offering alternative viewpoints as 'disinformation', 'misinformation' or 'crap' that needs to be kept out of the public domain.[29]

In one of the emails, Phil Jones, Director of CRU, suggested to Michael Mann that 'Kevin [Trenberth] and I will keep them out somehow – even if we have to redefine what the peer review literature is!'[30] Jones was referring to two peer-reviewed papers. One, by Ross McKitrick and Patrick J. Michaels, cast serious doubt on the quality of the data used by CRU, arguing that it was highly contaminated by non-climatic temperature effects which give it a strong warming bias despite assurances by the IPCC in all of their Assessment Reports that these 'inhomogeneities' had been taken into account and adjusted for. The other questioned the IPCC's claim that the MWP was cooler than the present. Both papers were accepted for publication in the journal *Climate Research* by the climate scientist Chris de Freitas, who later came under attack for allowing it to happen. The Climategate emails reveal attempts by CRU scientists to tarnish the reputation of *Climate Research* and to get de Freitas dismissed from his post at Auckland University.[31] Jones wrote to Mann on 11 March 2003, warning 'I'll be emailing the journal to tell them I'm having nothing more to do with it until they rid themselves of this troublesome editor,' referring to de Freitas.

Mann replied the same day, 'I think we should stop considering Climate Research as a legitimate peer-reviewed journal. Perhaps we should encourage our colleagues . . . to no longer submit to, or cite papers in, this journal. We would also need to consider what we tell or request our more reasonable colleagues who currently sit on the editorial board.'[32] Mann wrote again later, telling Jones, 'I think the community should . . . terminate its involvement with this journal at all levels . . . and leave it to wither away into oblivion and disrepute.'[33]

Jones, meanwhile, was offered a job as IPCC's coordinating lead author, which meant he would be in the unique position of reviewing evidence that cast doubt on his own and other CRU scientists' work supporting the IPCC position, including evidence that the CRU data were contaminated with non-climatic forcing effects. McKitrick points out that it was the IPCC that placed him in this position. They needed

Someone to write a section of the report that examined Jones' papers as well as those of Jones' critics and then offer a judgment on whether Jones was right or not. So they asked Jones to write it. Even though Jones is a common last name, you would think they could have found at least one person on Earth to do that job whose last name was not Jones. And you would think that an agency bragging about having 3,000 brilliant scientists involved with it could figure out how to avoid such conflicts of interest.[34]

Apparently they couldn't.
McKitrick continues,

Nonetheless, once Jones accepted the invitation he gave up the right to be biased on behalf of the CRU. Yet in the email, sent a year before the IPCC Expert Review process would begin, he was already signalling his determination to block any mention of a paper [by McKitrick and Michaels] that had provided significant statistical evidence that the data he supplied to the IPCC was potentially contaminated.

IPCC's lead author and climate researcher Benjamin Santer was so incensed by the CRU email leak he wrote to his 'colleagues and friends':

I am sure that by now, all of you are aware of the hacking incident which recently took place at the University of East Anglia's Climatic Research Unit (CRU). This was a criminal act. Over 3,000 emails and documents were stolen. The identity of the hacker or hackers is still unknown.

The emails represented private correspondence between CRU scientists and scientists at climate research centers around the world. Dozens of the stolen emails are from over a decade of my own personal correspondence with Professor Phil Jones, the Director of CRU.[35]

In one of these emails Santer said he wanted to 'beat the crap out of' the prominent sceptic and former Virginia State climatologist Patrick J. Michaels.[36] Santer, no doubt, was incensed by Michaels pointing out too many inconvenient truths, like Santer's carefully selected weather balloon data which gave a false impression of a close correlation between tropospheric temperatures and projections from climate models. Without such empirical agreement between the two models, any correlation was entirely speculative.

Something was needed and Santer obliged with a paper for *Nature* which appeared to show precisely this – a close correlation between the two.[37] Michaels writes, 'The Santer study used weather balloon data from 1962 through 1988. In fact, however, the weather balloon record was actually complete . . . from 1957 through 1995, and when the entire record was used, the correspondence vanished.'[38] Michaels says that after only a few hours' effort he and his colleagues 'determined that the entire result changed if *all* the data were used'.[39] The fallout from this embarrassing episode still reverberates today, says Michaels.[40]

Yet satellite measurements show clearly that the IPCC CO_2-centric model projections bear no resemblance to reality. It is specious for Santer to conclude that the models accurately follow observed satellite and radiosonde (weather balloon) temperature gradients. They do not. Of course, the longer the post-1998 (El Niño year) temperatures continue on their non-warming trend, as indicated by satellite and weather balloon measurements, the larger and steeper any subsequent upswing needs to be for the IPCC model projections to be vindicated. This is unlikely because any such positive upswing would require an astonishing amount of energy to be dumped into the climate system in a very short time frame (Figure 16). Where is this energy supposed to come from? From CO_2's *greenhouse* properties? Hardly. So the problem must be a real concern to the IPCC and CRU team, who insist that temperatures are on a positive trajectory and heading out of control.

They base this scenario on heavily adjusted, contaminated, ground-based measurements and entirely on the *assumption* that temperature necessarily follows increased CO_2 emissions. This follows from the *assumption* that the slight warming effect of CO_2 is strongly amplified by water vapour, that any apparent interruption in this ever-upward trend is due to short-term 'masking' and that anthropogenic warming is likely to return within twenty years. But this is simply not the case, as the satellite evidence shows. The physicist William Happer points out that 'The observed response of the climate to more CO_2 is not in good agreement with model predictions.'[41] And until CRU and the IPCC admit this, their models will continue to be meaningless and wrong.

Yet the disconnect between actual temperature trends and model projections has been well known by the CRU scientists, but was suppressed until the release of the Climategate emails. In a remarkable email to Phil Jones, dated 24 October 2008, Mick Kelly writes, 'Just updated my global temperature trend graphic for a public talk and noted that the level has really been quite stable since 2000 or so and 2008 doesn't look too hot . . . Be awkward if we went through a [*sic*] early 1940s type swing!'[42] Indeed it would. Stable temperatures or, worse, declining temperatures are a nightmare when you are trying to argue the case for catastrophic warming.

To date, the IPCC's four Assessment Reports have all been tailored to encourage the idea that late twentieth-century global warming has been caused mainly by humankind, terms such as 'likely' and 'very likely' notwithstanding. Each successive report is more alarmist and more assertive than the previous one. But the tacit

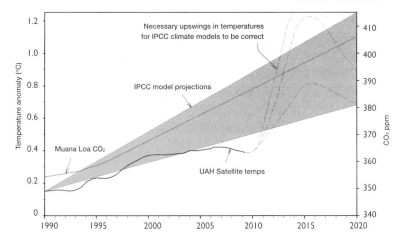

Figure 16. Actual temperature trend plotted against IPCC computer model projections (from low to high sensitivity, shown in the dark grey band). Note that temperatures fall below the lowest IPCC projection, bear no resemblance to the CO_2 trend (approximated) as measured at Mauna Loa and start heading in the opposite direction. For the IPCC model projections to be correct, temperatures must rise dramatically very quickly, becoming more severe and unlikely the longer actual temperatures remain on a non-warming trend line.[43]

political message is clear in each: late twentieth-century warming is our fault. There is no room for debate because the UN-sanctioned IPCC is held to be the absolute authority on which governments depend for their policy decisions. Questions and challenges to politicians on the subject are simply deflected by reference to the IPCC's pronouncements and Assessment Reports. Everything is tuned to support this mission statement to the extent that the IPCC has resorted to deleting or modifying entire passages written by unconvinced scientists from official reports if they do not comply with the political agenda.

Surprisingly, Santer openly admitted on Jesse Ventura television that he deleted sections of Chapter 8 of the 1995 IPCC Working Group I Report, which stated that humans were not responsible for climate change.[44] Christopher Monckton said of the incident, 'In comes Santer and re-writes it for them, after the scientists have sent in their finalized draft, and that finalized draft said at five different places, there is no discernible human effect on global temperature.' Monckton adds that Santer 'went through, crossed out all of those and substituted a new conclusion', which then became the official conclusion of the IPCC.[45] Unabashed, Santer defended his actions with the comment, 'Lord Monckton points to deletions from the chapter, and there were deletions from the chapter; to be consistent with the other chapters, we dropped the summary at the end.'[46]

The IPCC also came under attack in a report written by the Science and Environmental Policy Project (SEPP), headed by S. Fred Singer. The report claimed that Chapter 8 of the 1995 IPCC Working Group I Report, which dealt with human influence on global climate, had been heavily edited. Sections expressing uncertainty over humankind's impact on global climate had been expunged.[47] Singer says,

> Santer carefully removed any verbiage denying that human influences might be the major or almost exclusive cause of warming and substituted new language. There is no evidence that he ever consulted any of his fellow IPCC authors, nor do we know who instructed him to make these changes and later approved the text deletions and insertions that fundamentally transformed [the IPCC's Second Assessment Report].[48]

Similarly, in a 1996 article for *The Wall Street Journal*, Frederick Seitz protested,

> In my more than sixty years as a member of the American scientific community, including service as president of both the National Academy of Sciences and the American Physical Society, I have never witnessed a more disturbing corruption of the peer-review process than the events that led to this IPCC report.[49]

SMOKE AND MIRRORS

The IPCC is supported in this by CRU, which supplies most of the IPCC's adjusted temperature data and moral support. The two bodies are hardly distinguishable. Timothy Ball calls them 'the same corrupt organization'.[50] 'Most people, including the media, don't seem to realize the IPCC is the CRU,' says Ball, who also charges them with costing a fortune:

> It is time to total the massive amounts of money given to narrowly directed research, the cost of the impact on energy policy and economies; the lost jobs and opportunities from industries forced out of business; the unnecessary subsidies to research and businesses chasing unworkable alternate energies; the taxes and legislative restrictions on businesses and other activities.

Ball rails against the deception which 'has set world progress back at massive cost and it is time they are all held accountable'.

Marc Sheppard writes in the same vein, 'A glut of ongoing recent discoveries of systemic fraud has rocked that foundation, and the entire manmade global warming house of cards is now teetering on the verge of complete collapse.' He adds,

> Simply stated, we've been swindled. We've been set up as marks by a gang of opportunistic hucksters who have exploited the naïvely altruistic intentions of the environmental movement in an effort to control international energy consumption while redistributing global wealth and (in many cases) greedily lining their own pockets in the process.[51]

Donna Laframboise argues that the best way to bring the IPCC to heel is to cut its funding.[52] This also goes for the CRU. If the money dries up, so will the corruption.

But the fun doesn't stop there.

The idea of climate chaos due to manmade global warming during the twentieth century is implicitly implied in the infamous 'hockey stick' graph,[53] which first appeared in *Geophysical Research Letters* in a 1999 paper by Michael Mann, Raymond Bradley and Malcolm Hughes. It built on a 1998 paper by the same authors published in *Nature* which detailed their methodology for creating a proxy temperature reconstruction.[54] This graph was the ace up the sleeve of the IPCC in 2001 when it featured six times in their Third Assessment Report. It was remarkable for relying on tree ring temperature proxies for the early pre-industrial period with more modern thermometer records spliced onto the end for the later twentieth-century period. Yet another case of splicing together completely unrelated temperature proxies.

It appeared to be undeniable *scientific* proof of humankind's culpability for post-industrial warming[55] until it was unmasked by the mining engineer and mathematician Stephen J. McIntyre and his co-author Ross McKitrick as what appeared to be an outrageous smoke-and-mirrors trick designed to expunge the naturally occurring LIA and MWP from the history books. The new paradigm implied in Mann's graph and supported by the IPCC and CRU is that warming trends are the fault of humankind. In that case, how could there have been any such periods before the Industrial Revolution? So the LIA and MWP simply ceased to exist, and no one dared mention the even earlier Roman Warm Period. A hatchet job was done on hundreds of scientific studies proving the existence of the MWP and LIA,[56] and Mann's hockey stick reconstruction was adopted as the new, politically correct historical 'truth'.

The revelation by McIntyre and McKitrick of what appeared to be a scientific sleight of hand caused a furore and embarrassed the IPCC into gradually, but subtly, distancing itself from Mann's graph,[57] while, according to his critics, Mann himself took to hiding his data, preventing any close scrutiny by McIntyre and others who were suspicious of the methods he used to obtain such an unlikely shape in his graph.[58]

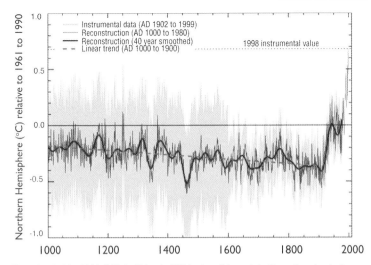

Figure 17. Article of faith.[59] Michael Mann's 1998 hockey stick graph for the northern hemisphere, with the LIA and MWP obliterated (IPCC, Third Assessment Report, 2001, p. 134).

After spending years trying to obtain access to Mann's data and computer code, while fighting obstruction and stonewalling tactics, McIntyre was able to disclose a multitude of serious errors, including truncated records, old data extrapolated forwards even when new data were available and gaps in the data being filled with spurious data, among many other issues.[60] Yet this graph, still tacitly endorsed by the IPCC, purports to show northern hemisphere 'average' temperatures trending slightly downward in a more or less straight line from 1000 AD to c. 1900 AD when they appear to soar, as though triggered by something wholly unnatural and out of place.

AGW advocates put this abrupt change down to CO_2 emissions since the Industrial Revolution and to industrial expansion during the twentieth century in particular. Of course they do. It could not possibly be due to selective datasets and biased programming. Or could it? As McIntyre's research indicated, Mann's model will produce a hockey stick shape no matter what data are used – even random data, or 'red noise', will produce the shape.[61] 'You could have entered last week's grocery list and still received "proof" of global warming!' explains Ian Wishart, an investigative journalist and author.[62] Yet the hockey stick is the *only* evidence that late twentieth-century warming is unprecedented. There is nothing else.[63]

The IPCC had in fact changed its tune in the years since the First Assessment Report was published in 1990. That report included an entirely different graph from the hockey stick and featured both the MWP and the LIA. Yet by 2001 they had vanished. This volte-face cannot be rationalized by arguing that new information or research came to light because the knowledge that these periods had occurred was available years before. It existed and was readily available. So why were these important periods obliterated from Mann's later graph?

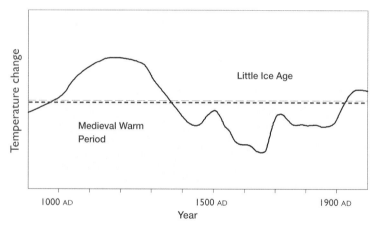

Figure 18. Global temperature since 900 AD (redrawn approximately from the original) which appeared in the IPCC First Assessment Report in 1990, but which originates from the work of the British climate researcher Hubert Lamb.[64]

As we saw earlier, the Medieval Warm Period (MWP) had become an embarrassment to the IPCC and CRU scientists who were trumpeting the alleged dangers of twentieth-century warming. Politics required that this alleged 'threat' be real and true, but it was also obvious that twentieth-century warming could hardly be 'dangerous' if there was evidence of pre-industrial periods that were even warmer. And that is why the MWP simply had to go – there was no place for it in the new political environment and modern warming was made to look more prominent instead. Hence the strange email sent to Deming in 1995, allegedly from Jonathan Overpeck, advising that 'We have to get rid of the Medieval Warm Period'. Mann, it seems, obliged with the hockey stick graph and all was well again. But a fabrication of staggering proportions was now being promoted by politicians and climate scientists and enthusiastically adopted by universities and schools as 'proof' that twentieth-century warming was unprecedented, dangerous and unnatural, and we all ought to be taxed to save the world from imminent climate chaos.

By 2008, however, things had moved on. Mann and his colleagues managed to breathe new life into the battered and discredited hockey stick with evidence that again appeared to support the twentieth-century upswing in temperatures. Mann had found new temperature proxies with a hockey stick shape that did not rely on tree rings, but on Finnish lake sediments instead, known as the Tiljander proxies. This was a major blow to the sceptics who had argued that using tree ring proxies in general was dubious while Mann's bristlecone pine dataset, used to produce the original hockey stick, in particular was hopelessly flawed and would always produce a hockey stick shape. Even the BBC trumpeted the return of Mann's 2008 version of the hockey stick, while *Nature* magazine boasted that Mann's critics would finally be silenced because he could now prove a hockey stick shape was produced even if the tree ring proxies were removed.

It didn't take long, however, for scientists and academics around the world to uncover more serious problems. McIntyre again found that Mann's statistical techniques could create a hockey stick with random data or 'red noise'.[65] Others found that part of Mann's work 'was mathematically impossible', while one statistician 'discovered how Mann padded future data with past data in reverse'.[66] All the usual suspects were back, including the biased bristlecone pine data, plus a few more that also conveniently led to hockey stick shapes. These included the Tiljander lake sediment proxies, which again seemed to suggest a sharp twentieth-century upswing in temperatures and no MWP.

But it turned out that the Tiljander proxies for the post-industrial period, especially for the twentieth century, were *not* related to temperature at all, but were due to increased agricultural activity and ditch-digging, a fact pointed out by Tiljander herself. This was later acknowledged by Mann, but he claimed it didn't matter because the hockey stick shape remained *without* the Tiljander proxies. Mann argued that if he removed the tree ring proxies, the hockey stick shape was still found and that if he removed the Tiljander lake sediment proxies, it was also there, which seemed to prove the validity of the graph's shape. But, as McIntyre points out, this was circular reasoning because *both* flawed proxies created hockey stick shapes. So when Mann removed the tree rings, the hockey stick shape came from the Tiljander proxies, and when he removed those, the shape came from the bristlecone pine tree rings. It was pointless to remove only one flawed set and then claim it proved something. 'You had to watch the pea under the thimble,' McIntyre said. Furthermore, explains John Dawson, even though 'Tiljander had explained that higher x-ray scores indicated lower temperatures, Mann had interpreted higher x-ray scores as indicating *higher* temperatures. So it was this upside-down graph that had demolished the Medieval Warm Period (which had been acknowledged by Tiljander) and replaced it with a hockey stick.'[67]

There is perhaps no other graph or image used by the IPCC or any climate research institute that has been the cause of so much controversy. As detailed by A.W. Montford in his extremely detailed and thorough analysis *The Hockey Stick Illusion: Climategate and the Corruption of Science*, Mann's hockey stick graph has been thoroughly discredited, dismantled and dismembered in all its aspects and found to be deeply flawed. If Mann's critics are right, his graph must be one of the greatest scientific frauds in history.[68] It smacks of a bad joke foisted on an unsuspecting public in order to promote a political agenda.

But Mann's bristlecone pines are not the only proxy tree ring series selected with a strong bias toward a hockey stick shape. Another series called the Polar Urals were also used by climatologists which likewise supported a hockey stick shape. In Keith Briffa's Polar Urals chronology, published in 1995, he claimed that the year 1032 was the coldest of the millennium, a statement that again implied the Medieval Warm Period was a non-event and late twentieth-century warming unprecedented. However, Andrew Montford points out in *The Hockey Stick Illusion*, that Briffa's statement was 'based on cores taken from just four trees',[69] a very small sample from which to draw a conclusion that contradicted numerous other studies suggesting precisely the opposite. Furthermore, three of the four trees Briffa used to justify his statement on the year 1032 turned out to have been incorrectly dated while the rest of the Polar Urals cores were beset by quality problems including large and frequent gaps, rendering them useless for drawing any kind of sensible conclusion.[70] It was now clear that Briffa's claim of a cold eleventh century came not from the tree samples themselves, which actually showed the opposite, but from poor and incorrect interpretation of the cores.

But worse was to come. In 2005, Steve McIntyre came across a little-known update to the original Polar Urals dataset used by Briffa. The updated data came from tree ring samples collected in 1999, but it had been buried and forgotten until McIntyre uncovered it six years later. Had the update been published at the time, it would have turned Briffa's reconstruction on its head. Instead, it was quietly shelved while an alternative that might suggest another hockey stick was urgently sought. As Montford writes, 'This must have represented something of a problem for the Hockey Team, but in the end the solution was simple enough: the issue was bypassed by the simple expedient of not publishing the update.' But it also meant that any new chronologies would also have to avoid using it, 'making hockey sticks much harder to manufacture'.[71] McIntyre's research into the newer data revealed not only a pronounced MWP, but that it was *warmer* even than the twentieth-century, all of which meant Briffa's original chronology was spurious, as were all other temperature reconstructions that had relied on the same dataset.

The now poisonous Polar Urals chronologies were almost immediately superseded by another regional chronology called Yamal, published again by Briffa in 2000. It was taken to by paleoclimatologists like 'crack cocaine' says McIntyre on climateaudit.com, presumably because it once again killed off the irksome Medieval Warm Period and restored the late twentieth-century uptick, the characteristic hockey stick shape favoured by the CRU team. But like Briffa's original Polar Urals chronology and Mann's bristlecone pine dependence, with their strong hockey stick biases, Briffa's Yamal chronology was undone by what appeared to be deliberate cherry-picking for anything that might generate a hockey stick shape. The late-twentieth-century period in Briffa's Yamal chronology was supported by only twelve cores, again a very small sample, with the uptick coming from a *single* tree, which would normally be dismissed as an outlier, while thirty-four cores taken from the nearby Khadtya River region that provided no evidence at all of a twentieth-century surge in tree-ring growth (and by implication, a corresponding increase in temperatures) were completely ignored. After McIntyre tested and analysed Briffa's data by replacing the twelve Yamal cores with the thirty-four Khadtya River cores, the hockey stick 'blade' vanished, being replaced by what appeared to be a *decline* instead.[72] This issue of a lack of trees showing the expected twentieth-century increase in ring widths was a major issue for the CRU and led to the now infamous 'hide the decline' email, about which more later.

However, no other event better demonstrates the scale of corruption festering within the climate science community, and in particular CRU, than the Climategate scandal. The release of over 1,000 emails by an unknown whistleblower, or 'hacker', exposes how far some individuals are prepared to go in order to prevent other scientists reviewing or even seeing their data and results. Climategate concerns a secretive, very small cabal of climate scientists, based predominantly at CRU and Pennsylvania State University, who controlled the data flow, the very temperature record used by the IPCC in its reports and on which the whole global warming edifice was constructed.[73] McKitrick makes the case that 'the IPCC used false evidence to conceal an important problem with the surface temperature data on which most of their conclusions rest'.[74] The Climategate scandal has opened a Pandora's box of horrors as scientists employed by CRU attempted to thwart all reasonable efforts to expose these problems with the surface temperature data.

However, the emails are also about McIntyre whose unfailing instincts told him early on that things were not as they seemed with the surface temperature record – let alone Mann's hockey stick graph – and who repeatedly tried to obtain data and computer code in order to understand how the official record had been achieved. He was turned down with the excuse that he was not an 'academic'. McIntyre therefore asked his colleague McKitrick from the University of Guelph to request access to the data. He also was denied.[75] And so it went on. Obfuscation, brick walls and silence.

Yet there was ample reason for McIntyre and McKitrick, or anyone else, to doubt the veracity of the temperature record the CRU and IPCC were using because McKitrick, like the climate scientist Patrick J. Michaels, had shown that the quality of the land-based records 'is so poor that the warming trend estimated since 1979 . . . may have been overestimated by 50 per cent. Webster, who received the CRU data, published studies linking changes in hurricane patterns to warming (while others have found otherwise).'[76] So CRU must have been aware of the issues and why anyone would be interested in obtaining the original data.

Nevertheless, McIntyre and McKitrick, among others, including Warwick Hughes and Willis Eschenbach, posed a serious problem to CRU scientists thanks to the Freedom of Information Act (FOIA), which obliged them to release their data to anyone who requested it. This was because it was owned not by CRU or the University of East Anglia, or indeed by the World Meteorological Organization, but by the British and American public whose taxes paid the scientists' salaries. The data are public information owned by the public so the tax-paying public of those countries at least have a right to access it.

Yet CRU closed ranks and used intimidation and stonewalling tactics to prevent open scrutiny of any data or source code they held. And in any case, according to Jones, some data were lost. The *adjusted* data exist, but the raw data *prior to* adjustment do not. In an email to Roger Pielke Jr., of the University of Colorado, who had also asked for the raw data, Jones claimed that 'Data storage availability in the 1980s meant that we were not able to keep the multiple sources for some sites, only the station series *after* adjustment for homogeneity issues. We, therefore, do not hold the original raw data but only the value-added (i.e. quality controlled and homogenized) data'[77] (emphasis added). If nothing else, CRU's failure to store the original data on which hangs the entire manmade global warming argument is either negligence or incompetence, perhaps both.

CRU is not the only climate research institute to 'lose' data. New Zealand's National Institute of Water and Atmospheric Research (NIWA) was challenged by the New Zealand Climate Science Coalition (NZCSC) to produce the Schedule of Adjustments for their raw data. NIWA adjusted the raw data, then claimed, on the strength of the result, that New Zealand has warmed at *twice* the global rate, a staggering 0.92°C for the twentieth century. This is odd as the raw data for 1853–2009 show little or no trend – at most +0.3°C – even according to NIWA, and almost no trend at all according to the New Zealand Meteorological Service. However, the details and rationale disappeared for how the adjustments were made. Richard Treadgold of the NZCSC said at the time, 'NIWA has admitted in writing that it lost the original data.'[78] Significantly, although the raw data show very little trend since 1850 (statistically insignificant at +0.06°C per century), nearly *all* the adjustments to the temperature record lead to strong warming.[79] That in itself is unlikely, unless by a fluke every monitoring station except one (Dunedin) is affected by an identical quantifiable bias. The only reasonable conclusion that can be drawn is that the apparent temperature rise is an artefact of the *adjustments* rather than any natural warming trend these stations measured.

Exacerbating the problem is the fact that, while the New Zealand Meteorological Service record shows almost *no* warming over the past century, 'NIWA has adopted a series of invariably downward adjustments in the period prior to World War 2.'[80] These downward adjustments inflated the apparent warming trend for the twentieth century, a ploy not unique to NIWA. GISS came under fire for a similar practice. According to the journalist Christopher Booker, GISS 'was forced to revise many of its figures when it was shown that wholesale "adjustments" had been made, revising older temperatures downwards and post-2000 figures upwards'[81] – hence the sustained and persistent questioning by NZCSC as to why NIWA had done the same thing. But, says Bryan Leyland, consulting engineer and member of NZCSC, 'NIWA refuses to accept that there are serious problems with the adjustments. In fact, no one has been able to explain exactly how they were arrived at.'[82]

Without the Schedule of Adjustments it was impossible to check, replicate or verify the accuracy of the final product or to justify the pre-1940s downward adjustments. This led to a court challenge brought by the NZCSC under the auspices of the NZ Climate Science Education Trust to compel NIWA to release the details. After so much pressure from the NZCSC and the Climate Conversation Group, NIWA surprisingly 'abandoned the official national temperature record and created a new one',[83] while also distancing themselves from the responsibility of ownership of the official New Zealand Temperature Record. Ironically, NIWA stated in their Statement of Defence[84] that 'there is no "official" or formal New Zealand Temperature Record', as though such an admission exonerates them from the responsibility of maintaining it and providing open and ready access to the adjustment records. After all, it is partly on the strength of these records that the New Zealand Government imposed an emissions tax.

NIWA's website now allows access to the raw data, the final post-adjusted data showing the enormous warming trend *and* their newly created Schedule of Adjustments, giving the impression that all is now well. Unfortunately, despite their efforts to restore public confidence in their claim that New Zealand has warmed at the *twice* the global average, their new Schedule of Adjustments has been shown by the NZCSC to be flawed because NIWA did not follow the adjustment methods they claimed and that had they done so, 'the resultant trend for the seven-station temperature series for New Zealand would have been significantly lower than the trend they obtained'.[85] In other words, had they followed their own rules, the 0.92°C temperature rise would have been just 0.34°C.

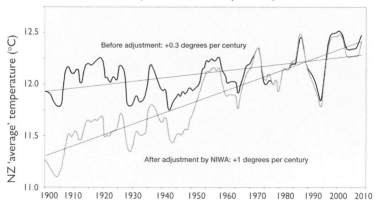

Approximate NZ temperature record 1900–2008
(before and after adjustment)

Figure 19. New Zealand temperature record for 1900–2008. The unadjusted trend line indicates at most a +0.3°C trend. After adjustment it increases to almost +1°C, or *twice* the global average. Graph courtesy Bryan Leyland.[86]

The recent High Court decision dismissing the case brought against NIWA by the NZ Climate Science Education Trust raised some questioning eyebrows. As pointed out by science writer Jo Nova, the Trust lost its case not because NIWA came up with the answers and not because they came up with the contentious missing data, but because the sceptics were not 'qualified' to question it. Nova argues that, 'If non-experts protested unfairly at the NIWA results, surely NIWA would find it easy to explain why they were wrong, and a judge would be more than capable [of] understanding [the science], but if NIWA is not even expected to answer those questions then no justice has been done . . . And again, we get the line that NIWA is OK, because it's just as bad and incompetent as all the other agencies around the world which adjust data without detailed explanations, and which lose data ad hoc.'[87] Dismissing the case on the grounds that the sceptics were shown to be wrong would settle it once and for all. But they weren't.

So the New Zealand public are no better off and have as much reason to doubt NIWA's temperature record as before. As Eschenbach said, 'when those guys "adjust", they don't mess around'. He was referring in this case to the Australian temperature record where he found precisely the same issues, but orders of magnitude worse.

Eschenbach analysed monitoring stations in Northern Australia, most notably for Darwin, and discovered that a natural −0.5°C cooling trend in the raw data had been turned into a very pronounced warming trend of a staggering 6°C after adjustment! Eschenbach was flabbergasted and writes, 'They've just added a huge artificial totally imaginary trend to the last half of the raw data . . . They've adjusted it 8 standard deviations from the average of the raw data . . . impossible.' Eschenbach continues, 'Those, dear friends, are the clumsy fingerprints of someone messing with the data Egyptian style . . . they are <u>indisputable evidence that the GHCN 'homogenized' data has been changed to fit someone's preconceptions about whether the earth is warming</u>'[88] (underlining in original).

In any case, as similarly pointed out by the Australian statistician Jonathan Lowe, there are serious flaws in the way temperature data are collected. Lowe claims that the warming interpreted from the land-based dataset for the past sixty years has been exaggerated by 45 per cent as a result of the methods used to take minimum and maximum readings, which tends to add a warm bias. But it gets worse because Lowe discovered that most of this warming has occurred approximately between sunrise and noon[89] due to decreased cloud cover during the day. This is a startling conclusion and suggests that not only do the adjustments after the fact appear to be corrupt, but the methods and techniques used are also suspect and bedevilled by bias.

According to an independent audit carried out on the Australian Bureau of Meteorology (BoM), around 90 per cent of Australian temperature recording sites prior to 1972 failed to comply with their own standards. Furthermore, some 25 per cent 'of all the measurements back then were rounded or possibly truncated' and that these 'sloppy' rounding errors may have led to an artificial warming trend.[90] The BoM responded by creating an entirely new temperature series, ACORN, but this too was found by one of the auditors, Ed Thurstan, to be full of mistakes, including nearly 1,000 cases where the maximum temperatures were recorded as being *lower* than the minimum temperatures for the same day. The Australian temperature history, like New Zealand's, is in a shambles. They both lack complete records and details on how the adjustments were carried out and they both therefore lack reliability for long-term trends to be determined with any accuracy, let alone policy decisions made on their basis.

A similar analysis carried out by Anthony Watts and colleagues at the US Historical Climatology Network (USHCN) uncovered huge positive biases in the adjusted data, demonstrating that reported temperature trends from 1979 to 2008 'are spuriously doubled, with 92 per cent of that over-estimation resulting from erroneous NOAA [National Oceanic and Atmospheric Administration] adjustments of well-sited stations upward'. The paper shows that from 1979 to 2008 there was a biased 'trend of +0.155°C per decade from the high quality sites, a +0.248°C per decade trend for poorly sited locations, and a trend of +0.309°C per decade after NOAA adjusts the data'. It was already known from an earlier study that around 90 per cent of the monitoring stations have been compromised by artificial heat sources and heat sinks, from airport tarmac to air conditioning heat exchangers. Among many other issues, the researchers found that 'Poorly sited station trends are adjusted sharply upward, and well-sited stations are adjusted upward to match the already-adjusted poor stations.' Meanwhile the well-sited 'rural stations show a warming nearly three times greater after NOAA adjustment is applied'.[91]

In an ironic twist on this problem, meteorologist Jeff Masters of Weather Underground explained that the 'all-time hottest temperature of 58°C (136.4°F) measured . . . at El Azizia, Libya on September 13, 1922' has now been dismissed by the World Meteorological Organization (WMO) as inaccurate due to errors in measurement and poor siting of the station near artificial heat sources. The record has since been given to Death Valley, California with a temperature of 56.7°C, measured on 10 July 1913.[92]

Clearly then, CRU is not alone in having dubious data, in having lost its records and in refusing to provide access to data it does hold. In an email to Phil Jones in February 2004, Warwick Hughes requested data used by CRU and the IPCC to support the claim that global temperatures had increased by 0.6°C over the last century. This claim was based primarily on the surface station temperature record whose accuracy, especially for Western Australia, Hughes doubted because of contamination by urban heat island (UHI) effects. Hughes's initial request opened an email exchange that increased in hostility on Jones's part. Jones eventually replied in February 2005, 'Even if WMO agrees, I will still not pass on the data. Why should I make the data available to you, when your aim is to try and find something wrong with it?'

This is an astonishing outburst from a senior figure in the climate science community who should know that it is not how the scientific method works. For it relies on testing, questioning and replicating the results of others. And yet it was Jones himself who said, 'Climate scientists should think about data quality more often so that there is no opportunity for incorrect data to sow seeds of doubt in people's minds about the reality of climate change.'[93] Hence Hughes's emails. As Michaels commented, Jones's email was 'breathtaking in its anti-scientific thrust. In fact, the entire purpose of replication *is* to "try and find something wrong". The ultimate objective of science is to do things so well that, indeed, nothing is wrong.'[94]

But the real hero of the Climategate story is the whistleblower. Someone who was familiar with the detailed workings of CRU and the data they control 'realised the implications of what was going on and was able to place all these emails on an obscure Russian website'.[95] They were released with the comment, 'We feel that climate science is, in its current situation, too important to be kept under wraps'.

That single act blew the lid off the global warming hoax being perpetrated by CRU, the IPCC and their colleagues and vindicated the suspicions of thousands of sceptics around the world that CRU is the architect of the biggest scientific fraud in history. The only problem is that the media almost completely ignored it. This is baffling considering the scale and implications of the scandal, which one might reasonably assume would be taken up eagerly by the media, which thrives on controversy. However, for the media to pay too much attention to the scandal would also mean having to debunk the hobgoblin of the century: human-induced climate chaos and global warming, which are supposedly threatening the planet. Such a message reads well in the press and makes great television with images of collapsing ice cliffs, wild fires in Australia and sweltering heat waves in Russia. Disaster porn. Climategate was nothing in comparison to the planet on the brink of Armageddon, so it faded into the background.

The email that broke the story appeared in Lucia Liljegren's blog 'The Blackboard' (also known as 'Rank Exploits') on 19 November 2009. Steven Mosher had stumbled on the link to the emails on the 'Airvent', a blog run by Jeff Id. Mosher then posted an explosive comment on Liljegren's blog explaining:

Found this on the airVent.
Posted on Lucia. This is huge.

Lucia,

Found this on JeffIds site:

noconsensus.wordpress.com . . . en-letter

It contains over 1000 mails. IF TRUE . . . 1 mail from you and the correspondence that follows.

*. . . you get to see somebody with the name of **phil jones** say that **he would rather destroy the CRU data than release it to McIntyre**.*

*And lots lots more, including **how to obstruct or evade FOIA requests**. and guess who funded the collection of cores at Yamal . . . and transferred money into a personal account in Russia.*

And you get to see what they really say behind the curtain . . . you get to see how they 'shape' the news, how they struggled between telling the truth and making policy makers happy.

*You get to see what they say about Idso and pat michaels, **you get to read how they want to take us out into a dark alley**, it's stunning all very stunning. **You get to watch***

> *somebody named phil jones say that John Daly's death*
> *is good news* . . . *or words to that effect.*
> *I don't know that its [sic] real.*
>
> *But the CRU code looks real.*

[Bold added].

It *was* real. The late John Daly, mentioned in the email, was the author of *The Greenhouse Trap* and a prominent sceptic. He was also a thorn in the side of the CRU gang. Daly's personal biography on his blog reads, in part:

> . . . for the last 9 years [I] have been one of the numerous 'sceptics' speaking out publicly against the Global Warming scare, which makes exaggerated claims that the earth will warm by +1.5 to +6 deg. C. due to an enhanced Greenhouse Effect.
>
> Climate and climate change has been a lifelong study of mine since my early days as a ship's officer in the British Merchant Navy. I have lived through and traced the progress of the 'ice age' scare of the 1970's, the 'nuclear winter' scare of the 1980s, and now the 'global warming' scare of the present. All these scares have advanced the interests of what was a small academic discipline 30 years ago to become a mammoth global industry today. It is my view that this industry has, through the 'politics of fear' which it has promoted, acted against the interests of the public.[96]

But there was discord in the ranks.

Keith Briffa did not entirely agree with Mann's temperature reconstruction for the past 1,000 years. During a meeting of IPCC authors held in Tanzania in 1999, there was huge disagreement over whether Mann's graph should be the one to appear in the

IPCC's 2001 report since Jones and Briffa had an alternative reconstruction which Briffa thought came closer to the truth.[97] However, Chris Folland, IPCC lead author, thought Jones and Briffa's graph 'dilutes the message rather significantly'[98] because it suggested a *downturn* in northern hemisphere temperatures after 1960 due to a significant decline in tree ring widths and densities, which appeared to contradict the opposite trend from the thermometer record. This discrepancy undermined both the message of unprecedented twentieth-century warming *and* the reliability of tree rings as a temperature proxy, which of course cast even more doubt on Mann's hockey stick and CRU's insistence that the MWP was either a local event or, better, did not occur at all. Yet evidence from a team of scientists led by the geochemist Zunli Lu at Syracuse University demonstrates that the MWP and LIA not only were real but were global phenomena. But CRU needed the tree ring proxy reconstruction to support the contention that late twentieth-century warming was unprecedented and that the MWP was a non-event, thus allowing the long, flat, gradual decline in global temperatures until the beginning of the twentieth century, which Mann's hockey stick purports to show. Anything that undermined this view was a serious problem for the upcoming IPCC Third Assessment Report which required a consistent message. Yet that is precisely what the sudden post-1960 decline in Briffa's reconstruction was doing. It had to go.

However, Briffa was not convinced and wrote an impassioned email, dated September 22 1999, defending his reconstruction:

I know there is pressure to present a nice tidy story as regards 'apparent unprecedented warming in a thousand years or more in the proxy data', but in reality the situation is not quite so simple . . . For the record, I believe that the recent warmth was probably matched about 1,000 years ago . . .[99]

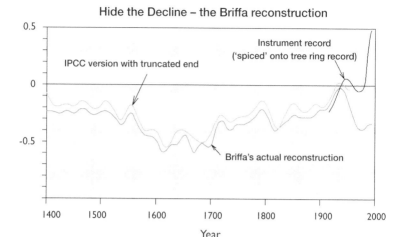

Figure 20. Comparing Briffa's reconstruction (black line), showing a decline, with the IPCC version truncated (grey line).[100]

This was like a slap in the face. Briffa was acknowledging that the MWP was at least as significant as the late twentieth century. Mann, however, thought Briffa's interpretation was a 'problem and a potential distraction/detraction' because it showed a post-1960 *decline* in tree ring widths, the opposite to what was required politically and which also contradicted the thermometer record. This was not acceptable.

Mann, therefore, as the lead author on this chapter of the IPCC report, deleted the embarrassing post-1960 portion of Briffa's reconstruction,[101] as it 'would raise a conundrum', which would be difficult to explain without admitting a weakness in the hypothesis that late twentieth-century warming was unusual. Briffa was not happy with the decision but Jones, on the other hand, thought deleting it was a good idea and wrote, 'I've just completed Mike's *Nature* trick of adding in the real temperatures to each series for the last twenty years (i.e. from 1981 onwards) and from 1961 for Keith's to hide the decline' by which he meant hiding the decline shown in Briffa's reconstruction, thus solving Mann's 'conundrum'. After sceptics took him to task for this 'trick', Jones's defence was that it 'was taken out of context'. But Steve McIntyre argues that it is even worse when taken *in* context. 'I'm not sure that it's in their interests that this email be placed in context,' he says, 'because the context leads right back to a meeting of IPCC authors in Tanzania, raising serious questions about the role of the IPCC itself in "hiding the decline" in the Briffa reconstruction.' The 'trick' was in merging the thermometer data onto the tree ring data at the point where they started to diverge, just as Mann had done earlier.

Mann was worried that if the sceptics knew of the problem with the tree ring proxies, and Briffa's decline in ring widths, it would 'undermine faith in the paleoestimates' for the MWP which naturally meant that his own hockey stick graph would be spurious. Public knowledge of the decline would also cast doubt on unprecedented twentieth-century warming which was not acceptable politically. Mann wrote in another email that the sceptics would have a 'field day casting doubt on our ability to understand the factors that influence these estimates' and that he'd 'hate to be the one to have to give it fodder!' By the following day however, writes Steve McIntyre of the affair, 'matters seem to have settled down, with Briffa apologizing to Mann for his temporary pangs of conscience.'[102]

And therein lies the crux of the matter. The actual evidence said something different from what they wanted so it had to be manipulated or trimmed. Although the 'decline' mentioned in Jones's email was referring specifically to tree ring widths and densities after 1960, and not actual temperature as many critics have thought, it was still a problem because if allowed to pass intact it would allow the observer to *infer* a corresponding decline in temperatures for the twentieth century because of the assumption that tree rings are accurate temperature proxies. This was a vital element in their argument upon which the entire AGW hypothesis hinges. Without the tree ring proxies for the pre-industrial period and without the thermometer record for the late twentieth century, they have nothing. Only an upward trend during the twentieth century would find its way into the IPCC's Assessment Reports and any suggestion of the opposite would have to be engineered out of existence.

And so it was that the IPCC 2001 version of Briffa's reconstruction had the offending decline omitted and the thermometer record seamlessly spliced onto the hacked ends of the tree ring proxies. Two entirely different datasets seamlessly merged in order to give a consistent image palatable to the IPCC and believable by politicians. Strangely, Briffa seems to have foreseen the coming problems with the divergence issue two years before because in 1997 he emailed Gordon Jacoby at Columbia University warning, 'I think we have to somehow adjust recent tree growth records or not use recent data in the calibrations!' This suggests that he was, at one point at least, in favour of ignoring the issue.

But it was not just the post-1960 decline that was removed. Briffa also trimmed off 148 years prior to 1550. As McIntyre pointed out in his blog, 'The day before yesterday, I reported that Briffa and Osborn . . . had not just deleted the post-1960 decline . . . [they] had deleted the pre-1550 portion as well – the deletions contributing to an unwarranted rhetorical impression of consistency between the reconstructions.'[103] When restored, the pre-1550 portion suggests that temperatures were also much lower during those years, rising sharply from around 1402. If this were allowed, it would be difficult to argue for a flat MWP and unnaturally high twentieth-century temperatures. So that had to go too.

The disagreement between Briffa, Mann and Jones over the post-1960 decline was started innocently by a colleague. 'Unfortunately for them,' writes John Costella in his detailed analysis of the affair, 'the game fell apart when one of their colleagues . . . went to check that their main "temperature proxy" – the tree ring data – agreed' with the actual temperature measurements. 'And what did they find?' asks Costella, that, while the thermometers showed increased temperatures, the tree ring proxies in the same areas showed the opposite,[104] which meant that the '*tree rings had been proved to be completely unreliable thermometers*' (emphasis added).[105] This should not have come as a surprise because it was widely known that *tree ring growth is affected by many environmental factors besides temperature*. Changes in rainfall, humidity, soil nutrients, sunlight and atmospheric CO_2 all affect tree ring growth. Even chopping down one tree will affect the growth profile of a nearby one if that alters the amount of sunlight falling on it over time.

In addition, as Daly pointed out, 'Tree rings only record the climate of the growing season, not the whole year. Tree rings are also influenced by rainfall, access to light, and other environmental variables, and are thus not an exclusive indicator of annual temperature as the tree ring researchers would have us believe.'[106] But Mann's hockey stick graph, based largely on biased bristlecone pines, assumed that temperature alone affected ring growth even though there existed an apparent and unexplained divergence between tree ring growth and temperatures over recent decades.[107] But the problem for the CRU was twofold. On the one hand, tree ring evidence definitely revealed the existence of the MWP (agreeing with many other proxies, including lake bed sediments, stalactites and ice cores, as well as written anecdotal evidence of the time), while on the other, they contradicted the thermometer evidence for unprecedented late twentieth-century warming. So they were on the horns of a dilemma.

All temperature proxies, including tree rings, dating from the MWP consistently show it to be similar to the RWP and even warmer than the twentieth century. The tree ring divergence problem however appears to have occurred gradually but dramatically during the early part of the twentieth century, as Briffa shows. And it was this decline that was causing all the trouble for presenting 'a nice tidy story'.

Andrew Montford demonstrates that 'The issue [of divergence] had been recognised for some years' and that Briffa himself had written two papers on the subject, the first of which studied 'tree rings across the world and presented a picture of how their growth patterns had changed across the centuries. His results clearly showed a marked decline in ring width density in the twentieth-century.'[108] But the cause of this twentieth-century divergence is not fully understood, being put down to a variety of assumed causes. Briffa and the rest of the CRU team had no explanation for it so they merely *assumed* that humankind was somehow responsible for that as well. They could not, must not, doubt the thermometer record, the *only* instrumental evidence in existence for late twentieth-century manmade global warming. And to doubt this would undermine the entire scientific argument which was politically unpalatable. So if the tree ring record started to contradict it, the tree ring record for this period simply had to go. There was no alternative. Nevertheless, the CRU scientists went to great lengths to hide the problem in the IPCC publications.[109] These issues of course meant that tree ring proxy data had to be carefully selected in order to give a consistent picture of temperature stability immediately prior to the twentieth century, followed by a sharp upswing. Any large divergence from a flat line up to that point would undermine faith in the message of 'unprecedented warming' caused by industrial CO_2 emissions. Tree rings were taken to be accurate thermometers when they appeared to corroborate the AGW hypothesis, and discarded as unfit when they didn't. Yet not only was the offending twentieth-century decline hidden, Briffa's post-1960 data was also 'deleted from the archive', write Mosher and Fuller in *Climategate – the Crutape Letters*, 'thus ensuring that anyone who used this data in the future would not have access to the inconvenient truth.'[110] Sadly for the CRU team, they never imagined it would turn up again embedded in the Climategate emails, allowing Steve McIntyre to reconstruct it and discover what they had done.

Yet, as we saw earlier, there was every reason to doubt the thermometer record as well. The sparsely sited land-based thermometers were themselves contaminated by Urban Heat Island (UHI) effects and so were equally unreliable. As anyone who lives in a city knows, roads and buildings tend to bias temperatures upward. And it was this very problem of positive bias with the land-based temperature record that initially sparked the interest of

Hughes and McIntyre. The surface station record was not to be trusted because monitoring stations were typically positioned near car parks, asphalt areas, airport runways where they are affected by jet wash, air-conditioning vents and even furnaces.[111] They have also been subject to warm biases from changes to the screens (including painting with rubber-infused paints), changes to the local environments, in addition to a bias that appears to have come from large reductions in their numbers during the 1990s.[112] Yet it is the land-based temperature record specifically that is used by CRU and the IPCC to conclude that there is an 'unprecedented twentieth-century warming'.

After Briffa admitted that today's temperatures may be no different from those of the MWP, Mann was not very happy. 'I walked into this hornet's nest!' he responds. Mann then 'engineers what became the infamous "green graph" – the green tree-ring line in the graph in the IPCC Report that mysteriously passes behind the other lines at the year 1961 – and never emerges on the other side,' writes Costella.[113] But in order to achieve this, he had to 'fiddle the data, to make sure that the lines all cross at [the] right place'.[114] And thus the embarrassing decline has vanished while the utterly unreliable thermometer record, fatally compromised by UHI effects biasing temperature readings upward, is relied on to emphasize late twentieth-century warming.

In spite of so much disagreement between the scientists over how to dispose of the embarrassing post-1960 decline in tree ring widths – the stonewalling, intimidation, data manipulation and deleting of emails to cover their tracks; the siting of monitoring stations near artificial heat sources – the IPCC *still* sees no reason not to trust the data. One cannot even question it without suffering a barrage of outrage. And on the strength of that manipulated, untrustworthy data, the citizens of most Western countries are being taxed in order to 'fight climate change'. The CRU's antics are reminiscent of the *Keystone Cops*, a mad comedy of errors, and it would indeed be hilarious were it not for the fact that the madness is threatening so many Western economies. Nevertheless, the greatest gift to the world from the climate science community, and CRU in particular, is Climategate. That more than anything else reveals the lengths some scientists will go to in order to perpetuate the AGW myth and hide the evidence that contradicts it. None of this matters however because the hockey stick graph was packaged so nicely and sold to the IPCC with a smile. And the IPCC in turn have sold it on to Western governments, who use it as 'proof' of manmade global warming for which we must all be taxed to 'save the planet'. But save it from what?

So if tree rings for the twentieth century *and* the ground-based temperature record cannot be trusted, what other indicators do we have that give a reliable and truly global temperature picture? The satellite record is the only source not under the tyrannical control of the IPCC but only goes back to the late 1970s. Nevertheless, as Singer pointed out in 1998, the satellite record is still an embarrassment to the IPCC because it shows 'a global *cooling* trend during the past nineteen years',[115] not Mann's hockey stick warming trend.

Satellite data also contradict the ground-based thermometer network on which the CRU hockey stick team relies for their message of climate doom. There is no hint in the satellite record of Mann's late twentieth-century 'unprecedented' temperature rise. There is no evidence of it *anywhere* except the infamous and controversial 'hockey stick' graph.

Furthermore, the satellite record is vindicated by measurements made by radiosondes attached to weather balloons which have 'returned data wholly consistent with the satellite record'.[116] It is for this reason that the IPCC avoids or dismisses this evidence as much as possible. In the Summary for Policymakers, the section most read by journalists and government officials, 'there is not one mention of the word "satellite",' says Michaels, 'because they are at variance with the ground-measured temperature trends', and since they are at variance, it was effectively decided by the so-called consensus that the inconsistency should not be revealed.[117] Yet according to data from Mauna Loa, CO_2 levels have been rising steadily since around 1959 which, if the global warming alarmists are right, should be forcing global temperatures ever upward.

Why then do the satellite datasets, which cover the whole globe, show only a slight warming trend to 1998, which was caused by the El Niño event, and *no* warming at all for the next thirteen years until 2011?[118] Because the hockey stick graph is wrong and because CAGW is simply quasi-religious dogma masquerading as science which its adherents believe can be 'proved' by other means than observation and experiment. Faced with this evidence, it is not surprising the UK Met Office 'quietly released' data in 2012 that showed there had been no global warming for sixteen years. According to journalist David Rose in *Mail Online*, 'The figures, which have triggered debate among climate scientists, reveal that from the beginning of 1997 until August 2012, there was no discernible rise in aggregate global temperatures' and that the data proving it was released 'quietly on the internet, without any media fanfare'.[119]

But desperate times call for desperate measures. Despite satellite and radiosonde evidence suggesting no warming, and even a slight cooling trend for the past two decades, CRU and the Hadley Centre still managed to conclude the opposite. They announced that temperatures since 1998 have continued to increase slightly due to CO_2 emissions and that, according to Louise Gray of the *Telegraph*, 'the world is warming even more than previously thought'.[120] This supports the politically correct view that 2010 ended the hottest decade on record. But in order to extract a warming signal from one that, if anything, appears to be going the other way, it appears that the CRU and NASA GISS scientists who compiled the data were obliged to employ the statistical smoke-and-mirrors tricks we saw before, including a series of cumulative 'adjustments', nearly all of which lead to warming. Amazingly, the adjustments also allowed 1934 – the previously warmest year in the last century – to swap places with 1998.[121] Their latest CRUTem4 dataset now indicates a slight warming trend *despite* the satellite evidence to the contrary, *despite* record low winter temperatures in both the northern and southern hemispheres and record snowfalls in those same years.

That feat was achieved largely by adjusting the earlier temperatures *downward*, thus suggesting a continuously positive upward slope in the data. This is an old ruse resorted to by CRU – 'business as usual' says Anthony Watts.[122] The most CRU will concede is that the apparent warming trend they magically extracted from the post-1998 trendless data is 'statistically insignificant'.[123] Why mention it then? If it's 'statistically insignificant', nothing at all can be inferred from the data. But even this small concession is an unintentional admission that the climate system is being driven by something other than industrial CO_2 emissions. If our increasing CO_2 emissions are supposed to be responsible for most of the warming over the last 100 years, that it is 'catastrophic' and given that a tipping point based on that premise is likely, how can temperatures after 1998 be 'statistically insignificant'? They should be continuing their ever-upward climb to catastrophe, but now even the CRU team has to admit that this is not happening, as does the UK Met Office.

8.   Sacred Cows and Heretics

> It does not matter who you are, or how smart you are, or what title you have, or how many of you there are, and certainly not how many papers your side has published, if your prediction is wrong then your hypothesis is wrong. Period.
>
> *Richard Feynman*

> Fiction is obliged to stick to possibilities. Truth isn't.
>
> *Mark Twain*

'The time for debate is over. The science is settled,' quipped Al Gore to the lawmakers.[1] Gore, however, was not really joking, so no one laughed. They should have.

This claim has been made frequently by proponents of the 'dangerous manmade global warming' theory in order to deny the existence of any contrary evidence or argument that might undermine this politically charged idea. If you go along with the proposition, you free yourself from the principles and disciplines of scientific veracity. You may then pursue your own agenda in the manner of Jonathan Swift's reformers. Mark Twain and Richard Feynman would have been in fits of laughter at such a hilarious remark because, as Feynman pointed out, 'If you thought that science was certain – well, that is just an error on your part.' Galileo also was wise to this four centuries ago when he observed in a letter to the mathematician astronomer Benedetto Castelli, 'Who would dare assert that we know all there is to be known?'

The nature of scientific enquiry is to assume that nothing in science is beyond debate, regardless of merit, because it is precisely this openness to questioning that allows for progress and the pursuit of knowledge. History's scientific landscape is littered with the carcases of dead theories all at one time or another held to be the 'consensus' view, yet many undone by a single 'heresy'. It takes just one inconvenient fact wielded by a lone 'heretic' ahead of his time to destroy the most elegant and time-honoured theory.

Only religious beliefs are settled and only politics is done by consensus. Science is indifferent to both because it is necessarily impartial to vested interests. Religion and politics require advocacy. Science does not. Mark Twain understood human nature and the tendency of those with vested interests to distort the facts and trim their data to fit preconceived ideas. This is where religion and bad science merge until they are indistinguishable. Thus the claim that the science of manmade global warming is 'settled' and that 'the debate is over' smacks of aggressive ignorance allied with tyranny. The Church exhibited these traits for centuries to the cost of many a 'heretic' who tried to bring enlightenment to the world. Little has changed since then.

The scientific establishment similarly relies on ideas that become so entrenched they are accepted without question. And to question scientific orthodoxy and science fashion is to invite ridicule and even hostility because you are seen to be throwing mud in the eye of respectability. Modern science has many sacred cows, so one might be forgiven for thinking today's scientific establishment is indistinguishable from the early Church with its dogmas and high priests. Like the early Church, the science establishment is peopled by fundamentalists who defend the faith and condemn anyone who questions it as a heretic. The heretics are free-thinkers like Copernicus, Galileo, the anatomist Vesalius and many others in the past, followed by Velikovsky more recently. Ted O. Thackrey, editor and publisher of New York City's newspaper *The Daily Compass*, reminded Harlow Shapley of this in a letter defending Velikovsky's right to have his book published, that 'such contributors to the field of scientific knowledge as Leeuwenhoek, the untutored church janitor who discovered and proved the existence of microbes' had infuriated 'the then existing practitioners of medicine' who refused to believe such tiny 'animalcules' could possibly exist. They couldn't be seen with the naked eye, therefore they didn't exist. Anton van Leeuwenhoek, who flourished in the seventeenth and early eighteenth centuries and who advanced the development and use of microscopes, was ridiculed by the establishment. He was dismissed as a charlatan and a fool.[2] These 'heretics' challenged the so-called consensus view of the world, yet they also advanced the course of science to where it is today. Without their single-minded efforts we would be floundering in superstition. But in their day, their heresies met the armour plate of religious conviction and authoritarian ignorance.

In the 1930s, the naturalist William Beebe and engineer Otis Barton unwittingly demonstrated the myth of 'consensus' science when they too were ridiculed by the scientific establishment for their outlandish descriptions of deep sea creatures seen from the early Bathysphere submersible. Mainstream science was sceptical of their discoveries because the consensus was that such creatures could not possibly exist – they were far too weird, too different from what we were familiar with at the surface; an exact repeat of Leeuwenhoek's experiences, but more than two centuries later as though nothing had been learned. Yet the creatures they witnessed do indeed exist, and the 'consensus' view that they didn't was disproved.

There are many such cases of scorn and ridicule from the establishment, of ideas and discoveries that were later proved to be correct. The history of science is littered with their sad remains. But the Leeuwenhoek and Beebe and Barton episodes reveal how meaningless a scientific consensus really is. The *only* thing a consensus proves is that a group of like-minded individuals happen to agree on an idea, which may or may not be correct, which is politics, not science. They may *believe* it to be correct, but what does that prove?

Science is not done by a show of hands, nor by advocacy, but by observation and experimentation. Why then is the term 'consensus' used to determine which idea is right and which wrong?

Why is a moral imperative attached to the idea of the majority vote, as though merit always lies with greater numbers? The history of science itself suggests precisely the opposite.

The last few decades have seen many plausible theories widely accepted and popularized by media hype.[3] Each was thought to be crucially important and promoted by the academic community as irrefutable. Most have since faded into obscurity. We have been threatened by another ice age, the Jupiter effect, nuclear meltdown, ozone depletion, the millennium bug, weapons of mass destruction, SARS (severe acute respiratory syndrome), global warming, climate change, bird flu and swine flu. Affluent Western societies, fearful of 'obesity epidemics', overpopulation and African killer bees, expect such calamities to overtake them. We live in constant fear of impending disaster as though God were targeting the human race. We are running out of oil and water and soon there will be standing room only, again. The end is always nigh and caused by man. The science is always settled. And the moon is made of green cheese.

Whether or not these predicted calamities had any merit at the time, they all died a natural death due largely to overexposure and a lack of anything happening. Whenever this occurs, alarm fatigue understandably takes root and it becomes difficult to separate fact from fiction so that real threats tend to be ignored.

This is a point well made by the geologist Bob Carter with respect to the very real threat of another mini ice age, based on the currently 'quiet' sun, which is being overshadowed by alarm over alleged manmade warming. Carter writes, 'the greatest damage that has been inflicted by those whipping up the hypothetical threat of human-caused global warming is that the subsequent hysteria has overwhelmed mature consideration of the much greater and proven threat of *natural* climate change' (emphasis in original).[4] The opposite precautions should be taken,[5] but no one is paying attention, least of all the politicians and the media who are utterly hoodwinked by the current warming hysteria. We will be unprepared for another long-term cooling phase like the last Little Ice Age. Unfortunately, the 'boy-who-cried-wolf' syndrome sets in and no one believes anything. The point is, none of these earlier fads materialized into what was supposed by the champions of habitual alarm, despite the hype. And manmade global warming is proving to be no different, except for the fact that it has become a Frankenstein monster and seems to be out of control. It is the best funded politically-driven pseudo-scientific scam in history and represents far more of a threat to the world in terms of lost freedoms, corrupted education and stunted progress than it ever did to the earth's climate.

Ignoring alarm fatigue, Sir John Houghton, first chairman of the IPCC, went so far as to suggest that disasters may be necessary if we want to save the planet – an astonishing concept that flies in the face of common sense. Piers Akerman writes in 'Malicious Bullets Fired by the Global Warmists' Guns',

> Yesterday I was forwarded an article published in the *Sunday Telegraph* (UK) on September 10, 1995, in which Houghton told writer Frances Welch: 'If we want a good environmental policy in the future we'll have to have a disaster.'

That appears to be the *modus operandi* of the IPCC and twenty-first-century politics – fostering fear and alarm in order to bring about widespread social change.

However, Stephen Schneider, lead author of the IPCC, worried no one would believe them, and with good reason considering the unenviable alarmist track record. As we saw in Chapter 1, Schneider thought it was important 'to capture the public's imagination' by offering 'scary scenarios', issuing 'simplified, dramatic statements' and making 'little mention of any doubts we might have'. Such deceitful pronouncements should be enough to raise doubts about anthropogenic global warming even without the physical evidence against the theory. Such statements should disconcert any self-respecting scientist or politician who currently endorses the theory. They should provoke suspicion of the true agenda of the IPCC. Yet they do not, or at least not for the passionately committed and the unsuspecting public. Why not? The answer lies in the vested interests that allowed the carbon cult to gain such powerful traction in the first place. It now has such inertia despite the problems with the science which are legion, as we have already seen.

Yet these issues are ignored by the media and politicians alike. According to Joanne Nova, 'The US government has spent over $79 billion since 1989 on policies related to climate change'[6] and she complains that 'In this scientific debate, one side is gagged while the other side has a government–funded media campaign.'[7] Lindzen similarly argues, 'Ambiguous scientific statements about climate are hyped by those with a vested interest in alarm, thus raising the political stakes for policy makers who provide funds for more science research to feed more alarm to increase the political stakes.'[8]

On top of this, according to the *Wall Street Journal* writer Bret Stephens, HSBC estimated that $94 billion had been spent globally on 'green stimulus' alternative energy schemes in 2009, in addition to hundreds of millions spent on climate research grants around the world.[9] The reason, according to Stephens, is that the millions from charitable trusts and the billions in government grants encourage 'universities, research institutes, advocacy groups and their various spin-offs and dependents' to emerge 'from the woodwork to receive them'.

It is all about spin and selling an idea. 'That spin is then dispersed into the public realm through conferences, through the education system and through the media,' writes Carter.[10] It is about *selling* the message, not what's *in* the message. The message itself can be a lie, but that doesn't matter if the public swallow it. According to Nick Pidgeon of Cardiff University, it is incumbent on climate scientists to ally themselves with psychologists from the 'social and decision sciences' in order to convince the public that action is needed to fight climate change.[11] The theory is called 'the science of communicating science' to the public, which apparently requires psychologists not scientists because 'scepticism' of manmade global warming is a sickness to be treated.[12] 'Resistance at individual and societal levels must be recognized and treated before real action can be taken to effectively address threats facing the planet from human-caused contributions to climate change' reads the message from a University of Oregon climate group, led by Kari Norgaard for the Planet Under Pressure Conference held in London in March 2012.[13]

It seems that while scepticism is a malady, it is ethical to falsify data in order to sell the message of climate doom, especially if the message is delivered with slick professionalism. Al Gore is a master of media presentation. This was seen in his recent Climate Reality Project[14] which included a video demonstration titled 'Climate Change 101', an easy experiment suitable for high school students and narrated by the popular American TV presenter Bill Nye, 'the Science Guy', which supposedly demonstrates the impressive greenhouse heating effect of atmospheric CO_2. 'You can replicate this effect yourself in a simple lab experiment,' says Nye. 'Here's how.' He then shows two identical glass jars containing identical thermometers placed under identical heat lamps at identical distances. The only difference between the two jars is that one includes a hose from which CO_2 is supposedly pumped into the interior. It all looks very plausible. Nye then explains, 'Within minutes you will see the temperature of the bottle with the carbon dioxide in it rising faster and higher.'

Then the scene changes to a split-screen close-up, apparently showing the two thermometers, one with rapidly rising mercury, of around 2°F 'within minutes'. This is a huge increase in temperature from such a small volume of enclosed CO_2 and must leave the uninformed audience with the impression that CO_2 is indeed a potent greenhouse gas. Just imagine what it is doing to the planet! However, according to Anthony Watts (of science blog wattsupwiththat.com), who replicated Gore's experiment, the demonstration was rigged. 'The scene with the split screen thermometers [was] edited to appear as if the temperature in the jar of elevated CO_2 level was rising faster than the jar without elevated CO_2 level.'[15] It turns out that the thermometers shown in the split-screen close-ups were not the ones in the jars. The scene is actually two juxtaposed images of just *one* thermometer, filmed and edited in time sequence to suggest rapidly rising CO_2 in one, while the other remains static. The two images are then arranged to make it appear to the viewers that they are seeing the original two thermometers in the jars.

Watts further explains, 'It turns out that the thermometers were *never in the jar recording the temperature rise presented in the split screen* and the entire presentation was nothing but stagecraft and editing. This was proved beyond a doubt by the Photoshop differencing technique used to compare each side of the split screen. With the exception of the moving thermometer fluid, both sides were identical.' Watts concludes:

> Mr. Gore's Climate 101 experiment is falsified, and could not work given the equipment he specified. If they actually tried to perform the experiment themselves, perhaps this is why they had to resort to stagecraft in the studio to fake the temperature rise on the split screen thermometers.

Not only was Gore's experiment 'faked in post-production', the premise on which it was based was also false.

So much for Gore's 'Climate Change 101', with the media playing its essential role in convincing the public that the earth's climate system is in peril due to their 'carbon emissions'. Yet it is the politicians who have allowed themselves to be bullied by the science and environmental lobbies to an extent that they have the potential to hamstring a country's economy and the welfare of its citizens by enacting damaging legislation. Naturally such legislation is always sold as being in the interests of the environment or the welfare of citizens, but this interest might also be a synthetic veneer disguising alternative political agendas. There is nothing new or unusual in this because such subterfuge is the bread and butter of practical politics. Why then should AGW as a *cause célèbre* be any different? The problem facing politicians is that they must always *appear* to be fighting the good fight for the good of the public, who will then reward them with their votes.

The 'good fight' is whatever happens to be the latest hobgoblin seizing the collective mind of the fashionably frightened. Today it is manmade global warming – now called 'climate change' or 'climate disruption', to deal with global temperatures going up or down. Tomorrow it will be something else that can be blamed on humankind in general and the Western world in particular. We are mining too much iron ore perhaps and unbalancing the earth's magnetic field. The science of course will be deeply flawed, supported only by speculation and computer models, but sufficiently obscured by arrogant insistence that the debate is over and the science is settled. And a team of compliant scientists will again be eager to 'prove' the case with a thin gloss of science to lend it just enough respectability to satisfy an ignorant public desperate once again to be saved. The mainstream media will of course be fully on board, broadcasting the new alarm into every living room while an assortment of celebrities write catchy ditties about the 'dangers' of mining iron ore and chain themselves to diggers and rigs. And environmental protection agencies will then classify Fe as a harmful substance.

Politicians must always appear concerned, ready to respond to the latest fad irrespective of their personal views on the issue. Failure to be seen on the latest bandwagon chanting the new mantra may translate into lost votes at the next election or lost authority and position within their party, especially when the voters are moved by weighty concerns like 'saving the planet'. What could possibly be bigger than saving the planet from an imagined menace? As we saw earlier, Henry Louis Mencken fully understood this when he observed that it is in the interests of politicians to 'keep the populace alarmed' and 'clamorous' so that they may be saved from imagined harm.

Today, environmentalism itself is the social cause and manmade global warming the latest hobgoblin in a long line of hobgoblins. Thus we need to be saved from ourselves and environmentalism is the path to redemption achieved through more social controls and more taxation designed to modify our behaviour in the interests of saving not only ourselves, but the entire planet.[16] Who needs good science when the future of the planet is at stake? Mencken also observed, 'The urge to save humanity is almost always a false front for the urge to rule.'

For the government, saving the planet is also about securing popular support and hanging on to power. So it takes a brave politician to swim against the tide even if s/he smells a scam like AGW. The mainstream media fan the flames of fear by bombarding the uncritical masses with one side of the issue – the side with the more exciting story to tell. This is why few if any media providers are willing to publish more than a token number of articles sceptical of human-induced climate change. To do so would be tantamount to admitting there is nothing to worry about. It goes against the grain, runs counter to media philosophies. Danger and disaster sell. Mundane normality does not.

Situated between the politicians and the media, scientists play piggy in the middle. Motivated by the promise of research grants and the potential kudos that comes from being involved in the latest scientific fashion, many scientists have made their careers out of trying to prove what the politicians require and what the media will publish. Yet the science behind AGW is so flawed it is amazing the alarmist politicians have managed to get away with it for so long and have been able to impose carbon taxes in various countries on its dubious merits. The scientists and government ministers must surely know the science is broken and that AGW is a monumental scam. But they appear not to care and are thus unmoved by conflicting evidence like global temperatures trending *downward* for the past decade while CO_2 emissions increased. Manmade global warming must be the only theory in history that cannot be disproved by contrary evidence. Confronting the alarmists with evidence that questions their science is 'denial' and 'heresy' and so it is ignored.

These issues should give any scientist worth his salt some pause. But it fails even to dent their pride, let alone their confidence in reiterating the AGW myth to an uncritical public. The politicians are immune, the electorate are preoccupied by environmental issues and 'saving the planet' by using low-energy light bulbs and shunning plastic shopping bags, and the scientists remain blind to the truth all the while the politicians are willing to dish out research grants to 'prove' how well-justified are the public's concerns.

Truth and good science have little or nothing to do with it. To the politicians, it is about power; to the climate scientists, it is about funding; to the media, it is a marketable commodity; and to the environmentalist extremists, it is akin to a religious conviction or a need to impose socialist controls – the 'green shackles' as put succinctly by the Czech President Václav Klaus.[17] The only people who care about the truth are the sceptics because scepticism, especially of any 'consensus' is the lifeblood of good science. That is how science works. But they are dismissed as cranks and heretics hell-bent on ruining the fun of everyone else. All four interest groups are like parasites feeding off each other while they also support our collective subconscious need for a surrogate devil to fear. They thrive on the madness because they have vested interests in keeping it alive: money, power, kudos and influence.

But the love of money is the root of corruption. The money tree's branches grow in all directions, supporting not only the scientists with research grants that encourage them to bend the science to the will of the politicians, but also the huge carbon market that sprang from the hysteria. Dozens of interest groups and investment companies immediately recognized the potential for trading in the new global currency: carbon credits and 'carbon offsets'. These latter-day 'indulgences' allow air travellers to absolve their guilt for future carbon sins. Buy carbon offsets today so you may fly tomorrow with a clear conscience for your increased carbon footprint. There are many entrepreneurial schemes available to make your trip guilt-free, including so-called 'carbon-neutral' companies promoting 'sustainability' – the new buzzword – companies that kindly plant a pine sapling on your behalf. You merely purchase the sapling online for a paltry $17 and you are ready to fly. Or, for those vexed by yet more carbon guilt, a modest $35 will buy you a Scotch pine that grows twice as fast.[18] The new tree will offset the CO_2 your travel has released into the already overburdened atmosphere. Or so the story goes.

Not surprisingly, many canny entrepreneurs soon saw the potential for making very large sums of money out of the hysteria and the ensuing 'carbon' phobia, relying on the general ignorance and naivety of the travelling and energy-using public. 'Carbon' suddenly became a dirty word: carbon emissions, carbon pollution, carbon miles – all of which can be offset by the buying and selling of carbon indulgences, or by taxation. We need to be 'carbon-neutral' if we are to achieve respectability. CO_2 needs to be controlled because it has become a noxious substance, an idea encouraged by the US Environmental Protection Agency (EPA), which moved to classify CO_2 as a harmful substance under its Endangerment Finding. Carbon is dirty and dangerous to the planet, so get rid of it. Or control it. Or trade in it. And a huge financial investment industry emerged from the mire which encourages the mania to continue. In reference to Al Gore's Climate Reality Project on Anthony Watts' science blog wattsupwiththat.com, Willis Eschenbach makes the general point that, 'if you are making a quarter of a million per year based on the idea that CO_2 is dangerous, you are very strongly motivated by the money to spread that meme to as many people as possible. If people stop believing that CO_2 is the magical control knob for the climate, you're out of a job.' So it's in the interests of investors in this new market to demonize 'carbon', meaning CO_2, in order to support an industry based on it.

Entire economies are now structured around carbon trading 'cap-and-trade' schemes where industries and companies unlikely to meet their emissions reduction targets set by the Kyoto Protocol must purchase credits or 'offsets' to make up the difference. These credits may then be sold on to others if the company ends up with a surplus. But the very structure encourages fraud, as noted by the Canadian Foreign Minister Greg Sheridan, '[Carbon trading] is like a pyramid marketing scheme. You don't have to actually sell the dog food, you just have to get ten of your friends to do it and you'll get royalties.' Sheridan adds, 'the international trading scheme [in greenhouse gases] lies halfway between a fantasy and a fraud and is never going to make a serious contribution to diminishing greenhouse gases.'[19] Some companies, notably in the UK, managed to sell their carbon credits in order to balance their books which might otherwise not have been possible during the European economic recession. However, the recession also led to falling energy use as consumers and industry cut their costs by using less, thus leaving many companies with a large surplus in carbon credits or permits to emit CO_2. That surplus became a convenient short-term cash cow. Deutsche Bank's carbon analyst Mark Lewis complained that carbon credits were seen as a source of 'cheap short-term funding options in the face of a credit crunch meltdown'.[20] The practice attracted the interest of financial speculators and led to a fall in the price of 'carbon' by up to 60 per cent after €1 billion worth of permits were traded in a few months. The result was that the burning of fossil fuels became cheaper rather than more expensive, the very opposite of what was intended under the rules set by the Kyoto Protocol.[21] It reinforced the view of the sceptics that the entire scheme is a farce.

The intention of many investors of course was not to 'fight climate change' or to save the planet, but to make money. In October 2008, an event was held in London under the banner 'Cashing in on Carbon'. The advertising flyer boasted that the conference was not concerned 'with broader climate change issues', but was 'aimed squarely at investment banks, investors and major compliance buyers and is focused on how they can profit today from an increasingly diverse range of carbon related investment opportunities.'[22] Many investors and buyers of carbon credits were banks such as Barclays, Goldman Sachs and JP Morgan, none of which has large emissions to worry about.[23] So why, one might ask, are they playing in the carbon market? According to the *Telegraph*, in January 2011 the European Commission threatened to stop transactions in carbon trading after €7 million worth of carbon credits were stolen on the Czech carbon register. The incident threatened to disrupt €2 billion in carbon trades across Europe while the entire system 'has been plagued by fraud' which, according to Europol, accounted for up to 90 per cent of the trading in some European countries in 2009.[24]

Among the investment companies set up to trade in 'carbon' is none other than Al Gore's own Generation Investment Management (GIM), for which Gore also acts as chairman, an enterprise specializing in buying and selling shares in companies that meet Gore's definition of sustainability.[25] Many critics argue that GIM allows Gore to buy carbon offsets essentially from himself,[26] thus deflecting criticism that his jet-setting world tours – promoting global warming alarmism – increase his own carbon footprint. But it also allows him to deflect criticism for the energy consumption of his mansion in Nashville, which, according to many commentators, uses far more energy than the average US citizen does, who is under pressure to *reduce* energy consumption to save the planet.[27] Purchasing his carbon offsets through GIM allows Gore to claim that his lifestyle is 'carbon-neutral'. Clearly, there is money to be made from global warming alarmism and no one is in a better position to do so than Gore himself.[28] According to Ellen McGirt, senior writer for *Fast Company* magazine, GIM commanded nearly $1 billion in investments by 2007 from companies investing in the new 'green' economy.[29] And it is this involvement in firms investing in the new green economy that has earned Gore accusations of a conflict of interest.[30]

Other high-profile political figures have been accused of having an interest in the carbon trading market conflicting with their political role. *Fox News* revealed that, before becoming

President, Barak Obama sat on the board of a Chicago-based charity called the Joyce Foundation which granted around $1.1 million in seed money to a carbon exchange he later pushed through Congress. It has been argued that this exchange would have benefited hugely from his proposed cap-and-trade scheme had it succeeded in becoming law.[31] Between 2000 and 2001, Obama's charity gave these grants for 'developing and launching the privately-owned Chicago Climate Exchange [CCX]'.[32] But critics of the scheme complain that CCX had ties to the investment bank Goldman Sachs which owned shares, the business magnate George Soros who had ties to the Joyce Foundation,[33] Al Gore whose GIM was apparently the largest shareholder, and the entrepreneur Maurice Strong; and, according to one of its founders, Richard Sandor – named by *TIME* magazine as the 'father of carbon trading' – would one day be worth $10 trillion a year.[34] Such confidence in the fortunes to be had from trading in the carbon market provides a valuable insight into how these high-level investors were thinking. The huge potential returns were irresistible to other would-be investors too who climbed on the bandwagon to make their millions.[35] However, the window of opportunity was fast closing, especially for those not considered among the top elite as investment in Gore's GIM was restricted to individuals 'of select high net worth'.[36] The average income earner could not afford to play on Gore's terms and was excluded,[37] but must still play a part in the financial game by paying emissions taxes on energy use designed to modify the public's behaviour as 'carbon emitters'.

As a presidential candidate, Obama was unapologetic that under his 'plan of a cap and trade system, electricity rates would necessarily skyrocket'.[38] Despite widespread opposition to the scheme, Obama still had reason to be confident it would work. Investors later flocked to the CCX expecting Congress would approve it. The House of Representatives passed a Bill proposed by Democrats Henry Waxman and Ed Markey which, if passed in the Senate, would have seen Obama's scheme made law. Fortunately for the American consumer, the Waxman-Markey Bill was narrowly defeated in the Senate by a Republican counterattack. Nevertheless, the attempt caused widespread outrage and investors started backing away. According to *Fox News*, 'In the last week, following the . . . Republican takeover of the House of Representatives, the slide became an avalanche. Investors in CCX, including Sandor and former Vice President Al Gore, sold the exchange to a company involved in commodities trading. Sale records show that Sandor cleared more than $90 million for his 16 per cent stake in the company.'[39]

It is not surprising, then, that the CCX collapsed in 2010 when the bottom finally fell out of the market. The collapse was also helped by growing public scepticism and a suspicion that the politicians and scientists were not being entirely honest. These suspicions were augmented by the Climategate email scandals – Climategate I released onto the internet in 2009, and Climategate II released in 2011 – and other revelations of corruption in the climate science community, with the University of East Anglia and Pennsylvania State University playing key roles. And so ended a beautiful dream and many jobs as massive layoffs followed due to the free-fall of their only commodity product: carbon emissions.[40] 'Carbon credits have collapsed, failing like any pyramid scheme without a product,' says Timothy Ball, 'but like all such schemes those in early made money. The problem with carbon credits was those who built the pyramid were also in control of the science and the politics. They controlled their value.'[41] *Investors' Business Daily* similarly noted, 'As the case for global warming and cap-and-trade has collapsed, so too has the market that was to exploit this manufactured crisis for fun and profit. The climate-change bubble has burst.'[42]

Suddenly 'carbon', in terms of CO_2 emissions, was worthless, having fallen from around $7 per tonne in 2008 to 10 cents per tonne in 2010.[43] The hopes and dreams of many investors were destroyed along the way, as always happens when such poorly conceived investment bubbles burst. But just why anyone thought there was a glorious financial future to be had in such a worthless commodity is itself a mystery. The artificial value of 'carbon' (a euphemism for atmospheric CO_2 in purely negative terms) depended entirely on perception, the assumption that it had an intrinsic value like gold which is controlled by the law of supply and demand. As we have seen, this perception was encouraged and supported by corrupt pseudo-science designed to convince the gullible media and punters lower down the food chain that carbon dioxide in the atmosphere was a pollutant and that carbon trading based on this concept was necessary, a good investment if you could afford it and, furthermore, a means of 'saving the planet'. Who could resist it?

Of course, the concept is absurd because 'carbon' itself is a naturally occurring solid, one of the most common substances in the universe, whereas the 'carbon market' is based on the idea that *emissions* of CO_2 have an intrinsic value which can be measured and weighed and then charged for by trading permits on an arbitrary market controlled by politics. It is a nonsense and a misnomer. Yet the very existence of the CCX in particular relied on the assumption and hope that Obama's cap-and-tax legislation – ostensibly designed to reduce CO_2 emissions by hugely increasing the cost of energy – would make carbon trading both compulsory *and* profitable[44] – profitable, that is, for the elite. Everyone else would be paying more for everything affected by higher energy costs.

With the introduction in New Zealand of the emissions trading scheme (ETS) in 2010, the National Party government launched a charm offensive to convince citizens that the emissions trading pill would be good for them, despite the unpalatable cost of living increase that came with it. To aid in the campaign, the Prime Minister's chief science adviser, Sir Peter Gluckman, participated in a series of lectures at Victoria University proclaiming the virtues of the ETS and the dangers of AGW. The lectures had the dual aim of selling the science to an increasingly sceptical public and of dealing with the so-called 'climate deniers' who maintain there is no global warming problem and therefore no need for an emissions tax to solve it.

But the government had a problem because the public was aware of temperatures appearing to trend *downward* despite all the hype to the contrary. The release by the National Institute of Water and Atmospherics (NIWA) of record low temperature data for July 2010 only emphasized the point. Furthermore, the only evidence for human-induced global warming was politically tainted by the IPCC. As an entity of the UN, the IPCC is dominated by political agendas which, according to its nemesis, the Nongovernmental International Panel on Climate Change, predispose it to champion the manmade global warming hypothesis. The IPCC therefore talks down contradictory evidence while promoting alarmist scenarios produced by computer models, as we have seen. These are then used to formulate government policy decades into the future. Yet every other indicator suggests either declining temperatures or statistically insignificant trends, a fact evinced by thousands of scientists worldwide. However, these scientists are Gluckman's politically incorrect 'climate deniers' so they are ignored in New Zealand and Australia where Prime Minister Gillard has staunchly defended and promoted her own brand of emissions tax after first stating, 'There will be no carbon tax under the government I lead.'[45]

Gillard though is not the only politician to make a U-turn on the idea of a CO_2 tax. In 2005, New Zealand's National Party was also hostile to the idea of a carbon tax. At the time, Opposition MP Nick Smith attacked the then Labour government saying,

> The madness of the Government's new carbon tax is that New Zealanders will be the only people in the world paying it. It will drive up the costs of living and undermine the competitiveness of New Zealand business for negligible environmental gain.[46]

Smith dismissed the idea of a carbon tax as absurd and worried that it would drive up the cost of energy, especially oil and electricity, and that these cost increases would 'flow right through the economy to basics like food', which would in turn drive up interest rates and the value of the NZ dollar. Smith correctly argued that none of these measures and cost increases would 'make one iota of difference to New Zealand's emissions'. Nor would they make the slightest difference to the climate or indeed to global warming. Yet it is on this very issue that the emissions tax was predicated, a point later admitted by Gluckman after he was appointed as the Prime Minister's climate adviser. In 2005, Smith's view of the Labour government's carbon tax was apocalyptic: he considered it utterly destructive of New Zealand's economy and for good reason.

Then, like Gillard, on becoming the new Environment Minister when the National Party ousted Labour in the polls, Smith changed his tune and decided CO_2 emissions must be taxed after all. He attempted to get around this blatant about-turn by arguing that the ETS is not really a tax, because it 'completely ignores the carbon credits flowing to forest owners',[47] as though this argument makes a difference to the consumer. If the ETS is not a tax, as Smith argued, what is it? A 'levy' perhaps? In short, a tax by any other name. But the ETS is a tax to the consumer and to claim otherwise is to play with words. Yet for all the good taxing CO_2 would do for global temperatures – which is precisely nothing – it would make more sense to tax *steam* since water vapour is by far the most important greenhouse gas, if that is indeed what they are all worried about. Another absurd proposition of course, but at least there would be more validity to the argument. Water vapour dwarfs everything else in the atmosphere for its warming effects, yet politicians focus on CO_2, that few *thousandths* of a per cent by volume, and think that by taxing it, we may save the planet from a heat-related catastrophe, after first saying the tax will have no effect whatsoever.

The public in both Australia and New Zealand are witnessing a contest between computer models and empirical evidence that contradicts them. The computer modellers win, however, because of contagion by political and financial investments that have allowed them to hijack the scientific process and dilute the criticism coming from Gluckman's so-called 'denier' scientists. Therefore to overcome the scourge of scepticism, both governments appeal to the public's respect for their authority. Forget what you are seeing; trust them and the IPCC instead. They know what they are doing because there is a 'consensus'.

Even New Zealand's Deputy Prime Minister, Bill English, in a rare slip, admitted that lowering carbon emissions was a 'fad'. In an article for the *National Business Review*, English states, 'I think it does show that being driven by a fad, which at the time was to have lower carbon emissions, means that you can make decision[s] – which were made by the previous government – turn out more expensive than they expected.'[48] Although English was defending the National Party government's rationale for purchasing BMWs for their vehicle fleet rather than cheaper alternatives with lower 'carbon emissions', his comment is nevertheless revealing and suggests political discord at high levels.

Nevertheless, since Gluckman and others similarly inclined use the term 'climate change deniers' to describe the sceptical scientists, they are obliged to define it so that their target audience can appreciate the moral argument as much as the scientific one.[49] Surely this much is essential if the politicians expect sympathetic compliance and a willingness to accept their word that global warming is a problem worth fixing through taxation.

So what does it mean to 'deny climate change'? The term is fraught with emotive hostility, akin to Holocaust denial, as though the two are related by denial of a moral truth. But using such a phrase to describe scepticism of the AGW hypothesis is to drag the climate debate out of the realm of science, where it rightly belongs, and into the realm of ethics, where it rubs shoulders with religious fundamentalism. You are either a believer or a denier, an apostle or a heretic to be harried into compliance. It is now considered immoral to 'deny' the reality of climate change just as it is considered immoral to deny the Holocaust. Robert F. Kennedy Jr., at the 2007 Live Earth concert in East Rutherford, NJ, declared that all climate change sceptics were enemies of the United States and the human race. 'This is treason,' he declared, 'and we need to start treating them now as traitors.'[50] *The New York Times* columnist Paul Krugman agrees and argued that politicians who do not subscribe to the idea of manmade global warming as a 'crisis' are guilty of 'treason against the planet'.[51] Krugman rebuked the 'irresponsibility and immorality of climate-change denial' as an unforgivable sin because it mocks the so-called consensus that global warming is a manmade catastrophe of unprecedented proportions. Not to be outdone, the prominent American climate campaigner Joe Romm even suggests that climate deniers should be 'strangled in their beds',[52] and the NASA scientist James Hansen wanted the chief executives of fossil fuel companies to be 'tried for high crimes against humanity and nature',[53] while on ABC Radio National's *The Science Show*, Robyn Williams likened AGW sceptics to paedophiles and drug pushers.[54]

Their extreme attitudes are reminiscent of the time when heretics were persecuted for questioning Church dogma. If Galileo, Copernicus and many others had not survived such oppression, Gluckman in New Zealand and Ross Garnaut in Australia, among others, would not be employed as government science advisers because science would have withered and died under the hot glare of tyranny long ago. They owe the so-called 'heretics' and 'deniers' a debt of gratitude. Scientific intolerance is no different from religious intolerance. Both stand in the way of knowledge. Both retard development. Both would keep us in the dark. Lindzen fully understood the implications of this for climate science when he wrote of a 'willingness [by alarmist scientists] to debase climate science into a triangle of alarmism'. Lindzen further explained,

> there is a more sinister side to this feeding frenzy. Scientists who dissent from the alarmism have seen their grant funds disappear, their work derided, and themselves

libelled as industry stooges, scientific hacks or worse. Consequently, lies about climate change gain credence even when they fly in the face of the science that supposedly is their basis.[55]

Yet the term 'climate change denier' underscores a curious deceit because it ignores the important distinction between natural climate change and manmade climate change. Only a fool would 'deny' climate change as though the earth's climate system was forever fixed and immutable. But only a mischief-maker would deliberately imply that deniers of manmade climate change were also deniers of natural climate change. However, AGW apologists like Gluckman and Garnaut are careful to avoid making a distinction between the two. It is a cheap shot intended to make the sceptics look like the enemies of reason, and help the emissions taxes go down without us gagging on it. Forget the scandals, the contrary evidence and the politics behind the ETS because 'the science is settled'.

The point of the government's charm offensive was to encourage New Zealanders to buy into the alarmism so that persuading them to accept the ETS would be that much easier. However, as the NASA astronaut and scientist Walter Cunningham pointed out, the real science doesn't matter because the alarmists 'continue to embrace more regulation, greater government spending, and higher taxes in a futile attempt to control what is beyond our control: the Earth's temperature'. The science can do what it likes, argues Cunningham, because the aim of the alarmists is to 'stampede governments into committing huge amounts of taxpayers' money before their fraud is completely exposed – before science and truth save the day'.[56]

Global warming hysteria eventually will subside, like so many earlier such scares that never materialized, leaving a strange legacy for future generations to ponder.

Conclusion

By investigating the origins of the anthropogenic global warming (AGW) hypothesis, we discovered its turbulent scientific course from the ideas of John Tyndall in the nineteenth century to the founding of the IPCC in the later twentieth century. We also unmasked its weak scientific foundations on the one hand and its fortuitous appeal to the political agenda of Thatcher's government on the other. Furthermore, we discovered that the theory meshed perfectly with the environmental movement after the fall of Soviet-style socialism. It is clear that the theory that humankind is heating the planet to a dangerous degree by emitting CO_2 has a corrupt pedigree, poisoned by politics and vested interests. Indeed, in the words of Philip Stott, Emeritus Professor of Biogeography at the University of London, climate change by dint of manmade global warming is a 'politico-pseudoscientific construct'.

In an article for the *Daily Telegraph* (10 June 2005) Stott went further and challenged its scientific foundations:

> Climate change has to be broken down into three questions: 'Is climate changing and in what direction?' 'Are humans influencing climate change, and to what degree?' And: 'Are humans able to manage climate change predictably by adjusting one or two factors out of the thousands involved?'

Most importantly, Stott then asks if it's even possible for humans to 'manipulate climate predictably' and whether or not reducing CO_2 at the margins will result in 'a linear, predictable change in climate?' The answer is 'No' he says, because 'in so complex a coupled, non-linear, chaotic system as climate, not doing something at the margins is as unpredictable as doing something. This is the cautious science; the rest is dogma.'

Despite Stott's already devastating argument, we still gave the theory a fighting chance by holding a blowtorch to its fundamental scientific principles. This task was actually quite simple: first, any scientific theory must be testable and verifiable by unambiguous evidence which must not contradict it and this is simply not the case for catastrophic AGW; secondly, the idea that twentieth-century global warming was caused predominantly by emissions of CO_2 depends on the validity of a few basic assumptions. The failure of any one of these is sufficient on its own to undermine the entire hypothesis, yet they are so important to its survival as a theory of merit that each one is in effect an article of faith.

These assumptions can be summarized as follows:

- Atmospheric CO_2 acts as a climate driver capable of forcing global temperatures to increase with increasing concentrations. From this first assumption we can infer that CO_2 drives temperature and not the other way round.

- The climate system is highly sensitive to small forcings, such as changes in CO_2 levels, and an atmospheric positive feedback mechanism exists to amplify the warming effect of CO_2.

- The warming effect of atmospheric CO_2 is amplified with increasing concentration to the extent that a 'tipping point' will ultimately be reached and any subsequent reduction in CO_2 to reverse the trend will have limited or no effect. The unstated but widely understood definition of 'tipping point' is thermal runaway, a situation that will ultimately lead to conditions similar to those found on Venus which is used as an example of a planet experiencing a 'runaway greenhouse effect' based on CO_2.

- Current levels of atmospheric CO_2, at approximately 0.0395 per cent, are unnaturally high and are rare in the history of the earth. High concentrations of atmospheric CO_2 are always accompanied by high temperatures, and vice versa.

All of these assumptions have been shown to be wrong. Their failure necessarily implies that the theory is corrupt. Consequently, all political policy decisions, including CO_2 emissions taxes like New Zealand's ETS, that have been made on its basis are unsound and should be overturned. Similarly, since the science supporting CAGW/climate change is fatally and fundamentally flawed, all research grants for investigating anthropogenic global warming as a 'problem to be solved' should be diverted into more deserving scientific research. The IPCC and the University of East Anglia's Climatic Research Unit, the CRU, should be disbanded.

Unfortunately, before this happens, much damage will be done to Western economies and the welfare of citizens, as draconian measures are taken to fight a non-existent problem. If the tide of corrupted science and superstitious ignorance is not turned, the cost of energy will continue to rise through fossil-fuel phobia and carbon mania, increasing the cost of living in all areas of society. Social freedoms will be further encroached upon with strictures and taxes placed on many otherwise normal activities. Carbon taxation will increase and evolve into 'carbon rationing' with the issuing of carbon 'debit' cards to anyone who buys energy or travels. Some British MPs have already argued that 'every adult should be forced to use a "carbon ration card" when they pay for petrol, airline tickets or household energy,' writes David Derbyshire in the *Mail OnLine*. These are the threats facing citizens of Western countries in particular. The mainstream media (MSM) of course continue to play a pivotal role in perpetuating the anthropogenic global warming myth by fostering alarm and aiding and abetting a highly politicized scientific crusade, denying sceptical scientists a fair and equal platform to put their case to the general public. The MSM turned a blind eye to the Climategate email scandals while playing down the dissenting voice, and will continue to do so while there is widespread belief and alarm in the AGW hobgoblin, and while there is money to be made in its maintenance.

From the above analysis, it is clear that something is wrong with the way we do science in the West. It is obvious that politics has poisoned the well, tempting scientists with ongoing lucrative research grants, provided they produce what is required by the politicians. The climate science community has been hijacked by vested interest groups, from politicians to environmentalist extremists, who are more concerned with advocacy for their causes than true unbiased scientific endeavour. We can only hope to have begun here to redress the balance, and to ask the questions which vested interests do not want asked.

Appendix I

From: Hal Lewis, University of California, Santa Barbara
To: Curtis G. Callan, Jr., Princeton University, President
of the American Physical Society

6 October 2010

Dear Curt:

When I first joined the American Physical Society sixty-seven years ago it was much smaller, much gentler, and as yet uncorrupted by the money flood (a threat against which Dwight Eisenhower warned a half-century ago).

Indeed, the choice of physics as a profession was then a guarantor of a life of poverty and abstinence–it was World War II that changed all that. The prospect of worldly gain drove few physicists. As recently as thirty-five years ago, when I chaired the first APS study of a contentious social/scientific issue, The Reactor Safety Study, though there were zealots aplenty on the outside there was no hint of inordinate pressure on us as physicists. We were therefore able to produce what I believe was and is an honest appraisal of the situation at that time. We were further enabled by the presence of an oversight committee consisting of Pief Panofsky, Vicki Weisskopf, and Hans Bethe, all towering physicists beyond reproach. I was proud of what we did in a charged atmosphere. In the end the oversight committee, in its report to the APS President, noted the complete independence in which we did the job, and predicted that the report would be attacked from both sides. What greater tribute could there be?

How different it is now. The giants no longer walk the earth, and the money flood has become the raison d'être of much physics research, the vital sustenance of much more, and it provides the support for untold numbers of professional jobs. For reasons that will soon become clear my former pride at being an APS Fellow all these years has been turned into shame, and I am forced, with no pleasure at all, to offer you my resignation from the Society.

It is of course, the global warming scam, with the (literally) trillions of dollars driving it, that has corrupted so many scientists, and has carried APS before it like a rogue wave. It is the greatest and most successful pseudoscientific fraud I have seen in my long life as a physicist. Anyone who has the faintest doubt that this is so should force himself to read the ClimateGate documents, which lay it bare. (Montford's book organizes the facts very well.) I don't believe that any real physicist, nay scientist, can read that stuff without revulsion. I would almost make that revulsion a definition of the word scientist.

So what has the APS, as an organization, done in the face of this challenge? It has accepted the corruption as the norm, and gone along with it. For example:

1. About a year ago a few of us sent an e-mail on the subject to a fraction of the membership. APS ignored the issues, but the then President immediately launched a hostile investigation of where we got the e-mail addresses. In its better days, APS used to encourage discussion of important issues, and indeed the Constitution cites that as its principal purpose. No more. Everything that has been done in the last year has been designed to silence debate.

2. The appallingly tendentious APS statement on Climate Change was apparently written in a hurry by a few people over lunch, and is certainly not representative of the talents of APS members as I have long known them. So a few of us petitioned the Council to reconsider it. One of the outstanding marks of (in)distinction in the Statement was the poison word incontrovertible, which describes few items in physics, certainly not this one. In response APS appointed a secret

committee that never met, never troubled to speak to any skeptics, yet endorsed the Statement in its entirety. (They did admit that the tone was a bit strong, but amazingly kept the poison word incontrovertible to describe the evidence, a position supported by no one.) In the end, the Council kept the original statement, word for word, but approved a far longer 'explanatory' screed, admitting that there were uncertainties, but brushing them aside to give blanket approval to the original. The original Statement, which still stands as the APS position, also contains what I consider pompous and asinine advice to all world governments, as if the APS were master of the universe. It is not, and I am embarrassed that our leaders seem to think it is. This is not fun and games, these are serious matters involving vast fractions of our national substance, and the reputation of the Society as a scientific society is at stake.

3. In the interim the ClimateGate scandal broke into the news, and the machinations of the principal alarmists were revealed to the world. It was a fraud on a scale I have never seen, and I lack the words to describe its enormity. Effect on the APS position: none. None at all. This is not science; other forces are at work.

4. So a few of us tried to bring science into the act (that is, after all, the alleged and historic purpose of APS), and collected the necessary 200+ signatures to bring to the Council a proposal for a Topical Group on Climate Science, thinking that open discussion of the scientific issues, in the best tradition of physics, would be beneficial to all, and also a contribution to the nation. I might note that it was not easy to collect the signatures, since you denied us the use of the APS membership list. We conformed in every way with the requirements of the APS Constitution, and described in great detail what we had in mind—simply to bring the subject into the open.

5. To our amazement, Constitution be damned, you declined to accept our petition, but instead used your own control of the

mailing list to run a poll on the members' interest in a TG on Climate and the Environment. You did ask the members if they would sign a petition to form a TG on your yet-to-be-defined subject, but provided no petition, and got lots of affirmative responses. (If you had asked about sex you would have gotten more expressions of interest.) There was of course no such petition or proposal, and you have now dropped the Environment part, so the whole matter is moot. (Any lawyer will tell you that you cannot collect signatures on a vague petition, and then fill in whatever you like.) The entire purpose of this exercise was to avoid your constitutional responsibility to take our petition to the Council.

6. As of now you have formed still another secret and stacked committee to organize your own TG, simply ignoring our lawful petition.

APS management has gamed the problem from the beginning, to suppress serious conversation about the merits of the climate change claims. Do you wonder that I have lost confidence in the organization?

I do feel the need to add one note, and this is conjecture, since it is always risky to discuss other people's motives. This scheming at APS HQ is so bizarre that there cannot be a simple explanation for it. Some have held that the physicists of today are not as smart as they used to be, but I don't think that is an issue. I think it is the money, exactly what Eisenhower warned about a half-century ago. There are indeed trillions of dollars involved, to say nothing of the fame and glory (and frequent trips to exotic islands) that go with being a member of the club. Your own Physics Department (of which you are chairman) would lose millions a year if the global warming bubble burst. When Penn State absolved Mike Mann of wrongdoing, and the University of East Anglia did the same for Phil Jones, they cannot have been unaware of the financial penalty for doing otherwise. As the old saying goes, you don't have to be a weatherman to know which way the wind is blowing. Since I am no philosopher, I'm not going to explore at just which point enlightened self-interest crosses the line into corruption, but a careful reading of the ClimateGate releases makes it clear that this is not an academic question.

I want no part of it, so please accept my resignation. APS no longer represents me, but I hope we are still friends.

Hal

Reprinted with permission.

calderup.wordpress.com/2010/10/10/hal-lewis-quits-aps
www.thegwpf.org/professor-hal-lewis-joins-the-gwpf

The late Harold Lewis was Emeritus Professor of Physics, University of California, Santa Barbara; former Chairman, Former member of the Defense Science Board; Chairman of the Technology Panel; Chairman of the DSB study on Nuclear Winter; Former member of the Advisory Committee on Reactor Safeguards; Former member of the President's Nuclear Safety Oversight Committee; Chairman of the APS study on Nuclear Reactor Safety; Chairman of the Risk Assessment Review Group; Co-founder and former Chairman of JASON (an independent group of scientists which advises the US government on science and technology); Former member of the USAF Scientific Advisory Board; served in the US Navy in the Second World War; author of *Technological Risk* (on technological risk) and *Why Flip a Coin* (on decision-making).

Appendix II

Useful Websites

www.appinsys.com/GlobalWarming/UnprecedentedWarming.htm
www.auscsc.org.au
www.australianclimatemadness.com
www.bishophill.squarespace.com
www.blogs.telegraph.co.uk/news/author/jamesdelingpole
www.calderup.wordpress.com
www.chiefio.wordpress.com
www.citizensforaconstitutionalrepublic.com/ball2-8-10.html
www.climateaudit.org
www.climateconversation.wordshine.co.nz
www.climatedebatedaily.com
www.climatedepot.comwww.climate-skeptic.com
www.climaterealists.com
www.climatescience.org.nz
www.co2science.org
www.dailybayonet.com
www.davidarchibald.info
www.ferdinand-engelbeen.be/klimaat/beck_data.html
www.foia2011.org (searchable database of the Climategate I and II emails, 2009 and 2011)
www.foia2011.org/index.php?id=5608 (Climategate II searchable database)
www.friendsofscience.org
www.grazian-archive.com
www.hidethedecline.eu
www.hockeyschtick.blogspot.com
www.icecap.us
www.jennifermarohasy.com
www.joannenova.com.au
www.joannenova.com.au/global-warming/ice-core-graph
www.lavoisier.com.au/index.php
www.mclean.ch/climate/global_warming.htm
www.nipccreport.org
www.noconsensus.org
www.nofrakkingconsensus.com
www.notrickszone.com/2012/04/10/50-top-astronauts-scientists-engineers-sign-letter-claiming-giss-is-turning-nasa-into-a-laughing-stock/50

www.numberwatch.co.uk/warmlist.htm
www.pielkeclimatesci.wordpress.com
www.prisonplanet.com
www.realclimategate.org
www.scienceandpublicpolicy.org
www.scienceandpublicpolicy.org/images/stories/papers/repring/climategate_
    analysis.pdf
www.sciencebits.com
www.solarscience.msfc.nasa.gov/predict.shtml
www.surfacestations.org
www.tomnelson.blogspot.com
www.velikovsky.info/Carl_Sagan
www.warwickhughes.com/blog
www.wattsupwiththat.com

Notes

Chapter 1

1. Vincent Gray, 'The Greenhouse Delusion', www.nzcpr.com/Research papers (5).pdf; www.john-daly.com/tar-2000/ch-1.htm.
2. wattsupwiththat.com/2010/12/19/model-charged-with-excessive-use-of-forcing.
    See also Thayer Watkins, 'The Errors of Arrhenius', www.applet-magic.com/arrhenius.htm.
3. Tim Ball, 'Canada Free Press', www.canadafreepress.com/index.php/article/6855.
4. Laurence Hecht, 'The Fraud of Global Warming: True CO_2 Record Buried Under Gore', rense.com/general75/0223_inconvenient_gore.pdf.
5. Redrawn from original by Zbigniew Jaworowski, 'Climate Change: Incorrect Information on pre-Industrial CO_2', www.mitosyfraudes.org/Calen5/JawoCO2-Eng.html. Statement written for the Hearing before the US Senate Committee on Commerce, Science and Transportation, 19 March 2004.
    See also www.warwickhughes.com/icecore.
6. Paper by Timothy Ball, 'Measurement of pre-Industrial CO_2 Levels', www.friendsofscience.org/assets/documents/FoS per cent20Pre-industrial per cent20CO2.pdf.
7. Ernst-Georg Beck, '50 Years of Continuous Measurement of CO_2 on Mauna Loa'*, Energy and Environment*, Vol. 19, No. 7, 2008.
    See also www.friendsofscience.org/assets/files/documents/C02 per cent 20Gas percent20Analysis-Ernst-Georg per cent20Beck.pdf; adog-namedkyoto.blogspot.com/2007/03/becks-138-year-long-record-of.html.
8. For a mathematical treatment of why Plass's calculations on infrared absorption by CO_2 were wrong see Thayer Watkins, 'Absorber Dispersion and the Absorption of Radiation', www.sjsu.edu/faculty/watkins/absorpdiff.htm.
9. James Rodger Fleming, 'Carbon Dioxide and the Climate – Gilbert N. Plass: Climate Science in Perspective', *American Scientist*, January –February 2010, www.americanscientist.org/issues/feature/2010/1/carbon-dioxide-and-the-climate/11.
10. Gilbert N. Plass, 'The Carbon Dioxide Theory of Climate Change', *Tellus*, Vol. 8, No. 2, 1956, p. 149.

11.   Jaworowski (2007), p. 16.
12.   Ibid.
13.   Jaworowski (19 March 2004).
      See also www.mitosyfraudes.org/Calen5/JawoCO2-Eng.html.
14.   Ibid.
15.   Zbigniew Jaworowski, 'C0$_2$: The Greatest Scandal of Our Time',
      21st Century Science & Technology, Spring–Summer 2007, pp. 17–19.
16.   Ibid., p. 19.
17.   Ibid., pp. 20–1.
18.   See Figure 2. Graph approximated from Jaworowski (2007), originally
      adapted from Freidli *et al* (1986) and Neftel *et al* (1985).
19.   Ibid.
20.   www.theworldforum.net/viewtopic.php?f=2&t=3133.
21.   US National Academy of Sciences, *National Research Council Report,
      1975.*
22.   Lowell Ponte, *The Cooling: Has the Next Ice Age Already Begun? Can
      We Survive It?* (Englewood Cliffs, NJ: Prentice-Hall, 1976).
23.   Ibid., p. 5.
      See also www.climatedepot.com/a/3213/Dont-Miss-it-Cl.
24.   Peter Gwynne, 'The Cooling World', *Newsweek*, 28 April 1975. *See
      also* denisdutton.com/cooling_world.htm.
25.   Marc Morano, 'Don't Miss it! Climate Depot's Factsheet on 1970s
      Coming "Ice Age" Claims', www.climatedepot.com/a/3213/Dont-
      Miss-it-Cl.
26.   Cited in the *Washington Times*, 12 June 1992.
      See also www.nationalcenter.org/dos7123.htm.
27.   Quoted by David L. Chandler of the *Boston Globe*, 23 January 1989.
      See also www.nationalcenter.org/dos7123.htm.
28.   Fred Warshofsky, *Doomsday: The Science of Catastrophe* (New York:
      Reader's Digest Press, 1977), pp. 189–90.
29.   Stephen Schneider, book jacket endorsement to Lowell Ponte's
      The Cooling: Has the Next Ice Age Already Begun? Can We Survive It?
30.   www.john-daly.com/schneidr.htm.
31.   Quoted in the *Washington Times*, 12 June 1992, www.nationalcenter.
      org/dos7123.htm.
32.   Quoted in the *Boston Globe*, 31 May 1992, www.nationalcenter.
      org/dos7123.htm.
33.   Interview, *Discover* magazine, October 1989. pp. 45–8.
      See also www.nationalcenter.org/dos7123.htm.
34.   'Global Warming? A New Ice Age? The Only Certainty is that
      YOU'RE Paying for the Hysteria of Our Politicians', www.dailymail.
      co.uk/debate/article-2011667/Global-warming-new-ice-age-YOURE-
      paying-politicians-hysteria.html.
35.   John P. Holdren and Paul R. Ehrlich, eds., *Global Ecology: Readings
      toward a Rational Strategy for Man* (New York: Harcourt Brace

Jovanovich, 1971), pp. 76–7.
See also www.zombietime.com/zomblog/?p=873.

36. Michael Krebs, 'Obama Discussing the Use of Pollutants to Stop Warming', April 2009, www.digitaljournal.com/article/270806. *See also* tierneylab.blogs.nytimes.com/2009/09/29/dr-holdrens-ice-age-tidal-wave.

37. Ibid. *See also* thinkprogress.org/romm/2009/04/09/203932/science-adviser-john-holdren-geoengineering-global-warmin/?mobile=nc.

38. Nicolas Ifft, American Consul to Norway, American Meteorological Society Monthly Weather Review, November 1922, docs.lib.noaa. gov/rescue/mwr/050/mwr-050-11-0589a.pdf.

39. www.chinatownconnection.com/global-warming-cooling.htm.

40. 3www.time.com/time/coversearch.

41. www.biomind.de/realCO2.

42. Beck (2008). *See also* www.friendsofscience.org/assets/files/documents/CO2 per cent20Gas per cent20Analysis-Ernst-Georg per cent20Beck.pdf.

Chapter 2

1. Ralph Juergens, in Alfred de Grazia (ed.), *The Velikovsky Affair* (London: Sidgwick & Jackson, 1966), p. 8. *See also* www.grazian-archive.com/quantavolution/vol_15/velikovsky_affair_01.htm.

2. Charles Ginenthal, *Carl Sagan and Immanuel Velikovsky* (New York: Ivy Press Books, 1990), p. 59, quoting Ben Bova, *The New Astronomies* (Worthing: Littlehampton Book Services, 1973), pp. 163–4.

3. Immanuel Velikovsky, *Stargazers and Gravediggers – Memoirs to Worlds in Collision*, Paradigma Ltd., new edition reprinted 2012 (originally published 1983 by William Morrow and Company, Inc., New York), p.137.

4. *Pensée: Immanuel Velikovsky Reconsidered* (Student Academic Freedom Forum, Lewis and Clark College, Portland, OR, 1972–75). *See also* www.velikovsky.info/Gordon_Atwater.

5. Ibid.

6. Juergens (1966), p. 21, www.grazian-archive.com/quantavolution/vol_15/velikovsky_affair_01.htm.

7. Ibid., p. 71.

8. James P. Hogan, *Kicking the Sacred Cow: Questioning the Unquestionable and Thinking the Impermissible* (New York: Baen Publishing Enterprises, 2004), pp. 168–70.

9. Ibid., p. 171.

10. Ibid., p. 178.

11. Ibid., p. 179, quoting Juergens (1966).

12. Warshofsky (1977), p. 42.

13. Hogan (2004), p. 183, quoting Juergens (1966).
14. Alfred de Grazia, *The Velikovsky Affair* (London: Sidgwick & Jackson, 1966), p. 1.
    See also www.grazian-archive.com/quantavolution/vol_15/velikovsky_affair_intro1.htm.
15. Immanuel Velikovsky, *Stargazers and Gravediggers – Memoirs to Worlds in Collision*, Paradigma Ltd., new edition reprinted 2012 (originally published in 1983 by William Morrow and Company, Inc., New York), p. 87.
16. Immanuel Velikovsky, 'My Discussions with Einstein (1946–54)', www.cesc.net/adobeweb/climate/velikovsky.pdf.
17. Warshofsky (1977), p. 40.
18. www.velikovsky.info/Carl_Sagan.
19. Ralph E. Juergens, 'Velikovsky and the Heat of Venus', *KRONOS*, Vol. I, No. 4, Winter 1976, fgservices1947.wordpress.com/2010/08/28/venus-greenhouse-effect-not.
20. Ibid.
21. S. Ichtiaque Rasool and Catheryn de Bergh, 'The Runaway Greenhouse and the Accumulation of CO_2 in the Venus Atmosphere', *Nature*, Vol. 226 (1970), pp. 1037–9.
    See also pubs.giss.nasa.gov/docs/1970/1970_Rasool_DeBergh.pdf.
22. Jno Cook, 'Recovering the Lost World, A Saturnian Cosmology', saturniancosmology.org/lost.php.
23. Isaac Asimov, *Asimov's New Guide to Science* (New York: Basic Books, 1984), p. 117.
24. Ginenthal (1990), p. 231.
25. Ibid., p. 219.
26. Ibid., p. 218. The list comprised the astronomers V.I. Moroz, G.V. Rosenberg, A. Dollfus, H. Spinrad and G. Kuiper.
27. wattsupwiththat.com/2010/05/06/hyperventilating-on-venus.
28. Wal Thornhill, 'Venus Isn't Our Twin', 22 April 2006, www.holoscience.com/news.php?article=9aqt6cz5.
29. Ginenthal (1990), p. 219.
30. www.theregister.co.uk/2010/06/25/venus_long_dead_aliens.
31. Ginenthal (1990), p. 224.
32. Ibid., p. 222.
33. U. Von Zahn, D. Krankowsky, K. Mauersberger, A.O. Nier and D.M. Hunten, 'Venus Thermosphere: In situ Composition Measurements, the Temperature Profile, and the Homopause Altitude', www.sciencemag.org/cgi/content/abstract/203/4382/768.
    See also Vladimir A. Krasnopolsky, *Photochemistry of the Atmospheres of Mars and Venus*, technical ed. Ulf von Zahn (New York: Springer, 1986).
34. Ginenthal (1990), p. 226.

35. Clark R. Chapman, *The Inner Planets* (New York: Charles Scribner's Sons, 1977), pp. 102–3.
    See also Charles Ginenthal, 'The Youthful Atmosphere of Venus', *AEON*, Vol. 1, No. 6, 1988, n-atlantis.com/venus%20atmosphere.htm.
36. Juergens (1976).
    See also fgservices1947.wordpress.com/2010/08/28/venus-greenhouse-effect-not.37.
37. V.A. Firsoff, in *Astronomy and Space Science*, Vol. 2, No. 3, 1973, quoted in Juergens (1976).
    See also www.holoscience.com/wp/venus-isnt-our-twin.
38. www.holoscience.com/news.php?article=9aqt6cz5.
39. wattsupwiththat.com/2010/05/06/hyperventilating-on-venus.
40. Juergens (1976).
    See also fgservices1947.wordpress.com/2010/08/28/venus-greenhouse-effect-not.
41. Anon., 'The Mystery of Venus' New Heat', *New Scientist*, Vol. 88, 13 November 1980, p. 437.
42. Ibid.
    See also Ted Holden, www.skepticfiles.org/neocat/equalib.htm; www.science-frontiers.com/sf014/sf014p03.htm.
43. Ibid.
44. Ibid.
45. Ibid.
46. Ibid.
    See also saturniancosmology.org/files/venus/venus.txt.
47. Hogan (2004).
48. Ibid.
49. Ibid., p 182, quoting Eric Larabee, 'Scientists in Collision', *Harper's*, August 1963.
50. Immanuel Velikovsky, *Stargazers and Gravediggers – Memoirs to* Worlds in Collision, Paradigma Ltd., new edition reprinted 2012 (originally published in 1983 by William Morrow and Company, Inc., New York), p. 172.
51. de Grazia (1966), p. 205.
52. See 'The Great Global Warming Swindle', Channel 4 documentary, 2007.
53. Richard Courtney, 'Global Warming: How it All Began', www.john-daly.com/history.htm.
54. Interview in 'The Great Global Warming Swindle', Channel 4 documentary, 2007.
55. Bob Carter, David Evans, Stewart Franks and William Kininmonth, Scientific audit of report from the Climate Commission, 'The Critical Decade – Climate Science, Risks and Responses', May 2011.

See also jonova.s3.amazonaws.com/debunk/climate-commission/cc-critical-decade-report-may-2011-audit-complete-file.pdf (quoted with permission).

See also Joanne Nova, 'Climate Commission Report Debunked', joannenova.com.au/2011/05/climate-commission-report-debunked.

56. Ibid. Quoted with permission; emphasis added. For more on these issues, see Chapter 7.

57. Iain Murray, 'Margaret Thatcher: A Free Market Environmentalist – Thatcher's Environmental Views from a New Perspective', *PERC Reports*, Vol. 22, No. 4, Winter 2004, www.perc.org/articles/article506.php.

58. See Roy Spencer, 'Global Warming: The Smoking Gun.', ff.org/centers/csspp/library/co2weekly/2005-05-12/smoking.htm.

59. Murray (2004).

60. Benny Peiser, CCNet 134/2009, 4 September 2009, www.staff.livjm.ac.uk/spsbpeis.

Chapter 3

1. Graph redrawn from newswithnumbers.com/2009/06/01/gores-graph-done-right.

2. Original from 'The Great Global Warming Swindle' Channel 4 documentary, 2007. Redrawn from original.
   See also joannenova.com.au/2009/12/carbon-rises-800-years-after-temperatures.

3. J.R. Petit *et al.*, 'Climate and Atmospheric History of the Past 420,000 Years from the Vostok Ice Core, Antarctica', *Nature*, Vol. 399, pp. 429–36 (June 1999), www.nature.com/nature/journal/v399/n6735/abs/399429a0.html.

4. Keith Sherwood and Craig Idso, 'Ice Core Studies Prove CO_2 is not the Powerful Climate Driver Climate Alarmists Make it out to be', *CO2 Science*, Vol. 6, No. 26., 25 June 2003, www.co2science.org/articles/V6/N26/EDIT.php.

5. Ibid.
   See also Joanne Nova, 'The 800 Year Lag – Graphed', joannenova.com.au/global-warming/ice-core-graph.

6. Nicolas Caillon *et al.*, 'Timing of Atmospheric CO_2 and Antarctic Temperature Changes across Termination III', *Science*, Vol. 299, 2003, pp. 1728–31.

7. Ibid.
   See also www.co2science.org/articles/V6/N26/EDIT.php.

8. See J. Hansen, Mki.Sata, P. Kharecha, D. Beerling, R. Berner, V. Masson-Delmotte, M. Pagani M. Raymo, D.L. Royer and J.C. Zachos, 'Target Atmospheric CO_2: Where Should Humanity Aim?', *The Open Atmospheric Science Journal*, Vol. 2, 2008, pp. 217–31.

9. Roy Spencer, *The Great Global Warming Blunder: How Mother Nature Fooled the World's Top Climate Scientists* (New York: Encounter Books, 2010), p. 30.

10. Roy Spencer, 'Ice Ages or 20th Century Warming, it All Comes Down to Causation', June 2009, www.drroyspencer.com/2009/06/ice-ages-or-20th-century-warming-it-all-comes-down-to-causation.

11. Ibid.

12. Ibid.

13. Wallace S. Broecker, 'Upset for Milankovitch Theory', *Nature*, Vol. 359, 1992, pp. 779–80.

14. Daniel B. Karmer and Richard A. Muller, 'A Causality Problem for Milankovitch', www.muller.lbl.gov/papers/Causality.pdf.

15. Ibid.

16. Broecker (1992).
    See also Sean D. Pitman, 'Milankovitch Cycles and the Age of the Earth', www.detectingdesign.com/milankovitch.html.

17. Gerald E. Marsh, 'Interglacials, Milankovitch Cycles and Carbon Dioxide', www.gemarsh.com/archives/143.
    See also arxiv.org/abs/1002.0597v2.

18. www.realclimate.org/index.php/archives/2007/04/the-lag-between-temp-and-co2, emphasis in original.

19. Spencer (2009).

20. Redrawn from Frank Lansner, 'CO_2, Temperatures, and Ice Ages', wattsupwiththat.com/2009/01/30/co2-temperatures-and-ice-ages.

21. Ibid.

22. Ibid.
    See also icecap.us/images/uploads/CO2,Temperaturesandiceages-f.pdf.

23. www.weatherexplained.com/Vol-1/El-Ni-o-La-Ni-a.html.
    See also jisao.washington.edu/pdo.

24. Graph derived from 'The Great Global Warming Swindle' documentary, www.greatglobalwarmingswindle.co.uk, and redrawn by the author.

25. Michael Asher, 'Solar Activity Diminishes; Researchers Predict Another Ice Age', 9 February 2008, www.freerepublic.com/focus/f-news/1967753/posts.

26. Jan-Erik Solheim, Kjell Stordahl and Ole Humlum, 'The Long Sunspot Cycle 23 Predicts a Significant Temperature Decrease in Cycle 24', 2012. Emphasis added.

27. Ibid.
    See also David C. Archibald, 'Solar Cycle 24: Expectations and Implications', *Energy & Environment*, Vol. 20, Nos. 1 and 2, 2009; David C. Archibald, *Climate Outlook to 2030*. www.climatechange 101.ca/assets/files/Archibald%20Graph.pdf.

28. IPCC Fourth Assessment Report: Climate Change 2007, www.ipcc.ch/publications_and_data/ar4/wg1/en/spmsspm-projections-of.html.

29. Christopher Booker, 'Crops under Stress as Temperatures Fall', *Telegraph*, 13 June 2009, www.telegraph.co.uk/comment/columnists/christopherbooker/5525933/Crops-under-stress-as-temperatures-fall.html.
   See also Hazel Muir, 'Sunspot Activity Impacts on Crop Success', *New Scientist*, 18 November 2004, www.newscientist.com/article/dn6680-sunspot-activity-impacts-on-crop-success.html.

30. Bo Christiansen, 'On Temperature Reconstructions, Past Climate Variability, Hockey Sticks and Hockey Teams', climaterealists.com/index.php?id=5814.

31. K. Lassen, 'Long-term Variations in Solar Activity and their Apparent Effect on the Earth's Climate', Danish Meteorological Institute, Solar-Terrestrial Physics Division, Lyngbyvej,100, DK-2100, Copenhagen, Denmark, www.tmgnow.com/repository/solar/lassen1.html.

32. E. Friis-Christensen and K. Lassen, 'Length of the Solar Cycle: An Indicator of Solar Activity Closely Associated with Climate', *Science*, Vol. 254, 1991, pp. 698–700.

33. Henrik Svensmark and Eigil Friis-Christensen, 'Variation of Cosmic Ray Flux and Global Cloud Coverage – A Missing Link in Solar-Climate Relationship'*, Journal of Atmospheric and Solar-Terrestrial Physics*, Vol. 59, No. 11, 1997, pp. 1225–32.
   See also Eigil Friis-Christensen and Henrik Svensmark, 'What Do We Really Know about the Sun-Climate Connection?', Solar-Terrestrial Physics Division, Danish Meteorological Institute, Copenhagen, Denmark, www-ssc.igpp.ucla.edu/IASTP/43.

34. blogs.reuters.com/environment/2008/05/16/so-what-happened-to-global-warming

35. 'Has Sulfate Pollution from Asia Masked a Decade of Warming?', blogs.nasa.gov/cm/blog/whatonearth/posts/post_1309955964133.html.
   See also errortheory.blogspot.com/2008/04/ocean-oscillations-are-not-masking.html

36. www.icrar.org/contact/staff_pages?image=1759068.

37. wattsupwiththat.com/2011/08/25/global-warming-is-killing-the-stars.

38. 'Scientists Examine Causes for Lull in Warming', Reuters, 25 February 2010, www.reuters.com/article/idUSTRE61O3O820100225.

39. climateaudit.org/2010/04/08/dealing-a-mortal-blow-to-the-mwp.

40. Andrew Montford, *The Hockey Stick Illusion: Climategate and the Corruption of Science* (London: Stacey International, 2010), pp. 27–30, 420–2.

41. Statement before the US Senate Committee on Environment and Public Works 12 June 2006, by David Deming, University of Oklahoma, College of Earth and Energy Climate Change and the Media, www.epw.senate.gov/hearing_statements.cfm?id=266543. Quoted with kind permission of Dr David Deming.

42. Jonathan Petre, 'Climategate U-Turn as Scientist at Centre of Row Admits: There Has Been No Global Warming Since 1995', 14 February 2010, www.dailymail.co.uk/news/article-1250872/ Climategate-U-turn-Astonishment-scientist-centre-global-warming-email-row-admits-data-organised.html?ITO=1490.

43. Ibid.

44. Based on Roy Spencer, www.drroyspencer.com/2001/01/dec-2010-uah-global-temperature-update-0-18-deg-c.

Chapter 4

1. Roy Spencer, *The Great Global Warming Blunder: How Mother Nature Fooled the World's Top Climate Scientists* (New York: Encounter Books, 2010), p. 68.

2. www.quadrant.org.au/blogs/doomed-planet/2009/08/ian-plimer. *See also* Ian Plimer, *Heaven + Earth – Global Warming: The Missing Science* (London: Quartet, 2009), pp. 148–235.

3. Ernst-Georg Back, www.biokurs.de/eike/daten/berlin30507/berlin2e.htm.

4. By their very nature, the feedback models themselves are subject to arbitrary parameter adjustments in order to cope with the myriad unknowns within the climate system. In this they resemble Ptolemy's universe of arbitrary epicycles, equants and deferents, one upon another: wheels upon wheels. The epicycles were Ptolemy's 'fudge-factors', designed to force the observed planetary movements into his vision of a geocentric universe, a universe he inherited from Aristotle but which did not exist. Whenever a new planetary motion was discovered, Ptolemy was obliged to add yet another epicycle to his already cumbersome model in order to account for it. But each successive epicycle was more complex and difficult to factor in than its predecessors because the entire system depended on a host of assumptions that were incorrect. The 'consensus' view in the second century AD, when Ptolemy was working, held that not only did all heavenly bodies orbit the earth, but that these orbits were perfectly circular and lay within a series of ethereal spheres, the movements of which created divine music audible only to God. This thinking was a by-product of the religious paradigm that the circle was divine and therefore perfect, and any deviation from it a small step towards evil. To contemplate a rational alternative to that perfect scheme was heresy. The consensus view, enforced by the early Church, prevented Ptolemy from considering the possibility of elliptical orbits, which meant that the planetary movements he observed never took the form he expected. There was therefore no alternative to his model based on epicycles and perfect circles to explain what he saw. The fact that Ptolemy's model of the universe failed to fit the observed data, requiring endless ad hoc fudges to make sense of it, should have signalled that his model was wrong. But – like the Lohmann team's

attachment to IPCC climate models – an unshakeable conviction in perfectly circular orbits within a geocentric universe prevented him coming to this conclusion and, without a better alternative, Ptolemy's model remained the scientific paradigm for the next 1,300 years until Nicolaus Copernicus turned the consensus view on its head with his sun-centred model. However, Copernicus's revised universe was still burdened with Aristotle's perfect circles. The heresy of elliptical orbits would have to wait until Johannes Kepler challenged the consensus of circular orbits in the seventeenth century.

5. Spencer (2010), pp. 64–103.
6. www.drroyspencer.com/2009/11/in-their-own-words-the-ipcc-on-climate-feedbacks.
7. 'Nature, not Human Activity, Rules the Climate', Summary for Policy-makers of the report of Nongovernmental International Panel on Climate Change, Science and Environment Policy Project, 2008, p. 14.
8. Minghua Zhang, 'Cloud-Climate Feedback: How Much Do We Know?' in Xun Zhu, ed., *Observation, Theory, and Modeling of Atmospheric Variability*, World Scientific Series on Meteorology of East Asia, Vol. 3 (Singapore: World Scientific Publishing, 2004), pp. 632–55.
    See also ftp:eos.atmos.washington.edu/pub/breth/CPT/zhang_cloud-feedback-04.pdf.
9. Roy Spencer and William D. Braswell, 'On the Misdiagnosis of Climate Feedbacks from Variations in Earth's Radiant Energy Balance', *Remote Sensing*, 2011, *3*, 1-x manuscripts, doi:10.3390/rs 30x000x.
10. Roy Spencer, www.drroyspencer.com/2010/04/the-great-global-warming-blunder-how-mother-nature-fooled-the-world's-top-climate-scientists. *See also* Spencer (2010, pp. 64–103).
11. Roy Spencer, 'A Layman's Explanation of Why Global Warming Predictions by Climate Models are Wrong', 29 May 2009, www.drroyspencer.com/2009/05/a-layman's-explanation-of-why-global-warming-predictions-by-climate-models-are-wrong. Emphasis added.
12. Ibid.
    See also Tony Cox and Joanne Nova, 'The Incredible Power of Clouds (and Roy Spencer's Work)', joannenova.com.au/2012/04/the-incredible-power-of-clouds-and-roy-spencers-work.
13. Richard Dawkins, 'Attention Governor Perry: Evolution is a Fact', *Washington Post*, 28 August 2011, www.informationclearinghouse.info/article28973.htm.
14. Patrick Frank, 'A Climate of Belief – The Claim that Anthropogenic CO_2 is Responsible for the Current Warming of Earth Climate is Scientifically Insupportable Because Climate Models Are Unreliable', p. 26, www.skeptic.com/reading_room/a-climate-of-belief.
15. Ibid.

16. Ibid.
17. Sebastian Lüning *et al.*, 'New AWI Research Confirms: Climate Models Cannot Reproduce Temperatures of the Last 6000 Years', April 2012, wattsupwiththat.com/2012/04/15/new-awi-research-confirms-climate-models-cannot-reproduce-temperatures-of-the-last-6000-years.
18. Ibid.
19. Ibid.
   See also Gerrit Lohmann *et al.*, 'A Model–Data Comparison of the Holocene Global Sea Surface Temperature Evolution', *Climate of the Past*, Vol. 8, 2012, pp. 1005–56, www.clim-past-discuss.net/8/1005/2012/; doi:10.5194/cpd-8-1005-2012.
20. Ibid.
21. Richard A. Lovette, 'The End for Small Glaciers: IPCC Estimates of Sea Level Rise Corroborated, but Large Ice Sheets Might Endure', January 2012, www.nature.com/news/2011/110109/full/news.2011.3.html#B1. Emphasis added.
22. Ibid.
23. Ibid.
24. 'The End for Small Glaciers or Anthropogenic Circular Reasoning?', wattsupwiththat.com/2012/03/19/the-end-for-small-glaciers-or-anthropogenic-circular-reasoning. See comment by Dave, 19 March 2012 at 1:33 pm.
25. Ileana Johnson Paugh, 'The UN Climate Change Summit in Durban', 13 December 2011, www.canadafreepress.com/index.php/article/43170.
26. www.drroyspencer.com/2009/11/in-their-own-words-the-ipcc-on-climate-feedbacks.
27. William Connolley, 'The IPCC: Dissolve it or Not?', scienceblogs.com/stoat/2010/02/the_ipcc_dissolve_it_or_not.php.
28. Andrew Orlowski, 'Would Putting All the Climate Scientists in a Room Solve Global Warming? Skeptics Meet Warmists at Cambridge', *The Register*, 13 May 2010, www.theregister.co.uk/2011/05/13/downing_cambridge_climate_conference.
29. For a detailed yet incomplete list of the huge number of variables affecting the earth's climate system, see 'The Ridiculousness Continues – Climate Complexity Compiled', wattsupwiththat.com/2012/01/21/the-ridiculousness-continues-climate-complexity-compiled/ by Wattsupwiththat regular 'Just the Facts'.
30. Warshofsky (1977), p. 189.
31. www.eastangliaemails.com/emails.php?eid=1048&filename=1255352257.txt.
32. Roger Pielke Sr., 'Candid Comments from Climate Scientists', *Climate Science*, 27 October 2011, pielkeclimatesci.wordpress.com/2011/10/27/candid-comments-from-global-warming-climate-scientists.

33. Kirk Myers, 'New research into greenhouse effect challenges theory of man-made global warming', February 2010, www.examiner.com/article/new-research-into-greenhouse-effect-challenges-theory-of-man-made-global-warming.

34. Henk Tennekes, 'He Was Right After All, Sacked KNMI Director Wiped the Floor with the Climate Know-it-Alls as Early as the 1990's', *De Telegraaf*, 13 February 2010, translation by Richard Sumner.

35. TakeOnIt: www.takeonit.com/expert/692.aspx.

36. Clark R. Carter, *The Inner Planets* (New York: Charles Scribner's Sons, 2011), p. 51.

37. Willem de Lange, Lecturer, Department of Earth and Ocean Sciences, University of Waikato and former IPCC reviewer, 'Why I am a Climate Realist', *NZCPR Guest Forum*, 2007, www.nzcpr.com/guest147.htm.

38. Ibid.

39. Richard S. Lindzen, 'Global Warming: The Origin and Nature of the Alleged Scientific Consensus', www.cato.org/pubs/regulation/regv15n2/reg15n2g.html.

40. 'On the Determination of Climate Feedbacks from ERBE Data', *Geophysical Research Letters*, Vol. 36, L16705, 2009, www.drroyspencer.com/Lindzen-and-Choi-GRL-2009.pdf.

41. www.drroyspencer.com/2009/11/in-their-own-words-the-ipcc-on-climate-feedbacks.

42. Patrick J. Michaels, *Meltdown: The Predictable Distortion of Global Warming by Scientists, Politicians, and the Media* (New York: Cato Institute, 2004), p. 24.

43. In an endorsement for Christopher C. Horner, *The Politically Incorrect Guide to Global Warming and Environmentalism* (Washington, DC: Regnery Publishing, 2007).

44. Michaels (2004), p. 25.

45. 'Does the Earth Have an Adaptive Infrared Iris?', *Bulletin of the American Meteorological Society*, 2001, ams.allenpress.com

46. www.worldclimatereport.com/index.php/2007/08/14/the-iris-opens-again.

47. Ibid.

48. R.W. Spencer, W.D. Braswell, J.R. Christy and J. Hnilo, 'Cloud and Radiation Budget Changes Associated with Tropical Intraseasonal Oscillations', *Geophysical Research Letters*, 2007, 34, L15707, doi:10.1029/2007/GL029698.

Chapter 5

1. NIWA scientist James Renwick in an email debate with the author, 11 September 2009.

2. Marc Morano, 'Laugh Riot: 190-Year Climate "Tipping Point" Issued – Despite Fact that UN Began 10-Year "Climate Tipping Point"

in 1989!', www.climatedepot.com.

3. 'Scientists "expect climate tipping point" by 2200', *Independent*, 28 June 2010, www.independent.co.uk/news/science/scientists-expect-climate-tipping-point-by-2200-2012967.html.

4. 'Just 96 months to save world, says Prince Charles', *Independent*, 9 July 2010, www.independent.co.uk/environment/green-living/just-96-months-to-save-world-says-charles-1738049.html.

5. news.bbc.co.uk/2/hi/uk_news/8313672.stm.

6. www.thestar.com/news/canada/article/607159.

7. www.australianclimatemadness.com/?p=979.

8. tomnelson.blogspot.com/2010/05/hay-festival-climate-change-is-long.html.

9. James Lovelock, 'The Earth is about to Catch a Morbid Fever that May Last as Long as 100,000 Years', January 2006, www.independent.co.uk/opinion/commentators/james-lovelock-the-earth-is-about-to-catch-a-morbid-fever-that-may-last-as-long-as-100000-years-52 3161.html.

10. Original by David Archibald, climatepolice.com/Climate_Outlook _2030.pdf.

11. David Archibald, 'Solar Cycle 24: Implications for the United States', International Conference on Climate Change, March 2008, www.warwickhughes.com/agri/Solar_Arch_NY_Mar2_08.pdf. *See also* www.davidarchibald.info/papers/Climate%20Outlook% 20to%202030.pdf.

12. Timothy Ball, 'Canada's Carbon Dioxide "Comedy of Errors" a Total Capitulation to Climate Change Dogma', *Canada Free Press*, 6 June 2007, www.canadafreepress.com/2007/global-warming060607.htm.

13. Sherwood B. Idso, 'C0$_2$-Induced Global Warming: A Skeptic's View of Potential Climate Change', *Climate Research*, Vol. 10, 1998, pp. 69–82.

14. Ibid.

15. www.quadrant.org.au/blogs/doomed-planet/2009/08/ian-plimer.

16. 'Climate and the Carboniferous Period', www.geocraft.com/WV Fossils/Carboniferous_climate.html.

17. David Bellamy, 'Global Warming? What a Load of Poppycock!', *Daily Mail*, 9 July 2004.

18. Interview with Helen Dowd, 7 March 2012.

19. Climate Depot, 'Special Report: More Than 1000 International Scientists Dissent over Manmade Global Warming Claims – Challenge UN, IPCC and Gore', www.climatedepot.com/a/9035/SPECIAL-REPORT-More-Than-1000-International-Scientists-Dissent-Over-ManMade-Global-Warming-Claims—Challenge-UN-IPCC—Gore.

20. William Happer, 'The Truth about Greenhouse Gases – The Dubious Science of the Climate Crusaders', *First Things*, www.firstthings.com/article/2011/05/the-truth-about-greenhouse-gases.

21. Lewis Page, 'New NASA Model: Doubled CO_2 means just 1.64°C Warming', www.theregister.co.uk/2010/12/08/new_model_doubled_co2_sub_2_degrees_warming.

22. Heartland Institute, June 2001, www.heartland.org/policybot/results/1069/IPCC_report_criticized_by_one_of_its_lead_authors.html.

Chapter 6

1. Temperature after C.R. Scotese; CO_2 after R.A. Berner 2001. Original source: www.mitosyfraudes.org/Calen9/MoncktonAPS.html.

2. Ian Plimer, *Heaven + Earth – Global Warming: the Missing Science* (Albany, NZ: Howling at the Moon Publishing, 2009), pp. 30–99.

3. Nicola Scafetta, 'Testing an Astronomically Based Decadal-Scale Empirical Harmonic Climate Model versus the IPCC (2007) General Circulation Climate Models', 2011, www.sciencedirect. com/science/article/pii/S1364682611003385.

4. Based on www.ianschumacher.com/img/ice_ages.png; newswith numbers.com/2009/06/01/gores-graph-done-right. *See also* www.iowalum.com/magazine/feb05/images/vostok_graph.jpg; www.lavoisier.com.au/articles/greenhouse-science/climate-change/evans2007-4.php

5. Plimer (2009), pp. 30–99.

6. Ibid.

7. For a detailed history of past Holocene climate events, see James S. ' Aber, 'Detailed Chronology of Late Holocene Climatic Change', academic.emporia.edu/aberjame/ice/lec19/holocene.htm.

8. *Mars Blast Puzzles Science: The Evening Citizen*, Ottawa, July 15 1952, quoting John J. O'Neill in the *New York Herald Tribune*, tinyurl. com/c2k3x2m.

9. Immanuel Velikovsky, *Stargazers and Gravediggers – Memoirs to Worlds in Collision*, Paradigma Ltd., new edition reprinted 2012 (originally published in 1983 by William Morrow and Company, Inc., New York), p. 115.

10. www.penttilinkola.com/pentti_linkola/ecofascism.

11. Andrew Bolt, 'Hamilton and the Green Totalitarians', August 2010, blogs.news.com.au/couriermail/andrewbolt/index.php/couriermail/comments/hamilton_the_green_totalitarians/.

12. Ibid.

13. Ibid.

14. Plimer (2009) p. 33.

15. Christian Gerondeau, *Climate: The Great Delusion – A Study of the Climatic, Economic and Political Unrealities* (London: Stacey International, 2010), p. 66.

16. Jonathan Adams, Mark Maslin and Ellen Thomas, 'Sudden Climate Transitions during the Quaternary', www.esd.ornl.gov/projects/qen/transit.html.

17. 'New Study Shows Greenland Ice Varied Greatly in the Past', wattsupwiththat.com/2011/09/11/new-study-shows-greenland-ice-varied-greatly-in-the-past.

18. Ibid.
    See also Don J. Easterbrook, 'The Looming Threat of Global Cooling – Geological Evidence for Prolonged Cooling Ahead and its Impacts', klimarealistene.com/looming-threat-of-global-cooling.pdf.

19. Brian Sussman, *Climategate – A Veteran Meteorologist Exposes the Global Warming Scam* (Los Angeles: WND Books, 2010), pp. 33–4.

20. Ross McKitrick, 'The Search for Warming in Global Temperatures: Data, Methods and Unresolved Questions', Department of Economics, University of Guelph, 2001, www.uoguelph.ca/~rmckitri/research/warming.pdf.
    See also Scafetta (2011) and Larry Bell, 'Global Warming? No, Natural, Predictable Climate Change', 2012, www.forbes.com/sites/larrybell/2012/01/10/global-warming-no-natural-predictable-climate-change.

21. John Daly, 'El Niño and Global Temperature', www.john-daly.com/soi-temp.htm.

22. 'Influence of the Southern Oscillation on Tropospheric Temperature', *Journal of Geophysical Research*, Vol. 114, 2009, D14104, doi:10.1029/2008JD011637, mclean.ch/climate/docs/McLean_deFreitas_Carter_JGR_2009.pdf.
    See also www.climatescienceinternational.org/index.php?option=com_content&view=article&id=220:mclean-de-freitas-carter-2009&catid=1:latest.

23. For example, Willis Eschenbach, 'Volcanic Disruptions', March 2012, wattsupwiththat.com/2012/03/16/volcanic-disruptions; www.pas.rochester.edu/~douglass/papers/2004GL022119_Pinatubo.pdf.

24. Chris de Freitas, 'Perspectives on Global Warming Science', aefweb.info/data/DeFreitas.pdf, p. 3.

25. Hubertus Fischer, Martin Wahlen, Jesse Smith, Derek Mastroianni and Bruce Deck, 'Ice Core Records of Atmospheric C0$_2$ Around the Last Three Glacial Terminations', Scripps Institution of Oceanography, Geosciences Research Division, University of California, San Diego, La Jolla, CA 92093-0220, ruby.fgcu.edu/courses/twimberley/EnviroPhilo/IceCoreRecords2.pdf.
    See also www.mendeley.com/research/ice-core-records-of-atmospheric-co2-around-the-last-three-glacial-terminations-1/#; www.nature.com/nature/journal/v399/n6735/abs/399429a0.html.

26. Gerondeau (2010) p. 66.

27. In an email to executive officer Kate Kirby, Giaever announces his formal resignation from the APS; see www.ibtimes.com/articles/214181/20110915/ivar-giaever-global-warming-climate-change-al-gore-ipcc-hoax-dissent-nobel-prize-winner-physicist-re.htm.

28. Andrew Bolt, 'Tim "1000 Years" Flannery Gives the Government a Millennium Bug', *Herald Sun*, 29 March 2011.

29. John Stokes, *The Canadian*, 11 November 2011, www.agoracosmo politan.com/home/Frontpage/2007/01/08/01291.html.

30. 'Most Idiotic Global Warming Headline Ever', May 2010, wattsup withthat.com/2010/05/18/most-idiotic-global-warming-headline-ever.

31. 'Climate Change Odds Much Worse than Thought', *Science Daily*, 20 May 2009, www.sciencedaily.com/releases/2009/05/0905191348 43.htm.

32. Dan Vergano, 'Climate Report Links Extreme Weather Events to Global Warming', *USA Today*, 8 September 2011, content.usatoday. com/communities/sciencefair/post/2011/09/climate-report-links-2011 -extreme-weather-events-to-global-warming/1.
    See also wattsupwiththat.com/2011/09/09/quote-of-the-week-wuebbles -weather-world.

33. www.windworker.com.au/qldcyclones.htm.

34. 'Known Floods in the Brisbane and Bremer River Basin', Australian Government Bureau of Meteorology, www.bom.gov.au/hydro/flood/ qld/fld_history/brisbane_history.shtml.

35. 'Deluges that have Gone Before: Floods in Australian History', www. abc.net.au/rn/rearvision/stories/2011/3130327.htm.

36. Lowell Ponte, *The Cooling: Has the Next Ice Age Already Begun? Can We Survive It?* (Englewood Cliffs, NJ: Prentice-Hall, 1976), p. 89.

37. V. Trouet, J. D. Scourse and C.C. Raible, 'North Atlantic Storms: Medieval Warm Periods vs. Little Ice Age', 2012, www.nipccreport. org/articles/2012/sep/11sep2012a4.html.

38. James A. Marusek, 'A Chronological Listing of Early Weather Events', 2010, www.breadandbutterscience.com/Weather.pdf.

39. phys.org/news/2010-11-satellites-reveal-differences-sea.html.

40. Immanuel Velikovsky, *Stargazers and Gravediggers*, p. 91, quoting Daly, *Our Mobile Earth*, 1926, pp. 177–179.
    See also www.varchive.org/ce/ocean.htm.

41. D. Bouziotas, G. Deskos, N. Mastrantonas, D. Tsaknias, G. Vangelidis, S.M. Papalexiou and D. Koutsoyiannis, 'Long-Term Properties of Annual Maximum Daily River Discharge Worldwide', European Geosciences Union General Assembly 2011, *Geophysical Research Abstracts*, Vol. 13, Vienna, EGU2011-1439, European Geosciences Union, 2011, itia.ntua.gr/en/docinfo/1128.

42. Roger Pielke Jr., 'A Decrease in Floods around the World?' April 2011, rogerpielkejr.blogspot.co.nz/2011/04/decrease-in-floods- around-world.html.

43. John Roach, *National Geographic News*, 1 August 2006, news. nationalgeographic.com/news/2006/08/060801-heat-waves.html.

44. www.whitehouse.gov/sites/default/files/microsites/ostp/jph-kavli- 9-2010.pdf.

45. Madhav L. Khandekar, 'Weather Extremes of Summer 2010: Global Warming or Natural Variability?', *Energy and Environment*, Vol. 21, No. 8, 2010, myexcellentopinion.com/wp-content/uploads/2010/12/mlk2010eegw-ew.pdf.

46. www.numberwatch.co.uk/warmlist.htm.

47. Spencer (2010), pp. 21–8.

48. After Dansgaard & Johnson 1969 and Schönwiese 1995. Redrawn from pgosselin.files.wordpress.com/2010/04/002-temparature_swings_11000-yrs1.jpg.

49. Zbigniew Jaworowski, 'C0$_2$: The Greatest Scandal of Our Time', *21st Century Science & Technology*, Spring–Summer 2007, pp. 15–16. *See also* www.sovereignty.net/p/sd/strong.html.

50. Maurice Strong, keynote speech, Rio Earth Summit, 1992. See James Delingpole, blogs.telegraph.co.uk/news/jamesdelingpole/100048217/government-decides-sustainable-development-commission-is-unsustainable-tee-hee. *See also* www.sovereignty.net/p/sd/strong.html.

51. Al Gore, 'There's Still Time to Save the Planet', June 2006, abcnews.go.com/GMA/GlobalWarming/Story?id=2110628&page=1, and 'Born Again', www.guardian.co.uk/film/2006/may/31/usa.environment.

52. Noel Sheppard, 'Hypocrisy Update: Al Gore's Home Uses 20 Times the Energy of Average American's', 26 February 2007, newsbusters.org/node/11073. *See also* freerepublic.com/focus/f-news/1792191/posts.

53. Robin Pagnamenta, 'Climate Chief Lord Stern: Give up Meat to Save the Planet', *Sunday Times*, 27 October 2009, www.timesonline.co.uk/tol/news/environment/article6891362.ece.

54. Ross Anderson, Interview, 'The Atlantic, How Engineering the Human Body Could Combat Climate Change', March 2012, www.theatlantic.com/technology/archive/2012/03/how-human-engineering-could-be the-solution-to-climate-change/253981.

55. Ibid. *See also* S. Matthew Liao, 'Human Engineering and Climate Change', www.smatthewliao.com/2012/02/09/human-engineering-and-climate-change.

56. Timothy Ball, 'The Great Global Warming Swindle', Channel 4 documentary, 2007.

57. Nigel Calder, 'The Great Global Warming Swindle', Channel 4 documentary, 2007.

58. Dennis T. Avery, 'Water Experts Find Earth's Warming, Rainfall Linked to Sun', July 2007, www.theweathervane.info/forums/f16/variability-sun-s-irradiance-global-warming-6271.html.

59. David Archibald, 'Solar to River Flow and Lake Level Correlations', July 2010, wattsupwiththat.com/2010/07/22/solar-to-river-flow-and-

lake-level-correlations.

60. John Gribbin, *The Case of the Missing Neutrinos: and Other Curious Phenomena of the Universe* (Mount Prospect, IL, Fromm International, 1998), p. 71.

61. Ibid., p. 72.

62. Ibid., p. 72.
     See also Jan-Erik Solheim, Kjell Stordahl and Ole Humlum, The Long Sunspot Cycle 23 Predicts a Significant Temperature Decrease in Cycle 24', February 2012, arxiv.org/pdf/1202.1954v1.pdf.

63. Paul Hudson, 'Met Office Wakes up to Solar Influence on Climate', 12 October 2011, www.bbc.co.uk/blogs/paulhudson/2011/10/met-office-finally-wakes-up-to.shtml.

64. www.freerepublic.com/focus/f-news/2651219/posts.
     See also James Delingpole, 'How the Doomed Met Office Tried to Spin its Way out of Trouble', January 2011, blogs.telegraph.co.uk/news/jamesdelingpole/100070451/how-the-doomed-met-office-tried-to-spin-its-way-out-of-trouble.

65. Hudson (2011).

66. Tim Cullen, 'The Problem with TSI', tallbloke.files.wordpress. com/2012/11/the-problem-with-tsi_v1.pdf.

67. Boris Johnson, 'The Man Who Repeatedly Beats the Met Office at its Own Game', 19 December 2010, www.telegraph.co.uk/comment/columnists/borisjohnson/8213058/The-man-who-repeatedly-beats-the-Met-Office-at-its-own-game.html.

68. Ibid.

69. Henrik Svensmark, *Cosmoclimatology: A New Theory Emerges*, Danish National Space Centre, Technical University of Denmark, 2007, ff.org/centers/csspp/library/co2weekly/20070213/20070213_07.html.

70. theresilientearth.com/?q=content/walk-clouds.
     See also Doug L. Hoffman, 'A Walk in the Clouds', 13 September 2011, climaterealists.com/index.php?id=8331.

71. Svensmark (2007).

72. Ibid.

73. www.drroyspencer.com/2009/06/epa-endangerment-finding-my-submitted-comments.

74. Redrawn from 'Variations in Cosmic Ray Intensity and Cloud Cover (1984–1994)', www.ourcivilisation.com/aginatur/cycles/fig9.htm, copied with permission.
     See also www.sciencebits.com/CosmicRaysClimate.

75. B.A. Laken, D.R. Kniveton and M.R. Frogley, 'Cosmic Rays Linked to Rapid Mid-Latitude Cloud Changes', 2010, www.atmos-chem-phys. org/10/10941/2010/acp-10-10941-2010.pdf.

76. www.drroyspencer.com/2011/05/indirect-solar-forcing-of-climate-by-galactic-cosmic-rays-an-observational-estimate.

77. Nigel Calder, 'CERN Experiment Confirms Cosmic Rays Can Influence Climate Change', August 2011, www.thegwpf.org/science-news/3699-cern-experiment-confirms-cosmic-rays-influence-climate change.html.
78. Ibid.
79. Ibid.
80. Andrew Orlowski, 'CERN "Gags" Physicists in Cosmic Ray Climate Experiment. What Do These Results Mean? Not Allowed To Tell You', July 2011, www.theregister.co.uk/2011/07/18/cern_cosmic_ray_gag.
81. Ibid.

Chapter 7
1. Clive James, 'The Golf Ball Potato Crisp – On Scepticism as a Duty', www.clivejames.com/point-of-view/series6/golfball.
2. Ross McKitrick, 'Circling the Bandwagons: My Adventures Correcting the IPCC', April 2010, scienceandpublicpolicy.org/images/stories/papers/reprint/Circling_the_Bandwagons_Correcting _the_IPCC.pdf.
3. Ibid.
4. *See also* Joanne Nova, 'The IPCC: 5,600 Small White Lies', joannenova.com.au/2010/04/the-ipcc-5600-small-white-lies.
5. 'Prime Time – The Cold Hard Truth', www.sunnewsnetwork.ca/video/featured/prime-time/867432237001/cold-hard-truth/1236389 234001.
6. Timothy Ball, 'IPCC Science Designed for Propaganda', March 2010, climaterealists.com/index.php?id=5315.
7. Joanne Nova, 'Pachauri Admits the IPCC Just Guesses the Numbers', joannenova.com.au/2010/09/pachauri-admits-the-ipcc-just-guesses-the-numbers.
8. sppiblog.org/news/global-warming-propagandist-slapped-down-by-wikipedia.
9. Timothy Ball, 'IPCC and CRU Are the Same Corrupt Organization – Legacy: Billions of Dollars and Unmeasured Loss of Lives', February 2010, www.citizensforaconstitutionalrepublic.com/ball2-8-10.html.
10. www.americanthinker.com/2010/01/climategate_just_sign_on_the_d.html.
11. Christian Gerondeau, *Climate: the Great Delusion – A Study of the Climatic, Economic and Political Unrealities* (London: Stacey International, 2010), p. 61.
12. Eric J. Steig, David P. Schneider, Scott D. Rutherford, Michael E. Mann, Josefino C. Comiso and Drew T. Shindell, 'Warming of the Antarctic Ice-Sheet Surface since the 1957 International Geophysical Year', *Nature*, Vol. 457, 22 January 2009, pp. 459–62. www.nature.com/nature/journal/v457/n7228/full/nature07669.html.

13. nsidc.org/arcticseaicenews.
14. Melanie Phillips, 'That Famous Consensus', November 2009, www.spectator.co.uk/melaniephillips/3332616/that-famous-consensus.thtml.
15. Ibid. Emphasis in original.
16. wattsupwiththat.com/2010/03/25/gisscapades.
17. Steve McIntyre, 'Dirty Harry 4: When Harry Met Gill', February 2009, climateaudit.org/2009/02/02/when-harry-met-gill.
18. Andrew Bolt, 'Going Cold on Antarctic Warming', blogs.news.com.au/heraldsun/andrewbolt/index.php/heraldsun/comments/going_cold_on_antarctic_warming; and Phillips (2009).
19. Ibid.
20. Nils-Axel Mörner, Interview with Gregory Murphy, 'Claim that Sea Level is Rising is a Total Fraud', June 2007, www.climatechangefacts.info/ClimateChangeDocuments/NilsAxelMornerinterview.pdf. Emphasis in original. Quoted with kind permission of Dr Nils-Axel Mörner.
21. Mark Jenkins, 'The Politics of Global Warming', 16 March 2007, www.thetrumpet.com/?q=3449.1796.0.0.
22. Robert M. Carter, *Climate: The Counter Consensus* (London: Stacey International, 2011), p. 194. Emphasis added.
23. Robert M. Carter, 'Knock, Knock: Where is the Evidence for Dangerous Human-Caused Global Warming?' *Economic Analysis and Policy*, Vol. 38, No. 2, September 2008, www.lavoisier.com.au/articles/greenhouse-science/climate-change/Carterknockknock.pdf.
24. See www.pbs.org/wgbh/pages/frontline/hotpolitics/etc/script.html; wattsupwiththat.com/2011/06/25/bring-it-mr-wirth-a-challenge1}.
25. joannenova.com.au/2011/11/breaking-more-emails-released-climategate-ii.
26. See John Costella, *The Climategate Emails*, The Lavoisier Group, March 2010, www.lavoisier.com.au/articles/greenhouse-science/climate-change/climategate-emails.pdf.
27. Steven Mosher and Thomas W. Fuller, *Climategate – the Crutape Letters* (CreateSpace, 2010), p. 7, www.createspace.com/3423467.
28. Ibid.
29. Steve Watson, '"Climategate": Peer-Review System Was Hijacked by Warming Alarmists', November 2009, www.infowars.com/climategate-peer-review-system-was-hijacked-by-warming-alarmists.
30. Ibid.
   See also www.theregister.co.uk/2011/09/05/remote_sensing_editor_resigns.
31. For more on this episode, see 'Climategate 2 – Salinger Puts the Boot into de Freitas', newzealandclimatechange.wordpress.com/2011/11/26/climategatte-2-salinger-puts-the-boot-into-de-freitas.
32. See Patrick J. Michaels, 'The Climategate Whitewash Continues', July 2010, www.cato.org/publications/commentary/climategate-whitewash-continues.

33. Ibid.

34. Ross McKitrick, 'Circling the Bandwagons: My Adventures Correcting the IPCC', April 2010, scienceandpublicpolicy.org/ images/stories/papers/reprint/Circling_the_Bandwagons_Correcting _the_IPCC.pdf.

35. Paul Chesser, 'Dear Ben Santer: Resign', spectator.org/blog/2009/12 /03/dear-ben-santer-resign.

36. www.eastangliaemails.com/emails.php?eid=1045&filename=12551 00876.txt. For more on Santer's outbursts, see climatedepot.com/s. asp?tag=ben santer.

37. B.D. Santer *et al.*, 'A Search for Human Influences on the Thermal Structure of the Atmosphere', *Nature*, Vol. 382, 1996, pp. 39–46, www.nature.com/nature/journal/v382/n6586/abs/382039a0.html.

38. Patrick J. Michaels, *MELTDOWN: The Predictable Distortion of Global Warming by Scientists, Politicians, and the Media* (Washington, DC: Cato Institute, 2004), p. 137.

39. Ibid., p. 138. Emphasis added.

40. Ibid.

41. William Happer, 'Global Warming Models Are Wrong Again', *Wall Street Journal*, March 2012, online.wsj.com/article/SB100014240527 02304636404577291352882984274.html?mod=googlenews_wsj.

42. See Costella, 'The Climategate Emails', p. 126.
    See also algorelied.com/?p=3184

43. Graph derived from Clive Best's original, with upswing added: clivebest.com/blog/wp-content/uploads/2011/06/overlayco2.png. For more on failed IPCC climate model projections
    See also www.c3headlines.com/2012/03/failed-climate-models.html.
    See also Girma Orssengo, 'Predictions of Global Mean Temperatures and IPCC Projections', April 2010, wattsupwiththat.com/2010/04/25/ predictions-of-global-mean-temperatures-ipcc-projections/; www. appinsys.com/GlobalWarming/GW_TemperatureProjections.htm.

44. Paul Watson, 'Lead Author Admits Deleting Inconvenient Opinions from IPCC Report', December 2009, quoting from Jesse Ventura's show: www.prisonplanet.com/exclusive-lead-author-admits-deleting -inconvenient-opinions-from-ipcc-report.html/print.

45. Ibid.

46. Ibid.

47. 'IPCC Controversy', www.colby.edu/sts/controversy/pages/ipcc_ controversy.htm.

48. Fred S. Singer, www.sepp.org/twtwfiles/2009/TWTW per cent 2012-26.pdf.
    See also 'It Didn't Start with Climategate', www.freerepublic. com/focus/f-news/2419548/posts.

49. Ibid.
    See also 'Were Key 1995 IPCC Scientists' Conclusions of

Manmade Global Warming Tampered with?', www.greenworldtrust. org.uk/Science/Social/IPCC-Santer.htm.

50. Timothy Ball, 'IPCC and CRU Are the Same Corrupt Organization – Legacy: Billions of Dollars and Unmeasured Loss of Lives', February 2010, www.citizensforaconstitutionalrepublic.com/ball2-8-10.html.

51. Marc Sheppard, 'IPCC: International Pack of Climate Crooks', February 2010, www.americanthinker.com/2010/02/ipcc_international_pack_of_cli.html.

52. Prime Time, 'The Cold Hard Truth', www.sunnewsnetwork.ca/video /featured/prime-time/867432237001/cold-hard-truth/1236389234001.

53. climateaudit.org/2005/04/08/mckitrick-what-the-hockey-stick-debate-is-about.

54. World Climate Report, 'Hockey Stick, 1998–2005, R.I.P.', www. worldclimatereport.com/index.php/2005/03/03/hockey-stick-1998-2005-rip.

55. Andrew Montford, *The Hockey Stick Illusion: Climategate and the Corruption of Science* (London: Stacey International, 2010), pp. 37–40.

56. Plimer (2009), pp. 88–9.

57. Spencer (2010), p. 10.

58. Ibid.
See also bishophill.squarespace.com/blog/2008/8/11/caspar-and-the-jesus-paper.html; joannenova.com.au/2009/12/fraudulent-hockey-sticks-and-hidden-data.

59. Redrawn from *Climate Change 2001: The Scientific Basis. Contribution of Working Group I to the Third Assessment Report of the Intergovernmental Panel on Climate Change* (Cambridge: Cambridge University Press), Figure 2.20. Reproduced with permission.

60. Matt Ridley, 'The Case against the Hockey Stick', *PERC Reports*, Vol. 2, No. 28, 2010, www.perc.org/articles/article1272.php.

61. Andrew Orlowski, 'Bishop Hill: Gonzo Science and the Hockey Stick Torturing the Climate Numbers Until They Confess', www. theregister.co.uk/2010/02/08/andrew_montford_interview.

62. Ian Wishart, *Air Con: The Seriously Inconvenient Truth about Global Warming* (Albany, NZ: Howling at the Moon Publishing, 2009), p.156.

63. Ridley (2010).

64. Montford (2010), p. 26.

65. Ibid., p. 366.
See also John Dawson, 'The Tree Ring Circus', July–August 2010, www.quadrant.org.au/magazine/issue/2010/7-8/the-tree-ring-circus.

66. Ibid.

67. Ibid.
See also Montford (2010) pp. 367–70.

68. For more on the hockey stick saga, see Peter Foster, 'Checking the Hockey Team – How a Small Group Botched and Manipulated Climate Science', opinion.financialpost.com/2010/07/09/checking-

the-hockey-team.
See also hockeyschtick.blogspot.com

69. Montford (2010), p. 271.

70. Montford (2010), pp. 272–75.

71. Montford (2010), p.275.

72. Bishop Hill, *The Yamal Deception*, www.bishop-hill.net/blog/2012 /5/9/the-yamal-deception.html.

73. Science and Public Policy Institute, 'The Climategate Emails', p. iv, scienceandpublicpolicy.org/images/stories/papers/reprint/climategate _analysis.pdf.

74. McKitrick (2010).

75. Patrick J. Michaels, 'The Dog Ate Global Warming – Interpreting Climate Data Can Be Hard Enough. What If Some Key Data Have Been Fiddled?' September 2009, www.nationalreview.com/articles/ 228291/dog-ate-global-warming/patrick-j-michaels.

76. Ibid.

77. Ibid.

78. Richard Treadgold, 'NIWA's Ghastly Blunders – Now Read the Official Letters', February 2010, www.climateconversation. wordshine.co.nz/2010/02/niwas-ghastly-blunders-now-read-the-official-letters.

79. NZCSC, 'Are We Feeling Warmer Yet?', November 2009, www. climateconversation.wordshine.co.nz/2009/11/are-we-feeling-warmer-yet.

80. The New Zealand Climate Science Coalition, 'High Court asked to Invalidate NIWA's Official NZ Temperature Record', 13 August 2010, probeinternational.org/library/wp-content/uploads/2010/10 /niwa.ct_.docs1_.pdf.

81. Christopher Booker, 'It's the "Hottest Year on Record", as Long as You Don't Take its Temperature', 18 December 2010, climaterealists. com/index.php?id=6878.

82. www.climatescience.org.nz/images/PDFs/niwa.ct.docs.pdf. For a more detailed analysis, see NZCSC (2009).

83. Climate Conversation press release, 'Climate Science Coalition Vindicated', 20 December 2010, www.scoop.co.nz/stories/SC1012/ S00054/climate-science-coalition-vindicated.htm.

84. nzclimatescience.net/images/PDFs/statement_of_defence.pdf.

85. NZCSC, 'Statistical Audit of the NIWA 7-Station Review' July 2011, www.climateconversation.wordshine.co.nz/2011/08/ what-warming.

86. Redrawn from wattsupwiththat.com/2010/08/16/new-zealands-niwa-sued-over-climate-data-adjustments.

87. Joanne Nova, joannenova.com.au/2012/09/nz-justice-shows-courts -are-useless-in-a-science-debate.

88. Willis Eschenbach, 'The Smoking Gun at Darwin Zero', December

2009, wattsupwiththat.com/2009/12/08/the-smoking-gun-at-darwin-zero.

89. Philip Bradley, 'Australian Temperatures', November 2011, www.bishop-hill.net/blog/2011/11/4/australian-temperatures.html.

90. Joanne Nova, 'Australian Temperature Records Shoddy, Inaccurate, Unreliable, Surprise!', joannenova.com.au/2012/03/australian-temperature-records-shoddy-inaccurate-unreliable-surprise.

91. wattsupwiththat.com/2012/07/29/press-release-2; wattsupwiththat.files.wordpress.com/2012/07/watts-et-al_2012_discussion_paper_webrelease.pdf.

92. www.wunderground.com/blog/JeffMasters/comment.html?entrynum =2230.

93. www.freerepublic.com/focus/f-news/2399271/posts.

94. Michaels (2009). Emphasis added.

95. Science and Public Policy Institute, 'The Climategate Emails', scienceandpublicpolicy.org/images/stories/papers/reprint/climategate _analysis.pdf.

96. www.john-daly.com/dalybio.htm.

97. Fred Pearce, 'Controversy behind Climate Science's "Hockey Stick" Graph – Pioneering Graph Used by IPCC to Illustrate a Compelling Story of Manmade Climate Change Raises Questions about Transparency', February 2010, www.guardian.co.uk/environment/ 2010/feb/02/hockey-stick-graph-climate-change.

98. Ibid.

99. For the full email exchange, see junkscience.com/2011/12/02/ climategate-2-0-briffa-current-warming-probably-matched-about-1000-years-ago.

100. Redrawn from original graph by Steve McIntyre, 'IPCC and the "Trick"', December 2009, climateaudit.org/2009/12/10/ipcc-and-the-trick.

101. Alexander Cockburn, 'Turning Tricks, Cashing in on Fear', December 2009, www.prisonplanet.com/turning-tricks-cashing-in-on-fear.html.

102. Alexander Steve McIntyre, 'IPCC and the "Trick"', December 2009, climateaudit.org/2009/12/10/ipcc-and-the-trick.

103. Steve McIntyre, 'Hide the Decline', *Sciencemag*, No. 3, March 2011, climateaudit.org/2011/03/23/13321.

104. John Costella, 'The Climategate Emails', scienceandpublicpolicy.org /images/stories/papers/reprint/climategate_analysis.pdf.

105. Ibid. Emphasis in original.

106. John L. Daly, 'IPCC's "TAR-2000" – A Discernible Political Influence', April 2000, www.john-daly.com/tar-2000/tar-2000.htm.

107. Montford (2010), p. 238.

108. Ibid.

109. Mosher and Fuller (2010), p. 29.

See also www.createspace.com/3423467; '"Hide the decline" – worse than we thought', wattsupwiththat.com/2011/11/30/hide-the-decline-worse-than-we-thought.

110. Mosher and Fuller (2010), p. 160.

111. www.surfacestations.org.

112. wattsupwiththat.com/2008/03/06/weather-stations-disappearing-worldwide.
See also Roy Spencer, 'McKitrick and Michaels Were Right: More Evidence of Spurious Warming in the IPCC Surface Temperature Dataset', March 2012, www.drroyspencer.com/2012/03/mckitrick-michaels-were-right-more-evidence-of-spurious-warming-in-the-ipcc-surface-temperature-dataset; Horst-Joachim Lüdecke, Rainer Link and Friedrich-Karl Ewert, 'How Natural is the Recent Centennial Warming? An Analysis of 2249 Surface Temperature Records', *International Journal of Modern Physics C*, Vol. 22, No. 10, doi:10.1142/S0129183111016798, 2011, www.eike-klima-energie.eu/uploads/media/How_natural.pdf.

113. Costella, 'The Climategate Emails'.

114. Ibid.

115. S. Fred Singer, 'Global Warming Is Not Happening', January 1998, naturalscience.com/ns/letters/ns_let06.html.

116. John Daly, 'IPCC's "TAR-2000" – A Discernible Political Influence', April 2000, www.john-daly.com/tar-2000/tar-2000.htm.

117. Michaels (2004), p. 23.

118. Ibid.
See also reasonabledoubtclimate.wordpress.com/2011/08/11/breaking-the-satellite-temperature-record-down.

119. David Rose, 'Global warming stopped 16 years ago, reveals Met Office report quietly released... and here is the chart to prove it', October 2012, www.dailymail.co.uk/sciencetech/article-2217286/Global-warming-stopped-16-years-ago-reveals-Met-Office-report-quietly-released--chart-prove-it.html.

120. Louise Gray, 'Met Office: World Warmed Even More in Last Ten Years than Previously Thought When Arctic Data Added', March 2012, www.telegraph.co.uk/earth/earthnews/9153473/Met-Office-World-warmed-even-more-in-last-ten-years-than-previously-thought-when-Arctic-data-added.html.

121. 'CRU's New CRUTem4, Hiding the Decline Yet Again', wattsupwiththat.com/2012/03/19/crus-new-hadcrut4-hiding-the-decline-yet-again-2.

122. Ibid. For another apparent example of this practice, see Paul Homewood, 'How GISS Has Totally Corrupted Reykjavik's Temperatures', January 2012, notalotofpeopleknowthat.wordpress.com/2012/01/25/how-giss-has-totally-corrupted-reykjaviks-temperatures.

123. Ibid.

Chapter 8

1. Andrea Seabrook, 'Gore Takes Global Warming Message to Congress', www.npr.org/templates/story/story.php?storyId=9047642. *See also* 'They Call This a Consensus? Only an Insignificant Fraction of Scientists Deny the Global Warming Crisis. The Time for Debate is over. The Science is Settled', www.canada.com/national post/financialpost/story.html?id=c47c1209-233b-412c-b6d1-5c755457a8af.

2. Immanuel Velikovsky, *Stargazers and Gravediggers – Memoirs to Worlds in Collision*, Paradigma Ltd., new edition reprinted 2012 (originally published in 1983 by William Morrow and Company, Inc., New York), p.98.

3. For other more recent false alarms, see thegwpf.org/false-alarms.html.

4. Robert M. Carter, *Climate: The Counter Consensus* (London: Stacey International, 2011), p. 211.

5. Ibid., p. 212.

6. Joanne Nova, *CLIMATE MONEY*, 21 July 2009, heartland.org/policy-documents/climate-money.

7. Ibid.

8. Richard Lindzen, 'Global-Warming Alarmists Intimidate Dissenting Scientists into Silence', www.libertymatters.org/newsservice/2006/faxback/2996_Climate.htm.

9. Bret Stephens, 'Climategate: Follow the Money – Climate Change Researchers Must Believe in the Reality of Global Warming Just as a Priest Must Believe in the Existence of God', *The Wall Street Journal – Global View*, December 2009.

10. Carter (2011), p. 162.

11. Lewis Page, 'Fight Global Warming with Asimov-Style Psychohistory – Profs – "Social Decision Sciences" to Adjust Dwindling Public Concern', April 2011, www.theregister.co.uk/2011/04/01/psychohistory_to_fight_climate_change.

12. Lewis Page, 'Climate-Change Scepticism Must Be "Treated", Says Enviro-Sociologist – Dubious on Warmo Peril? You're the Kind Who'd Own Slaves', March 2012, www.theregister.co.uk/2012/03/30/climate_scepticism_racism_slavery_treatment.

13. Ibid.
   See also 'Simultaneous Action Needed to Break Cultural Inertia in Climate-Change Response', uonews.uoregon.edu/archive/news-release/2012/3/simultaneous-action-needed-break-cultural-inertia-climate-change-response.

14. climaterealityproject.org; www.huffingtonpost.com/2011/09/15/al-gores-presentation-24-hours-reality_n_964846.html?ref=climate-change.

15. Anthony Watts, 'Al Gore and Bill Nye FAIL at Doing a Simple
    CO_2 experiment', wattsupwiththat.com/climate-fail-files/gore-and-
    bill-nye-fail-at-doing-a-simple-co2-experiment.
    See also wattsupwiththat.com/2011/09/28/video-analysis-and-scene-
    replication-suggests-that-al-gores-climate-reality-project-fabricated-
    their-climate-101-video-simple-experiment;
    wattsupwiththat.com/2011/10/18/replicating-al-gores-climate-101-
    video-experiment-shows-that-his-high-school-physics-could-never-
    work-as-advertised.

16. blog.labour.org.nz/index.php/2010/07/01/nick-smith-estranged-from
    -the-truth-and-from-kiwis-on-ets.

17. Václav Klaus, 'Blue Planet in Green Shackles', Competitive
    Enterprise Institute, 2007, www.realclearpolitics.com/articles/2008/
    05/blue_planet_in_green_shackles.html.

18. www.erasecarbonfootprint.com/planting-trees.html.

19. John Baird, 'Carbon Trading "a Pyramid Marketing Scheme"', *The
    Australian*, November 2011, www.australianclimatemadness.com/
    2011/11/carbon-trading-a-pyramid-marketing-scheme.

20. Terry Macalister, 'Britain's Big Polluters Accused of Abusing EU's
    Carbon Trading Scheme', January 2009, www.guardian.co.uk/
    business/2009/jan/27/industry-abusing-ets-carbon-trading.

21. Ibid.

22. Austen Naughten, 'Designed to Fail? – The Concepts, Practices and
    Controversies behind Carbon Trading', www.fern.org/sites/fern.org/
    files/FERN_designedtofail_internet_0.pdf, emphasis added.

23. Ibid.

24. Rowena Mason, 'European Carbon Market Suspended over Fraud
    Fears', January 2011, www.telegraph.co.uk/finance/newsbysector/
    energy/8269907/European-carbon-market-suspended-over-fraud-
    fears.html.

25. 'An Inconvenient Portfolio', 1 July 2007, www.fastcompany.com/
    magazine/117/features-gore-an-inconvenient-portfolio.html.

26. WorldNetDaily, 'Gore's "Carbon Offsets" Paid to Firm He Owns –
    Critics Say Justification for Energy-Rich Lifestyle Serves as Way
    for Former VP to Profit', March 2007, www.wnd.com/?pageId=40445.

27. Allison Linn, 'Market for Carbon Offsets Raises Questions –
    Growing Industry Has Few Standards: Buyers Need to Beware',
    May 2007, www.msnbc.msn.com/id/18659716/ns/business-going_
    green/t/market-carbon-offsets-raises-questions.

28. Noel Sheppard, 'Media Ignore Al Gore's Financial Ties to Global
    Warming', March 2007, newsbusters.org/node/11149.

29. Ellen McGirt, 'Al Gore's $100 Million Makeover', July 2007, www.
    fastcompany.com/magazine/117/features-gore.html?page=0 per
    cent2C3.

30. Ed Pilkington, 'Al Gore's Green Investments Prompt Conflict of Interest Row', *Guardian*, November 2009, www.guardian.co.uk/world/2009/nov/03/al-gore-conflict-of-interests.

31. Ed Barnes, 'Obama Years Ago Helped Fund Carbon Program He is Now Pushing Through Congress', March 2009, www.foxnews.com/politics/2009/03/25/obama-years-ago-helped-fund-carbon-program-pushing-congress.

32. Judi McLeod, 'Obama's Involvement in Chicago Climate Exchange – the Rest of the Story', March 2009, www.canadafreepress.com/index.php/article/9629; www.prisonplanet.com/research-reports-obama-intimately-tied-to-phony-environmental-movement.html.

33. judgepedia.org/index.php/Joyce_Foundation; www.examiner.com/orange-county-conservative-in-orlando/scandal-obama-gore-goldman-joyce-foundation-ccx-partners-to-fleece-usa.

34. McLeod (2009).
    See also www.prisonplanet.com/research-reports-obama-intimately-tied-to-phony-environmental-movement.html; lonelyconservative.com/2010/04/barak-obama-goldman-sachs-and-the-chicago-climate-exchange.

35. www.cmia.net/WhoisCMIA/tabid/170/language/en-US/Default.aspx.

36. Press release, 'Generation Announces Plans for New Investment Management Firm', www.generationim.com/media/pdf-generation-final-launch-release-08-11-04.pdf.

37. Dan Riehl, 'Al Gore's Inconvenient Loot', www.riehlworldview.com/carnivorous_conservative/2007/03/al_gores_inconv.html.

38. Ed Morrissey, 'Obama: I'll Make Energy Prices Skyrocket', November 2008, hotair.com/archives/2008/11/02/obama-ill-make-energy-prices-skyrocket.

39. Ed Barnes, 'Collapse of Chicago Climate Exchange Means a Strategy Shift on Global Warming Curbs', November 2010, www.foxnews.com/politics/2010/11/09/collapse-chicago-climate-exchange-means-strategy-shift-global-warming-curbs.

40. Patrick Henningsen, 'The Great Collapse of the Chicago Climate Exchange', August 2010, www.infowars.com/the-great-collapse-of-the-chicago-climate-exchange.

41. Timothy Ball, 'Ghost of Kyoto: Government Control by Any Means', www.lewrockwell.com/orig11/ball-t7.1.1.html.

42. 'The Crash of the Climate Exchange', September 2010, news.investors.com/Article/553236/201011091851/The-Crash-Of-The-Climate-Exchange.htm.

43. Patrick Henningsen, 'The Great Collapse of the Chicago Climate Exchange', August 2010, www.infowars.com/the-great-collapse-of-the-chicago-climate-exchange.

44. news.investors.com/Article/553236/201011091851/The-Crash-Of-The-Climate-Exchange.htm.

45. *Sydney Morning Herald*, 17 August 2010, www.smh.com.au/federal-election/climate/gillard-rules-out-imposing-carbon-tax-20100816-1270b.html.

46. NZCPR, 'Time to Make a Stand', 13 June 2010, www.nzcpr.com/weekly233.htm.

47. John Boscawen, 'ETS: Time for a Stock Take', speech to ETS public meeting, New Plymouth, NZ, 4 May 2010, www.act.org.nz/posts/ets-time-for-a-stock-take.

48. 'BMW Contract Signed by Labour Govt. – English', NBR, 16 February 2011, www.nbr.co.nz/article/bmw-contract-signed-labour-govt-english-ne-86105.

49. Richard Treadgold, 'Gluckman Stumbles on the Truth', July 2010, www.climateconversation.wordshine.co.nz/2010/07/gluckman-stumbles-on-the-truth.

50. Noel Sheppard, 'RFK Jr. Calls Rush Limbaugh, Sean Hannity and Glenn Beck Lying "Flat Earthers"', 9 July 2007, newsbusters.org/node/13977.

51. climaterealists.com/index.php?id=3655.

52. www.climatedepot.com/a/1096/Execute-Skeptics-Shock-Call-To-Action-At-what-point-do-we-jail-or-execute-global-warming-deniers–Shouldnt-we-start-punishing-them-now.

53. James Hansen, 'Try Fossil Fuel CEOs for "High Crimes Against Humanity"', June 2008, www.environmentalleader.com/2008/06/24/james-hansen-try-fossil-fuel-ceos-for-high-crimes-against-humanity.

54. ABC Radio National, 'The Science Show', 24 November 2012, www.abc.net.au/radionational/programs/scienceshow/climate3a-who-denies3f/4381756.
    See also joannenova.com.au/2012/11/breaking-skeptics-are-like-paedophiles-drug-robyn-williams-abc-time-to-protest.

55. Richard Lindzen, 'Global-Warming Alarmists Intimidate Dissenting Scientists into Silence', www.libertymatters.org/newsservice/2006/faxback/2996_Climate.htm.

56. news.heartland.org/newspaper-article/2010/06/05/politics-outweigh-science-global-warming-debate.

Bibliography

Arrhenius, Svante. *Die vermutliche Ursache der Klimaschwankungen*. Stockholm: Almqvist & Wiksells, 1906. *Worlds in the Making: the Evolution of the Universe*. New York, London: Harper, 1908

Asimov, Isaac. *Asimov's New Guide to Science*. New York: Basic Books, 1984

Beck, Ernst-Georg. '50 Years of Continuous Measurement of CO_2 on Mauna Loa', *Energy and Environment*, Vol. 19, No. 7, 2008 '180 Years of Atmospheric CO_2 Gas Analysis by Chemical Methods', *Energy & Environment*, Vol. 18, No. 2, 2007

Bova, Ben. *The New Astronomies*. Worthing: Littlehampton Book Services, 1973

Carter, Robert M. *Climate: The Counter Consensus*. London: Stacey International, 2011

Chapman, Clark R. *The Inner Planets*. New York: Charles Scribner's Sons, 1977

de Grazia, Alfred. *The Velikovsky Affair*. London: Sidgwick & Jackson, 1966

Firsoff, V.A. *Astronomy and Space Science*, Vol. 2, No. 3, 1973

Fleming, James Rodger. 'Gilbert N. Plass: Climate Science in Perspective', *American Scientist*, Vol. 98, No. 1, 2010

Gerlich, Gerhard and Ralf D. Tscheuschner. 'Falsification of the Atmospheric CO_2 Greenhouse Effects within the Frame of Physics', Version 1.0, 2007

Gerondeau, Christian. *Climate: the Great Delusion – A Study of the Climatic, Economic and Political Unrealities*. London: Stacey International, 2010

Ginenthal, Charles. *Carl Sagan and Immanuel Velikovsky*. New York: Ivy Press Books, 1990

Gray, Vincent. *The Greenhouse Delusion: A Critique of 'Climate Change 2001'*. Brentwood: Multi-Science Publishing, 2002

Gribbin, John. *The Case of the Missing Neutrinos: and Other Curious Phenomena of the Universe*. Mount Prospect, IL, Fromm International, 1998

Hogan, James P. *Kicking the Sacred Cow: Questioning the Unquestionable and Thinking the Impermissible*. Riverdale, New York: Baen Publishing Enterprises, 2004

Holdren, John P. and Paul R. Ehrlich. *Global Ecology: Readings Toward a Rational Strategy for Man*. New York: Harcourt Brace Jovanovich, 1971

Idso, Sherwood B. 'CO_2-induced Global Warming: a Skeptic's View of Potential Climate Change', *Climate Research*, Vol. 10, 1998, pp. 69–82

Jaworowski, Zbigniew. 'CO_2: The Greatest Scandal of Our Time', *21st Century Science & Technology*, Spring–Summer 2007, pp. 14–28

Juergens, Ralph E. 'Velikovsky and the Heat of Venus', *KRONOS*, Vol. 1, No. 4, Winter 1976, pp. 86–92

Khandekar, Madhav L. 'Weather Extremes of Summer 2010: Global Warming or Natural Variablity?', *Energy & Environment*, Vol. 21, No. 8, 2010

Langway Chester C. Jr. *The History of Early Polar Ice Cores*, Hanover, NH: Cold Regions Research and Engineering Laboratory, 2008

Michaels, Patrick J. *Meltdown: the Predictable Distortion of Global Warming by Scientists, Politicians, and the Media*. New York: Cato Institute, 2004

Montford, Andrew. *The Hockey Stick Illusion: Climategate and the Corruption of Science*. London: Stacey International, 2010

Mosher, Steven and Thomas W. Fuller. *Climategate – the Crutape Letters*. CreateSpace, 2010

Murray, Iain. 'Margaret Thatcher: a Free Market Environmentalist – Thatcher's Environmental Views from a New Perspective', *PERC Reports*, Vol. 22, No. 4, Winter 2004

Oyama, Vance I, G.C. Carle, F. Woeller, J.B. Pollack, R.T. Reynolds and R.A. Craig. 'Pioneer Venus Gas Chromatography of the Lower Atmosphere of Venus', *Journal of Geophysical Research*, Vol.85, December 1980, pp. 7891–902

Petit, J.R. *et al.* 'Climate and Atmospheric History of the Past 420,000 Years from the Vostok Ice Core, Antarctica', Nature, Vol. 399, pp. 429–36 (June 1999).
www.nature.com/nature/journal/v399/n6735/abs/399429a0.html

Plass, Gilbert. N. 'The Carbon Dioxide Theory of Climatic Change', Tellus, Vol. 8, No. 2, 1956, pp. 140–54

Plass, Gilbert N. 'Carbon Dioxide and the Climate: Climate Science in Perspective', *American Scientist*, January–February 2010

Plimer, Ian. *Heaven + Earth – Global Warming: the Missing Science*. Albany, NZ: Howling at the Moon Publishing, 2009

Ponte, Lowell. *The Cooling: Has the Next Ice Age Already Begun? Can We Survive It?* Englewood Cliffs, NJ: Prentice-Hall, 1976

Rasool, S. Ichtiaque and Catheryn de Bergh. 'The Runaway Greenhouse and the Accumulation of CO_2 in the Venus Atmosphere', Nature, Vol. 226, 1970, pp. 1037–39

Royal Meteorological Society. *Quarterly Journal of the Royal Meteorological Society*, Vol. 64, 1938

Singer, Fred, ed. *Nature, Not Human Activity Rules the Climate*, Summary for Policymakers Nongovernmental International Panel on Climate Change, Science and Environment Policy Project. Heartland Institute, 2008

Spencer, Roy. The Great Global Warming Blunder: *How Mother Nature Fooled the World's Top Climate Scientists*. New York: Encounter Books, 2010

Spencer, Roy W., W.D. Braswell, J.R. Christy and J. Hnilo. 'Cloud and Radiation Budget Changes Associated with Tropical Intraseasonal Oscillations', *Geophysical Research Letters*, Vol. 34, L15707, 2007

Sussman, Brian. *Climategate – A Veteran Meteorologist Exposes the Global Warming Scam*. Los Angeles, CA: WND Books, 2010

Tallbot, Stephen L. 'Immanuel Velikovsky Reconsidered VII', *Pensée Journal*, Vol. 4, No. 2, Spring 1974

US National Academy of Sciences, *National Research Council Report*, 1975, Washington, DC

Velikovsky, Immanuel. *Earth in Upheaval*. New York: Doubleday, 1956 – *Stargazers and Gravediggers: Memoirs to Worlds in Collision*. New York: William Morrow, 1983; 2012 edition published by Paradigma Ltd. – *Worlds in Collision*. New York: Macmillan, 1950

Warshofsky, Fred. *Doomsday: The Science of Catastrophe*. New York: Reader's Digest Press, 1977

Wishart, Ian. *Air Con: the Seriously Inconvenient Truth about Global Warming*. Albany, NZ: Howling at the Moon Publishing, 2009

Zhang, Minghua. 'Cloud–Climate Feedback: How Much Do We Know?' in Xun Zhu, ed., *Observation, Theory, and Modeling of Atmospheric Variability*, World Scientific Series on Meteorology of East Asia, Vol. 3. Singapore: World Scientific Publishing, 2004, pp. 632–55

Index